The FIRST
PET HISTORY
of the WORLD

DAVID COMFORT

•

A FIRESIDE BOOK
PUBLISHED BY SIMON & SCHUSTER
New York London Toronto Sydney Tokyo Singapore

FIRESIDE
Rockefeller Center
1230 Avenue of the Americas
New York, New York 10020

Designed by Pei Loi Koay
Manufactured in the United States of America

1   3   5   7   9   10   8   6   4   2

Library of Congress Cataloging-in-Publication Data
Comfort, David.
The first pet history of the world / David Comfort.
        p.   cm.
"A Fireside book."
Includes bibliographical references (p.   ).
        1. Pets—History.   I. Title.
            SF411.35.C65   1994
        636.088'7'09—dc20   94-1219
                    CIP
            ISBN: 0-671-89102-2

FOR KATHY

I would like to express my sincere thanks to my editor, Becky Cabaza, and to my agent, Nancy Yost. Their assistance on this project has been invaluable.

CONTENTS

III. THE DARK AGES

IV. THE RENAISSANCE

V. RUFFURMATION AND ROVERLUTIONS

VI. THE WILD AND WOOLLY AGE

VII. THE ROCK 'N' ROLL AGE

PREFACE

This is the first pet history of the world.

Why has it no precedent?

Do the pets of the last thirty thousand years not deserve the attention of the serious historian, much less the curious person?

Consider the words of a few famous animal lovers from the past:

> *I give thee every land in obeisance, I give thee all power like Ra.*
>
> **KING OSORKON II, INSCRIPTION ON THE EGYPTIAN CAT HALL OF BUBASTIS, 950 B.C.**

Qui me amat, amet et canem meum.[1]

> **ST. BERNARD, A.D. 1150, "SERMO PRIMUS"**

> *I speak Spanish to God, Italian to women, French to men, and German to my horse.*
>
> **HOLY ROMAN EMPEROR CHARLES V, 1519**

> *I was desperate. The swine who stole my dog doesn't realize what he did to me!*
>
> **HITLER, 1917, AFTER A RAILROAD WORKER IN ALSACE STOLE HIS TERRIER, FUCHSL**

---

[1] "Love me, love my dog."

I was an utter flop. . . . Well, at least I won the dog vote tonight.

**RICHARD NIXON, 1952, AFTER HIS CHECKERS SPEECH IN
REPLY TO DEMOCRATS WHO ACCUSED HIM OF
ACCEPTING $18,000 IN ILLEGAL CAMPAIGN
CONTRIBUTIONS, PLUS A COCKER SPANIEL**

We see from these documented remarks alone that at least as far as the architects of our history were concerned, their pets were far from unimportant.

Now let's look at a few amazing but true facts:

- Egypt, history's longest-lived civilization, was based on the worship of animals—dogs and cats in particular.
- Romulus and Remus, before founding the next great civilization, were suckled by a she-wolf.
- No political or military decision was made by any ancient tyrant before checking the flight of birds, the howling of dogs, and/or the vein patterns in a chicken's liver.
- In A.D. 40, Rome was run by consul Incitatus, Caligula's racehorse.
- If not for rat-killing cats, the entire human population of fourteenth-century Europe might have been annihilated by the Black Plague. As it was, only half was wiped out—fifteen million.
- Pets have been in every military engagement from Salamis to Shiloh, Dunkirk to Desert Storm. Alexander the Great named a city after his war dog, Peritas. Conquistador Balboa took Colombia with his mastiff, Leoncico, a lieutenant. In World War II, eight dogs, three horses, thirty-one pigeons, and one cat received the highest Allied animal decoration: the Dickin Medal for Valor.
- Long before Waterloo, Josephine's toy spaniel outflanked Napoleon in bed and got a piece of him.

• When the British burned Washington in 1814, First Lady Dolley Madison escaped the White House with our nation's two irreplaceable treasures: the Declaration of Independence and the First Parrot.

• The Soviet Samoyed bitch Strelka, piloting *Sputnik V,* was the first creature to survive orbital flight. Later, Khrushchev gave to Caroline Kennedy the canineaut's puppy Pushinka, and the Cold War began to thaw (though she was searched for bugs at Walter Reed by the CIA).

• In 1986, Morris the Cat made a serious run for the presidency as a Democrat.

In light of such facts, is it possible to any longer ignore our pets' paw in history?

We are about to meet the unsung heroes of the seven great epochs from the Pyramid Period through the Rock 'n' Roll Age:

Felines: from Cleopatra's Charmain, bitten by an asp and mummified with her mistress after Antony's defeat at Actium; to President Teddy Roosevelt's Tom Quartz, who chased Speaker of the House Joseph G. Cannon out of the White House; and many others.

Canines: from Frederick the Great's eleven greyhound bitches with whom the emperor was buried at Sans Souci Palace; to FDR'S Major, who ripped the trousers off Prime Minister James Ramsay MacDonald of Great Britain.

Equines: Henry VIII's Arabians, Canicida and Barbaristo, whom he loved more than his wives; Lady, the psychic Virginia mare, who predicted Harry Truman's victory in 1948; and so on.

Avians: Thomas Jefferson's mockingbird, Dick, who whistled along whenever the author of the Declaration of Independence played violin; McKinley's

yellow-headed Mexican parrot, Washington Post, who
sang "Yankee Doodle Dandy" and greeted all old ladies to the White House with "Oh, look at the pretty
girls!"

Nor will we forget Pope Leone I's dancing elephant, Annone,
painted by Raphael, life-size. Or Elizabeth I's favorite pit bears,
Sackerson, Great Ned, and Harry Hunks, who liked nothing
better than discussing religion with Catholics. Included, too, is
our first First Snake, Alice Roosevelt's Emily Spinach, so named
because she was "as green as spinach and as thin as my aunt
Emily." And many, many more.

As we see, then, pet history is a vast, many-faceted, until-now-
unexplored territory. For this reason *The First Pet History of the
World* will be using an all-new system of information gathering
and analysis: the Pet News Network, PNN.

PNN will interrupt regular programming in this text to pro-
vide in-depth, up-to-the-minute, hard-hitting reportage of important furry events and issues. The backbone of the network
coverage will be the "Pet Datelines" in each of the seven epochs. These will be supplemented by "Profiles in Currage,"
"PNN Eyewitness Extra!," "PNN Update," and other timely spe-
cials.

Now, without further ado, the historic pets, pet owners, and
marvelous events in pet history. . . .

I.
THE
PYRAMID
PERIOD

Am I a dog, that you come out against me with sticks!

**Goliath, the Philistine giant,
squaring off against the shepherd boy, David
(I Samuel 17:43)**

An overdressed woman is like a cat dressed in saffron.

Egyptian proverb

IN THE BEGINNING . . .

Pet history began with the Bone Age. Little is known of this wild and primeval period, but we feel certain that dogs and cats were already socializing with our species, or at least giving us a loose tail, in such important Old Bone locales as Peking, Java, Neanderthal, and Eden.

The Bone Age came to an abrupt end when the Almighty drowned everybody except a six-hundred-year-old vintner, Noah, and his pets. Noah was, according to reliable authority, a good and sober individual (though around harvest he was reportedly inclined to oversample his Bordeaux and pass out in front of his sons au naturel). He was also history's first animal rights activist.

One blustery evening, after perhaps a glass or two, the patriarch was shaken from a light slumber by a peal of thunder. Suspecting who this might be, he stepped right over to his window. The Almighty told him to build an ark of gopherwood, three hundred by fifty cubits, with three decks—lower, promenade, and solarium. Then the Lord explained the reason for the size:

> *Take with you seven pairs, male and female, of all beasts that are clean, and one pair, male and female, of all beasts that are not clean.*

Though six hundred years old—and in spite of initial skepticism from his wife and sons, too—Noah got down to work.

By the end of the week, the vessel complete according to

divine specs, the patriarch loaded up his family and their breeding stock and pulled anchor. Hardly had the ark disappeared in the downpour of cats and dogs than his neighbor, in poncho and rainboots, gleefully appropriated the madman's winery.

After the Flood, Noah, his kids, his pets, and all the descendants of the original cruise group headed directly for the Nile valley. It was said to be fine grazing down there and the real estate affordable.

Soon this bountiful land became the cradle of the greatest pet civilization the world has ever known.

PUPPIES OF ANUBIS, KITTENS OF PASHT

N oah's great-great-great-grandchildren, the Egyptians, worshiped all animals.

Canines were believed to be descended from the god Anubis, judge of the otherworld. Well-to-do Thebans kept kennels of two to three hundred saluki hounds. They called them by such names as Tekal, Tarm, Ken, Akna, and Abu (or "Blackie").

Felines were believed to be descended from the goddess Pasht, daughter of the moon. The sun god Ra was called the Great Cat. At the solar eclipse, Egyptians shook rattles to waken the Great Cat, who would then destroy Apeep, the serpent of darkness. Sacred felines were kept by priests and fed with sacred fish raised in holy Nile hatcheries.

Both species were provided every creature comfort. Cats wore gold earrings; dogs silver necklaces.[1] When family por-

---

[1] Other sacred pets also wore jewelry. The Greek historian Herodotus tells us that the divine crocodiles raised by the college of crocodile priests at Lake Shedit were decked with gold leg bracelets. The crocs rarely lost or damaged their jewelry since they didn't often move from their sunning spots on the lakeshore: the priests hand-fed them holy meat, bread, and honey water. The Lake Shedit crocodile gods were reportedly one of the greatest tourist attractions of the ancient world. When on occasion the braceleted beasts ate a tourist,

traits were done, pets were always included. Pharaoh Antifaa of the Eleventh Dynasty appears on a tablet with his four hounds, each with name above, plus praise for his divine qualities.

When a pooch or puss died, Egyptians shaved off their eyebrows, smeared mud in their hair, and wept bitterly for days. Even commoners spent great sums to embalm, mummify, and lay the departed to rest in one of the country's many canine and feline necropolises.[2] In this way they insured not only their pet's place in the otherworld, but their own.

The murder of a dog or cat, even a stray, was a capital offense. According to Diodorus Siculus, the Greek historian, a Roman soldier once killed a cat in Thebes, and the locals bludgeoned him to death.

Because of their supernatural origins, many superstitions were attached to Mesopotamian pets, dogs in particular. Being urinated on by a dog, for instance, was a portentous event for a Babylonian: if the pooch was black or white, this foretold hard times or doom itself; but if he was red, this assured happiness and prosperity. The Babylonians also kept a close eye on canine sexual activity, particularly anything offbeat. If a man saw one stud mount another, this meant that the woman closest to him would soon become romantically involved with another woman.

THE TAO OF BOW AND MEOW

Animals of the ancient Far East were also held in high regard and respected for their wisdom. At the end of the second millennium B.C., the Chinese emperor Wen Wang opened the world's first public zoo, a 1,500-acre complex called Ling-Yu, the Garden of Intelligence.[3]

---

the deceased automatically became a god, and only the Shedit priests were allowed to touch the remains. All funeral expenses were proudly borne by the state.

[2] See "Pet Mummies," page 42.

[3] Some centuries later, King Solomon opened a royal zoo, as did Assyrian king Ashurbanipal and Babylonian king Nebuchadnezzar. (Nebuchadnezzar later be-

Early Asians were especially partial to canines, believing that the Dog of Many Colors had created the world. By the Chou dynasty in 1028 B.C., Pekingese were being entombed with their emperors. Others were buried under city gates to ward off evil. Archaeologists have uncovered three ancient sacred dog cemeteries in China: the Ho Mu-du site, the Xia Wang-gang site, and the Ban-Po site.

Canine worship was still alive in the Orient little more than a century ago. When the British sacked Peking in 1860, the empress had all her Pekingese executed so that they would not fall into the hands of the "white devils."[4]

Cats were held in equally high esteem. Throughout the East it was believed that enlightened souls returned to earth in feline form. In ancient India, Sastht, the cat goddess of maternity, was worshiped. Throughout China Siamese were exchanged for pure silk. In Siam, when the emperor died, his cats were buried alive with him but provided with escape holes: when they emerged from them, this meant that the king's spirit had reached heaven.

---

came a member of his own zoo when God banished him from the throne "to live with the wild beasts": for seven years the former king "ate grass like an oxen . . . his hair grew long like a goat's and his nails like eagles' talons." Daniel 4:33)

[4] Some were confiscated and spirited to England. Later Mao ordered the extermination of "decadent" pets.

CAT CREATION

Three Conflicting Reports

ARABIAN LEGEND
An amorous monkey seduced a lioness on Noah's ark: she gave birth to a kitten.

MUHAMMADAN LEGEND
Rats were overrunning the ark, Noah passed his hand over a lioness: she sneezed out a kitten.

GREEK LEGEND

Apollo, the sun god, created the lion to scare his sister, Artemis, the moon. Artemis foiled him by turning it into a pet kitten.

THE PYRAMID PERIOD FOR POOCHES

The first great epoch of pet history was, as we might expect, preoccupied with the basics: animal domestication, breeding, and training. In the fourth and fifth millennia B.C., from the Tigris to the Nile, horses were broken, oxen yoked, sheep herded, and chickens brought to roost. Soon domestication in Egypt reached an unprecedented level: by 2500 B.C. baboons were waiting on the tables of the old kingdom courts of the Pepis.

As for dogs, they neither waited on tables nor begged at them. The Egyptians gave them pretty much anything they wanted since, as we have seen, pooches were believed to be gods. The Egyptians worshiped three canine deities besides Anubis himself: Upuaout, "the opener of pharaoh's paths"; Khentamentiu, dog of the dead; and Thoth, the jackal-headed baboon, guardian of art and science.

Here now, the milestone dates in the early history of our best friend:

Dateline	Milestone
3000 (B.C.)	Pharaoh Menes I, unifies Upper and Lower Egypt and begins breeding history's first pedigrees: greyhounds, afghans, and salukis.
2900	First veterinarians, Arab barbers, begin practice. Extensive bleeding of pooches and use of chants.

2697   Huang-ti, "Yellow Emperor" of China, breeds first imperial ch'ins, or "sleeve dogs," predecessors to the Pekingese.

2200   Cynopolis, the City of Dogs, dedicated to Anubis, is founded in Abydos.[5]

1800   The Temple of Higher Spirits, dedicated to Thoth, is built at Tuna el-Bebel. It features a thirty-seven-acre, trilevel underground animal necropolis, the largest in Egypt.[6]

1760   Code of Hammurabi enacted, ending *Lex Talonis,* or Law of the Claw. The code establishes fines for mad dogs: if a mad dog kills a free man, his master must pay forty shekels; if a slave—fifteen shekels.

1523   Twelve-sign pet zodiac developed in China during the Yin dynasty. Includes Sign of the Dog (honest but stubborn); the Tiger (courageous and candid); Horse (gregarious and sexy); Dragon (passionate and complex); and others.

1350   Pharaoh Tutankhamen dies, is mummified and laid to rest in the Valley of the Kings. A curse is associated with his tomb, over which Anubis, the guard dog of the dead, watches.

(In 1922 the tomb is disturbed by Egyptologist Howard Carter. For the climax of the story, see "Curse of the Pet Mummies," page 48.)

1150   Samson catches three hundred jackals, ties them tail to tail, sets tails afire, and drives them through Philistine fields. (Judges 15:4)

---

[5] The necropolis was later excavated by archaeologist T. E. Peet in 1900: the mausoleum chambers contained thousands of dog mummies, stacked ten high. See "Pet Mummies," page 42.

[6] This necropolis became one of the greatest tourist attractions of the ancient world. It was later excavated by Samuel Gabra of the University of Egypt. Gabra unearthed four million ibis, falcon, and flamingo mummies alone from the mausoleum's first level, Gallery A.

1100   King Ahab's bloody chariot is licked out by dogs. (I Kings 22:38) His wife, Jezebel, is eaten by the same pack. (II Kings 9:35)

500   Persian king Xerxes overruns Greece with his ferocious Indian war dogs, which Greeks believe are a cross between mastiff bitches and stud tigers.

330   Alexander the Great overruns Persia with his Greek war dogs. (See "Profiles in Currage," page 61.)

310   Alexander's son by Roxana, Ptolemy VII, restores Egypt's great pet necropolis, The Temple of Higher Spirits, at Tuna el-Bebel.

207   Ch'in Shih-huang-ti, emperor of China, installs an underground army of porcelain ch'ins around his tomb.

THE PYRAMID PERIOD
FOR PUSSIES

In 1983 archaeologist Alain le Brun unearthed the jawbone of a domestic cat in Khirokitia, Cyprus. The bone carbon-dated to 6000 B.C. Other feline remains have been found in Jericho. These test even earlier.

The cat, then, may have been our first domesticated pet. But the species was apparently no less mysterious or regally aloof than it is today. As we see from its early history, the divine feline was associated with magic and the afterlife from the outset:

Dateline   **Milestone**

2715 (B.C.) Pharaoh Cheops builds the Great Sphinx of Gizeh. Installs many stone pussies throughout Egypt, employing millions of otherwise unemployable Numidians.

2697   Huang-ti, the "Yellow Emperor," breeds sleeve Siamese.

2500   Cats sing at Egyptian banquets, accompanied by women with sistras—bronze musical instruments decorated with *maus*.[7]

1700   First bathrooms with running water in Minoan palace, Crete. Litter boxes are introduced.

1210   Construction of Lion Gate at Palace of Minos, Mycenae.

1125   Samson dismembers a cat with his bare hands; stumps the Philistines with the riddle of the honey in the lion carcass; then slays one thousand with the jawbone of an ass. (Judges 14–15)

1050   Twenty-first Dynasty Theban cat woman/priestess of Amen-Re, dies, is mummified, and laid to rest. A curse is associated with her remains. (Nearly three thousand years later, her mummy is shipped to the British Museum. For the climax, see "Curse of the Pet Mummies," page 48.)

950   Poppies, locoweed, and catnip are cultivated in Egypt.

850   King Solomon builds the lion throne.

595   Pharaoh's forces turn tail in the face of King Cambyses, Cyrus the Great's son, when the Persian nails sacred cats to the shields of his soldiers and attacks.

580   Daniel, Hebrew fortune-teller/dream interpreter/lion tamer/Babylonian POW, is thrown into the lions' den by Darius. The cats lie at Daniel's feet. The Babylonians convert to his religion.

---

[7] For later musical activities of the species, see "Musical Hairs," page 168.

Some speculate that *mau,* the Egyptian word for "cat," gave rise to the term for its musical cry "meow." The relation of these terms to later homonyms—Mau Mau, Maui, mouse, Mao Tse-tung—is still a source of debate among serious petymologists.

550   Aesop declares: "Who is to bell the cat? It is easy to propose impossible remedies." ("Belling the Cat")

483   Buddha dies. The cat and the snake are the only creatures that do not weep.

30   Cleopatra poisons her cats and puts an asp to her bosom after Augustus crushes her lover Antony at Actium.

PNN EYEWITNESS EXTRA!
GREAT CAT HALL OPENS—SEVEN HUNDRED THOUSAND ATTEND ORGY

950 B.C.—BUBASTIS-ON-THE-NILE, EGYPT.

On completion of its construction, Pharaoh Osorkon II held a ribbon cutting at the Great Cat Hall of Bubastis. The fertility gala was attended by seven hundred thousand people and nearly as many cats.

Prior to the orgy, men played flutes; women played cymbals, removed their clothing, and screamed off-color jokes.

In his welcome speech, Osorkon said he hoped this would become an annual event for the next thousand years.

IT DID.

PLUTOCATS AND PLUTOCRATS

Divine pets of the Pyramid Period were given royal privileges, and some were even allowed on the throne. Though in later ages many were not even allowed on the furniture, much less the throne, there have been some notable exceptions to the rule:

- Rome, A.D. 40: Emperor Caligula appointed his race-horse, Incitatus, consul of the Roman Empire.
- Turkey, 1425: King Matyas ruled with his favorite kuvasz dog as co-regent.
- Jaboatão, Brazil, 1954: Smelly, a goat, was elected to the city council.
- São Paolo, Brazil, 1959: A female rhino was elected to the municipal council by a landslide fifty thousand votes.
- Sunol, CA, 1981: Bosco, a black Lab-Rottweiler cross, was elected mayor. Every Halloween thereafter the retriever, wearing a red satin bow, led the town parade.
- United States, 1986: Morris the Cat, the former Animal Shelter stray, ran for the presidency as a Democrat. Former vice-president Mondale's daughter, Eleanor, endorsed the candidate: "Morris realizes that prejudices exist, but he believes that, like records, they are meant to be broken. Morris gives the examples of Harry S Truman, who became the first haberdasher to inhabit the Oval Office, and John Kennedy, who became the first Catholic."

ALL THE PRESIDENTS' PETS—I
POLICYMAKERS AND POWER BROKERS

Why is your turkey at the polls? Does he vote?

ABE LINCOLN, TO HIS SON TAD, ON SEEING TAD'S PET TURKEY, JACK, AT THE SOLDIER'S POLLING BOOTH OUTSIDE THE WHITE HOUSE, 1864

No. He's not of age yet.

TAD LINCOLN'S REPLY TO HIS DAD

Like the Egyptian pharaohs, our presidents have been, with few exceptions, great animal lovers. And with good reason. Herbert

Hoover clinched his 1928 presidential bid by circulating auto-
graphed photos of himself with his dog, King Tut, in begging
position. Later, Richard Nixon saved his career by going on TV
and telling the American people that he would keep Checkers,
a black-and-white cocker spaniel given to him under the table,
along with $18,000, by a Texas Republican.

In keeping with this historical tradition, many of our other
presidents, never underestimating the political influence and
savvy of their pets, have extended power to them.

- Ulysses S. Grant appointed his Newfoundland, Faith-
ful, the White House "steward."
- James Garfield, a Republican pitted against the forty-
seventh Democratic Congress, named the First Dog
"Veto."
- LBJ's Yuki, a mutt that daughter Luci picked up at a
Texas gas station, regularly attended cabinet meetings.
He also presided over the signing of the Wholesome
Meat Act, attended by Upton Sinclair, author of *The
Jungle*.

Some First Dogs have jumped into the political arena on their
own.

- FDR's Fala hopped into the limo for his master's
third inauguration and refused to get out. Later, the
Scottie was at the president's side on the USS *Augusta*
for the signing of the Atlantic Charter with Winston
Churchill and his poodle, Rufus.

Some First Pets have kept their masters' political allies and
opponents in line.

- FDR's German shepherd, Major, bit Senator Hattie
Caraway and ripped the trousers off Prime Minister
James Ramsay MacDonald of Great Britain.
- Theodore Roosevelt told this story about an encoun-
ter between his cat, Tom Quartz, and Joseph G. Can-

non, Speaker of the House, at the White House: "He spied Mr. Cannon going down the stairs, jumped to the conclusion that he was a playmate escaping, and raced after him, suddenly grasping him by the leg the way he does with Archie and Quentin when they play hide-and-seek with him; then, loosening his hold, he tore downstairs ahead of Mr. Cannon, who eyed him with iron calm and not one particle of surprise."

Other First Dogs have boosted their masters' popularity or rescued them from ruin.

• George Bush's spaniel, Millie, the best-selling authoress, received a public apology and yummies from *Washingtonian* magazine editor Jack Limpert after his publication voted her "Ugliest Dog." The president's approval ratings soared when he responded diplomatically on his bitch's behalf:

> Dear Jack:
> Not to worry! Millie, you see, likes publicity. . . .
> Seriously, no hurt feelings: you are sure nice to write.
> P.S. Arf, arf, for the dog biscuits.

• Warren Harding's Airedale, Laddie Boy, distracted public attention from his master's Teapot Dome scandal when he led the Washington ASPCA's Be Kind to Animals parade. Later, in an interview with the *Washington Star,* the First Terrier discussed Prohibition, Wilson's sheep, and reduction of work hours for guard dogs.

On the other hand, some First Dogs have unwittingly gotten the chief executive into dutch.[8]

---

[8] Presidents aren't the only politicians who have found themselves in the doghouse. According to a 1992 *New York Times* report (March 14), Maryland governor William Donald Schaefer, AKA "the King of Perks," has been charged not only with using taxpayer money to vet his dog, but with having the pooch housebroken by the Maryland State Police.

• When LBJ gave his beagle, Him, Washington, D.C., Tag #1, and Her #2, women's groups cried foul. Later, when the president picked up the beagles by their ears during a news conference, his ratings plummeted. His predecessor and fellow Democrat, Harry Truman, had to come to his aid: "What the hell are the critics hollering about? That's the way to handle hounds!"

Doggerel

ROVER RHETORIC

If a dog will not come to you after he has looked you in the face, you ought to go home and examine your conscience.

WOODROW WILSON

I love a dog. He does nothing for political reasons.

WILL ROGERS

One time Leader strolled into the busy hallways and was gone for about a half an hour. Finally, a guard called to tell us Leader was loose in the Capitol Rotunda. That ended our dog's free rein in the halls of Congress.

SENATOR BOB DOLE (R-KANSAS)

My dog can bark like a congressman, fetch like an aide, beg like a press secretary, and play dead like a receptionist when the phone rings.

CONGRESSMAN GERALD SOLOMON (R-NEW YORK)

continued

Basically a dog person. I certainly, though, wouldn't want to offend my constituents who are cat people, and I should say that being, I hope, a sensitive person, I have nothing against cats, and had cats when I was a boy, and if we didn't have two dogs might very well be interested in having a cat now.[9]

JAMES TALENT, NEW MISSOURI REPRESENTATIVE, WHEN ASKED BY *SPY* MAGAZINE, "ARE YOU A DOG OR A CAT PERSON?"

Dog person. If more of us were like dogs, we'd be better off.

JAY DICKEY, REPRESENTATIVE FROM ARKANSAS, RESPONDING TO THE SAME QUESTION

They say that dogs often take on the characteristics of their owners, and I must admit, Leader and I have quite a few similarities. We've both called press conferences (this is true), we're both intensely loyal, and we both bark at liberals from time to time.

SENATOR BOB DOLE

---

[9] Apparently sharing the same feeling, but in reverse, on May 11, 1992, President Clinton bid on a golden retriever puppy at an auction to benefit his daughter Chelsea's school, Sidwell Friends. Unfortunately the president was the under-bidder.

LEGENDARY DATES OF THE BONE AGE

As we have seen, the friendship of people, pooches, and pussies was forged in the very earliest epochs—in the Pyramid Period and even well before, in the Bone Age itself. The most important events of the Bone Age took place during what pet historians refer to as the Legendary Period. Supernatural felines and canines flourished then, particularly the latter.

What follows are the milestone dates of this marvelous epoch, foreshadowing later mythological, cultural, and political developments.

Dateline   **Milestone**

30,000
(B.C.)
Icarius, king of Attica, is murdered and buried under a tree. His daughter, Erigone, is led to the spot by his howling dog Maera. Erigone hangs herself. She, her dad, and Maera become constellations in heaven: the Virgin, the Wagoner, and Dog Minor.

29,000
Orion, the hunter, is shot by Diana and goes to heaven to become a constellation with his two dogs: Arctophomus (bear killer) and Ptoophagus (the glutton of Ptoon).

28,000
Actaeon accidentally spots Artemis in the buff: the goddess turns him into a stag, and he is devoured by his hounds, Raven, Snatcher, Bright Eyes, and Wolf Howl.

27,500
Leda makes it with a swan and lays an egg that hatches into Helen of Troy.

27,000
Freya, the Norse deity of fertility, drives a flaming chariot drawn by two black cats.

26,500
Queen Pasiphae, a neglected Cretan housewife, crawls inside a wooden cow in a Frederick's outfit and consummates with her husband King Minos's

stud bull. Nine months later she delivers a ninety-eight-pound six-ounce horned boy by C-section—the Minotaur.

26,000   Orpheus plays lyre for the guard dog of hell, Cerberus, lulling the pooch to sleep, rescuing his dead wife, Eurydice.[10]

25,000   Hercules dognaps Orthus, the two-headed canine of three-headed monster Geryon.

4,500   The Flood: God drowns everybody except Noah and his pets.

PROPHETS AND PETS

While dogs may have been worshiped elsewhere in the pagan Middle and Far East, they are generally depicted in less than a divine light by the authors of the Bible.[11] As far as house cats are concerned, the Good Book ignores them. Figuring more prominently are goats, asses, sheep, and lambs, especially the latter.

Still, as we see from the following chart, most of the holy men had fateful and (by and large) pleasant relations with animals.

Noah   Establishes Pet Club Med.

Abraham   A ram arrives just as he is about to sacrifice his only son, Isaac.

---

[10] Soon afterward, Aeneas feeds Cerberus drugged honey cakes, rescuing his dead father, Anchises. At around the same time Garm, the Icelandic Dog of Hell, also accepts kickbacks from visitors in the form of honey cakes.

[11] The authors of the Good Book were, by and large, Jehovah's Witnesses and no doubt had had some unpleasant experiences with the pets of idolaters and polytheists while circulating the *Watchtower* door-to-door Sunday mornings in the old Middle East.

Jacob   Spotted goat/brindled goat misunderstanding with his father-in-law, Laban.

Moses   Inflicts snakes, frogs, locusts, and all the rest on Pharaoh.[12]

Golden calf misunderstanding with brother, Aaron, at Mount Sinai after bringing down the Tablets.

Puts forth the Tenth Commandment: Thou shalt not covet thy neighbor's wife, slave, slave-girl, ox, or ass. (Exodus 20:17)

Gideon   Crushes the Midianites with an army of three hundred men "who lap like dogs." (Judges 7:5)

Balaam   Saved from the wrath of Yahweh by his talking ass. (See "The Smart Ass," page 40.)

Elijah   While on the run from bull worshipers Ahab and Jezebel (who are later eaten by dogs), the Tishbite is fed by ravens in Carmel. Later he is transported to heaven by flaming steeds.

Elisha   Sics she-bears on forty-two boys for calling him "Baldy." (2 Kings 2:25)

Jonah   Swallowed by a whale. Lives inside for three days till he sees the light.

Jesus   Drives Legion's devils into a herd of swine.
Rides a she-ass into Jerusalem on Palm Sunday.
Denounces Herod as "that fox."
Heals a Canaanite girl after her mother shrewdly likens herself to a dog.

[12] Because he did not threaten Pharaoh's sacred cats, it has been speculated by some pet historians that Moses, unable to forget his Egyptian roots completely, remained a closet cat lover.

JESUS: DOG LOVER
Two Tales

"LOST SHEEP AND DOGS"
(FROM MARK 7:28)

A Canaanite woman once asked Jesus to heal her sick daughter.

"I was sent only to the lost sheep of Israel," he replied. "It is not right to take the children's bread and toss it to the dogs."

"Yes, Lord, but even the dogs eat the crumbs that fall from their master's table," she countered.

"Oh, woman of great faith!" he exclaimed. "Your request is granted."

"THE EYE OF CHARITY"
(A PARABLE BY PERSIAN POET NIZAMI, A.D. 1203)

One day while Jesus was preaching in the marketplace, he noticed a crowd of people nearby backing away from something in horror.

"Detested creature!" cried one, holding his nose.

"He pollutes the earth and air!" declared another.

"The execrable cur was hung for theft!" a third.

Stepping over, Jesus found a dead dog. He beheld the creature kindly and, marveling, said to his disciples, "Even pearls are dark before the whiteness of his teeth."

MORAL
"No creature so accursed can be but some good thing a loving eye can see."

AFURISMS
2000 B.C. — A.D. 2000

During the ancient ages pet proverbs and idioms were common. Today we speak of "the straw that broke the camel's back," "killing two birds with one stone," "monkey see, monkey do," and so on. These phrases all hark back many centuries. The original coiners of pet proverbs, or afurisms, were Confucius, Aesop, and the authors of the book of Proverbs itself. Today, of course, we have added to these.

Here, now, are some of the all-time greats:

- He who lies down with dogs wakes up with fleas.
- You can't teach an old dog new tricks.
- Every dog has his day.
- Life is a bitch, then you die.

- The leopard can't change his spots.
- There's more than one way to skin a cat.
- While the cat's away the mice will play.
- Curiosity killed the cat. Satisfaction won him back.

- A bird in hand is better than two in the bush.
- Birds of a feather flock together.
- The rooster does all the crowing, but it's the hen who lays the eggs.[13]

Do's

- Let sleeping dogs lie.
- Take the bull by the horns.

[13] Attributed to Texas governor Ann Richards.

Don't's

- Don't cast your pearls before swine.
- Don't look a gift horse in the mouth.
- Don't change horses in midstream.
- Don't count your chickens before they hatch.
- Don't have a cow.

THE SMART ASS

In the ancient ages pets were quite bright, even donkeys. The Bible (Numbers 22:27–35) tells of a certain wise ass who saved her master's life.

King Balak, son of Zippor, offered Balaam, a sorcerer, a pot of gold to put a curse on the Hebrews who were invading his country. Balaam accepted the offer. On his way to the job, the sorceror stumbled upon an angel whom he didn't see but whom his she-ass did. She shied away from the winged gentleman three times. Balaam began kicking her furiously. At last she lay down in the middle of the road, crushing her master's foot:

> At that, Balaam lost his temper and beat the ass with his stick. The Lord then made the ass to speak.
>
> ASS *(to Balaam):* "What have I done? This is the third time you have beaten me."
>
> BALAAM *(to ass):* "You have been making a fool of me. If I had had a sword here, I should have killed you on the spot!"
>
> ASS: "Am I not still the ass which you have ridden all your life? Have I ever taken such a liberty with you before?"
>
> BALAAM *(seeing his ass has a point):* "No."
>
> Then the Lord opened Balaam's eyes. Seeing the angel standing in the road now, sword drawn, he fell flat on his face.

ANGEL *(to Balaam):* "What do you mean by beating your ass three times like this? I came out to bar your way, but you made straight for me, and three times your ass saw me and turned aside. If she had not turned aside, I should by now have killed you and spared her!"

Balaam apologized to the angel (but not his ass). He promised to turn back and hold his curse. As a result, the Hebrews conquered the Holy Land and had only one creature to thank for the acquisition.

Balaam's ass.

PNN UPDATE
THE NEIGH-SAYER

Besides Balaam's ass, many ancient animals also talked—Oedipus' Sphinx, Leda's swan, Pluto's dog, Artemis' cat, and others.

Most moderns believe that talking pets, especially talking horses, are, except in certain remarkable cases (Roy Rogers's Trigger, Flicka, Mr. Ed), a thing of the past. But this could not be farther from the truth.[14]

At the turn of the twentieth century, there were three German geldings, Muhamed, Zarif, and Clever Hans, who could do arithmetic and read music—but couldn't talk . . . at least not at first. The Elberfield Horses, as they were called, were owned and trained by Karl Krull, a wealthy jeweler. In the beginning, the horses communicated with Herr Krull by means of hoofing on a large custom-made checkerboard with numbers, letters, and German diphthongs. Using the checkerboard one day, Muhamed, the brightest of the Elberfield Three (he had recently calculated the square root of 614,656 for a team of university psychologists), said to Krull, using phonetic spelling:

[14] For more talking pets of the modern age, see "Woofers and Tweeters" (page 180), "Interview with the Parrot" (page 268), and "Smart Mouth Birds Overheard" (page 271).

"Igbb kein gud sdim!" ("I have a good voice!")

So Krull, with his assistant, Dr. Scholler, immediately set to the task of teaching Muhamed to speak. He began by showing the gelding photos of dogs opening their mouths to bark, by way of indicating that the jaws had to be *moved* to speak. After the demonstration, Krull had the following documented conversation with Muhamed:

> KRULL: "What must you do to speak?"
> MUHAMED *(stomping out letters on his checkerboard):* "Open mouth."
> KRULL: "Then why don't you open yours?"
> MUHAMED *(again, on the checkerboard):* "Because I can't."

Even so, Krull did not give up hope, nor did Muhamed. Persistence paid off in the end. After several more weeks of training, the horse was communicating orally in brusque, windy sentences.

At about this time the Belgian essayist Maurice Maeterlinck, winner of the Nobel Prize in literature for *The Intelligence of Flowers* (1907) among other great works, heard about Muhamed and made a pilgrimage to the famous stables of Elberfield.

Upon entering, he was greeted by Muhamed in a remarkable baritone.

"How do you do?"

Maeterlinck later recorded in his memoirs his reaction to the greeting: "It came like a breath from the abyss as my mind floundered for a reply. It was as if I had heard a voice from the dead!"

PET MUMMIES

Experts estimate that the Egyptians, between the First and Thirtieth dynasties, wrapped more than five hundred million mummies. A good percent were dogs, cats, gazelle, mongooses, ibis, falcons, flamingos, and crocodiles. Each sacred creature had designated necropolises where taxidermy and burial took place. The largest Caninopolis (or, as the Greeks knew it, "Cynopolis"), sacred to the dog god, Anubis, was situated in Abydos; the largest Felinopolis, sacred to the cat goddess, Pasht, was in Bubastis; the largest Crocodilopolis, sacred to the crocodile god, Sobek, was located just south of Cairo in Tebtynis.[15]

As we will see, in later ages theologians hotly debated whether an animal had a soul (in spite of the etymology of the word: animus = soul), much less whether one should be preserved for life in heaven. Egyptians would have considered such a question ridiculous, not to mention heretical. Also, practically speaking, to the pagan mind heaven wouldn't have been heaven without divine pets.

Preparing the body of a sacred pet for reunion with its soul in the otherworld was as long and painstaking a procedure as it was for a human. Mummification took seventy days. Long prayers were uttered between each of the prescribed physical steps: the extraction of the brain through the snout; the evisceration; the three ceremonial ablutions; the dehydration of the remains with natron; the stuffing of the abdominal cavity and brisket with sawdust, lichen, or bitumen; the application of resins; and then the wrapping itself. Up to three hundred yards of bandage were used on dogs and cats. More than four hundred yards have been found on crocodile mummies. The wrapping alone took fifteen days and was carried out by a priest wearing the mask of Anubis, the dog god of the dead.

Finally, the pet's eyes were inlaid with obsidian, and its head was covered with a bronze mask. Then the body was sealed in a painted wooden sarcophagus inscribed with hieroglyphics and poems and carried down to the mausoleums in a solemn procession.

Today only a fraction of the original five hundred million

---

[15] Two thousand croc mummies were unearthed here in the early 1900s. They were found carefully laid out in family groups—father, mother, and a few young, plus some eggs.

animal and human mummies remain. Some were burned by arsonists and grave robbers. Others were disinterred en masse and sold for fertilizer. But most were eaten.

CAT MUMMY AUCTION

In 1850 three hundred thousand cat mummies were discovered in the pyramids of Beni-Hassan, Egypt.
   Twenty tons of the ancient feline remains were shipped to Liverpool and sold to farmers for fertilizer.
   The price: $18 a ton.
   The auctioneer used the body of an embalmed cat for a gavel.

Mummy eating started in the Middle Ages.[16] The standard medical text from 1100 to 1500, *Canon of Medicine,* by the Islamic physician Avicenna, prescribed mummy as a cure-all for every ailment: from "abscesses, fractures, contusions, paralysis, migraine, and epilepsy, to coughs, palpitations, and disorders of the liver and spleen." Mummy eating reached its peak in 1300, when it was endorsed by the Linus Pauling of the age, El-Magar, a Jewish physician from Alexandria. Three hundred years later the noted French doctor Savary de Bruslon defined the ideal mummy for consumption as "the one the least shiny, really black, smelling pleasant, and which when burned has no odour of pitch."

But by this time supplies were dwindling and exorbitant prices were being paid for even unrecognizable mummy parts. Only royalty could afford what Christoph Harant, sixteenth-century drug merchant from the imperial court in Bohemia, called "the whole fellow."

So, Alexandrian mummy brokers soon began exporting pet parts up to Europe, unlabeled and without a discount. By the

---

[16] For more on Dark Age pharmacology, see "Pet Panaceas," page 119.

seventeenth century the Europeans were not getting any healthier, finally smelled something in Denmark, and the bottom fell out of the mummy-eating market. But not before most of the five hundred million specimens—man and animal—were largely exhausted.

The epilogue to this story involves the curse of certain mummies and tomb guardians. But, first, an update on modern memorials for pets. . . .

SNUFFED, STUFFED, AND FLUFFED
History's Pet Pantheon

No civilization has rivaled the Egyptian in love and care for pets both in life and in death. But, in more recent times, certain people have paid their last respects to their beloved in true Egyptian fashion. Petrarch, the fourteenth-century Italian poet, embalmed the cat of his deceased wife, Laura, and enshrined it over his doorway with the inscription *Second Only to Laura*. P. T. Barnum stuffed his favorite elephant, Jumbo, and installed him in Barnum Memorial Hall at Tufts University, after the 3½-ton giant was hit by a freight train in 1885. Here now, some other cases:

* King Tut I, the saluki mascot of Southern Illinois University, is entombed under a concrete pyramid at McAndrew Stadium, fifty yards from the north goalpost.
* Handsome Dan I, the progenitor of the 103-year Dan dynasty at Yale, is preserved behind glass in the trophy room of the university's gym.
* Roy Rogers' Trigger and Dale Evans's Buttermilk are mounted at the couple's museum in Victorville, California.

• In 1872 the people of Edinburgh installed a life-size statue of Grayfriars Bobby, a Skye terrier, who, after the death of his master, Jock, slept by his grave at the Grayfriars church for the rest of his life.

• In 1989 Texas A&M's mascot collie, Reveille IV, was interred with full military honors, twenty thousand mourners attending.

• University of Georgia's bulldogs UGA I, II, III, and IV are enshrined in the Sanford Stadium end zone. The epitaph on UGA I's red Georgia marble crypt:

UGA
A Real Georgia Bulldog
Georgia Mascot
1956–1967
"Damn Good Dog"

IN POOCHI REQUIESCAT?

Today pet mummification has been overtaken in popularity by other more practical alternatives. Glassman Box Company in Astoria, New York, offers a complete line of pet coffins and urns. Pet Rest, a southern California concern, offers economical memorial service packages, complete with sympathy card and flowers.[17] Preserv-a-Pet International, another West Coast operation, offers a freeze-dry, cryonic package.

Japan boasts numerous pet crematoria. One of the more popular, Jippo, Inc., has a fleet of radio-dispatched "Pet Angel Service Trucks." Each unit is equipped with a pink altar and a portable incinerator and is manned by a technician in a pink jumpsuit.

Jippo's mortuary in downtown Tokyo is equipped with a

---

[17] The price for a guinea pig package is $14.99.

$520,000 computer-generated planetarium reserved for deluxe services. To musical accompaniment, a trembling beacon of light in a pyramid, representing the pet's departing soul, is launched to the heavens.

"There," says the funeral director. "Fluffy has gone back to the land of the stars."

PNN HARD COPY!
LONG ISLAND PET CEMETERY

Between 1984 and 1991, the Long Island Pet Cemetery in Middle Island, New York, illegally disposed of up to 250,000 pets. Some were burned in mass incinerations, random ashes sent to unsuspecting owners; others were bulldozed into pits in the woods. On June 11, 1991, the FBI charged Long Island Pet Cemetery owner Alan Strauss with mail fraud. A demonstration was staged at the facility, attended by pet owners, animal rights activists, and celebrities such as singer LaToya Jackson, accompanied by her pet snake.

Soon afterward, owners of the Long Island Pet Cemetery were arrested by the FBI on new charges that they sold dog food that was bug-infested and contaminated with flea powder. Thousands of local dogs fell sick after eating the Strauss family's Professional Choice dog food featured in its ten Bow-Wow-Meow stores.

On January 17, 1992, Samuel and Alan Strauss, owners of the Long Island Pet Cemetery, were convicted of mail fraud for gouging pet owners. Individual civil suits followed. On September 1, 1992, Justice Stuart Ain of the New York State Supreme Court awarded Joyce Walp and Michael Bachman, owners of the late Ruffian, a ten-year-old English sheepdog, $600,000 each in compensatory and punitive damages against the Strausses.

On May 29, 1993, the federal government sold the cemetery to three Long Island entrepreneurs. Before resuming operations, the buyers agreed to renovate the twenty-seven-acre complex and to erect a memorial to the unfortunate pets.

THE FUR SIDE
CURSE OF THE PET MUMMIES

In his 1943 article *Chats sacres* ("Sacred cats"), Egyptologist J. Capart discussed ancient cat curses that were often used during the Pyramid Period. Most curses involved the drowning of a cat. During the process, this invocation was uttered:

> *Come to me, you to whom the appearance of Helios, the cat-headed god, belongs, and see how your adversaries so and so have maltreated you; take vengeance on them. Rise up for me, O cat-headed god, and carry out such and such. . . .*

After the cat was drowned, the corpse was mummified in papyrus on which the invocation to Pasht or Bastet, the cat goddesses, was written. Next, the deceased was sprinkled with the water in which it was drowned. Finally, its whiskers were thrown into the air, and the curse was repeated. . . .

In the Twenty-first Dynasty (c. 1050 B.C.), there lived a certain Theban priestess of Amen-Re, that is to say of the cat sun god. In the course of her professional career, it is likely that she delivered more than a few cat curses; and, on retirement, it is likely that her mummy, guarded as it was by feline mummies and amulets, had a cat curse associated with it.

Nearly three thousand years later, in 1880, three British tourists were on holiday in Thebes, looking for a souvenir to bring back home. They bought the cat priestess (mummy and case) from a local entrepreneur with underground connections. En route back to Cairo with the relic, the first tourist had to have an arm amputated after a fluke duck-hunting accident; the second vanished seemingly in thin air (some said he drowned); and the third unloaded the mummy in Cairo, then fled to England. The next three purchasers of the cat woman all died quite suddenly and mysteriously. She was shipped to London in 1888 and went through many hands there. Her first photographer perished within twenty-four hours of taking pictures. Months later she was purchased by a lady collector: all the windows in the woman's house were shattered the first night, and within days all her pets died, and she herself became seriously ill.

The mummy was then donated to the British Museum and became Exhibit No. 22542. While carrying the case into Exhibit Room One, one of the porters broke his leg. The other expired days later. Soon the museum nightwatchman reported peculiar activity in Exhibit Room One: he saw an apparition rise from Exhibit No. 22542 and described its face as "yellow green and wrinkled like a sheep's bladder." The day before the sighting, another photographer took a picture of the case, then committed suicide.

In 1889 Sir Ernest Alfred Wallace Budge, keeper of Egyptian antiquities at the British Museum, removed the priestess's mummy from her box and sold it to an American collector. The cadaver was loaded onto the *Empress of Ireland,* and the ship sank in the St. Lawrence. The story of the priestess's curse did not stop there, however. Some held it responsible for the sinking of the *Titanic* in 1912, as well as the HMS *Hampshire* in 1916. Just before retiring as curator of the British Museum in 1924, Sir Budge, a celebrated scholar and personal friend of Prime Minister Gladstone himself, confided to an associate:

"Never print what I say in my lifetime, but that mummy caused the War [World War I]."

The spirit of the cat priestess was exorcised by two British psychics in a secret ceremony at the museum on the evening of January 1, 1921.

In the autumn of the same year, the most historic discovery in modern Egyptology was made: Tutankhamen's tomb. When the director of the expedition, Howard Carter, arrived in Luxor[18] in October, he bought a pet to keep him company in his off-site house—a canary in a golden cage. When seeing the bird for the first time, Carter's Egyptian excavation foreman exclaimed, "Mabrook—it's a bird of gold that will bring luck. This year we will find *insh-Allah* [God willing] a tomb full of gold!" Indeed, within a week the crew uncovered the door to King Tut's tomb.[19]

Overjoyed, Carter telegrammed his expedition sponsor, Lord Carnarvon, in England. A short time later he went to meet Carnarvon in Cairo before proceeding with the dig. In his absence, Carter left his house and his pet canary with his right-hand man, archaeologist "Pecky" Callender. One afternoon Pecky, hearing a fluttering and squeaking in the next room, hurried in to find a king cobra consuming Carter's canary. Returning to Luxor to resume the dig, Carter was dismayed to hear the news of his canary and the cobra and became even more troubled when a number of his diggers refused to continue work. King cobras were the sacred guardians of the pharaohs, and their golden images were coiled on the headdresses of royal coffins.

A few weeks after the cobra-canary incident, on the night of November 26, 1921, Carter, Callender, and Carnarvon secretly penetrated King Tut's tomb. The relics they discovered were countless and dazzling. Lord Carnarvon later said he was particularly taken by "a beautiful little thing . . . a cat with a pink tongue. I could scarcely take my eyes off it." As for Carter, he reported being spellbound by the guardian statue of Anubis, the dog god, in front of the sealed treasury door.

Early the following March, Lord Carnarvon died from an infected insect bite to the face. At the moment of his passing, there was an electrical blackout in Cairo lasting three minutes, which the power company could not explain. At the very same time, back on Carnarvon's estate in England, according to his

---

[18] Centrally located a few miles from Thebes, hometown of the cat priestess; and a few miles from Abydos, the dog necropolis.

[19] In honor of their employer's pet, the diggers dubbed it "the Tomb of the Golden Bird."

son Lord Porchester, his dog uttered a terrible howl, sat up on his hind legs, and also expired.[20]

In the years that followed there were twenty-five more deaths that were attributed to the curse of Tutankhamen and his guardian pet gods. They ranged from the death of Arthur C. Mace, keeper of antiquities at the Metropolitan Museum of Art, who helped Carter break through the wall of the funerary chamber; to that of Dr. Evelyn White, also one of the first to enter the grave and who survived twenty years before hanging herself. Her suicide note read: "I have succumbed to a curse which has forced me to depart from this life."

The curse aroused famous skeptics and believers. In the second group was Sir Conan Doyle, Sherlock Holmes's creator, who twenty years earlier wrote that most famous ghostly dog story, "The Hound of the Baskervilles."

THE FURTHER SIDE
TAILS OF THE UNDEAD—I

Providing ample proof of the Egyptian belief in afterlife, many a mummy, as we know, has walked.

But not just human mummies.

Documented accounts of pet resurrection abound even to the present day.

> • 1983—U.S. Christine Harrison's Chihuahua, Percy, was run over by a car. Christine's father, Bill, buried Percy in his backyard. Three days later Bill's dog, Micky, disinterred Percy (with whom he, Micky, never got along before). He began licking the Chihuahua's body feverishly. Percy resurrected.

[20] One of the canine guardians in Tut's tomb was Upuaout—"The Opener of Paths" through Pharaoh's enemies, who is always depicted standing on his hind legs.

Micky was named Pet of the Year by the animal charity Pro-Dog.

• July 1983—Pleasanton, CA. A local vet put down Katrina, a tabby cat, by lethal injection. He placed Katrina's corpse in the deep freeze. Two days later Katrina showed up at her home two miles away. The vet had no explanation for the family.

• 1990—Saverna Park, MD. Mugsy, a four-year-old Jack Russell terrier, was run over by a car. His master, Glen Maloney, a restaurant worker, had no question about his condition: "He died in my arms. I know a dead dog when I see one. This one was real dead."

Maloney and his family buried Mugsy in a nearby woodlot that night. His little girl, Megan, said a prayer for the terrier.

The family was awakened by a racket at the door around dawn the next morning. Mugsy was standing there covered with dirt. "His little tail was wagging at ninety miles an hour," reported Maloney.

"Jack Russells are bred to burrow after foxes," his wife, Viola, later speculated for *People* magazine. "I guess when Mugsy woke up in that hole, he just thought it was another old hole, and he dug his way out, not knowing it was supposed to be his grave."

She gave the dog a bath. "After that, he acted perfectly normal," she said. "Except he slept all day."

(For more, see "Tails of the Undead—II," page 230.)

THE LAST PHARAOH

The last pharaoh of Egypt, H.M. King Farouk (1920–1965), had a few quirks, at least where animals were concerned. It seems that he was somehow haunted by his country's strange and magnificent pet history. He bred rabbits on his bed. His limousine was equipped with a special horn that did not honk but howled like a dog being run over.

And he suffered recurrent nightmares about cats. Big cats in particular.

One morning, after an especially frightful night in bed with his mares and his bunnies, Farouk limo'd directly to the Cairo Zoo and gunned down all the lions in their cages.

Shortly after the event he was deposed by Nasser.

Thus the Age of the Pharaohs and the Pyramid Period officially came to an end.

II.
THE GOLDEN
RETRIEVER
AGE

Man is the two-legged animal without feathers.

Plato, 390 B.C.

Here is your man.

**Diogenes (AKA the Dog), to Plato,
handing him a plucked cock**

THE EARLY GOLDEN
RETRIEVER AGE

The disposition of noble dogs is to be gentle with people they know and the opposite with those they don't know.... How, then, can the dog be anything other than a lover of learning since it defines what's its own and what's alien by knowledge and ignorance?

PLATO, *THE REPUBLIC*, BOOK II

Being pagans and pantheists, the Greeks and Romans were as crazy about animals as the Egyptians. Still, each group did have its preferences. The Egyptians, mysterious, aloof, and otherworldly, tended to be Cat People; the Greeks and Romans, reasonable, gregarious, and down-to-earth, tended to be Dog People and adjusted their legend accordingly.

The Greeks said canines were forged by Vulcan, the god of fire, and that their god of medicine, Asclepius, had been suckled by a bitch. The Romans, on the other hand, went one better: they insisted that their founder, Romulus, son of Mars, had been suckled by a she-wolf.[1]

---

[1] The tradition of divine babies with animal foster parents was ancient: Zeus himself was suckled by the she-goat Amalthea; Hippothoos by a mare; Thyro by cows; Telephus, son of Hercules, by deer; Iamos was fed honey by serpents. The tradition continues to the present day: in 1982 an infant orphan from the Philippines, Zoel Zacarias, was saved from starvation by a mongrel bitch who nursed him for more than a year. Historically, suckling has been a two-way street. During the Middle Ages virgins were said to have nursed unicorns. In the Far East, the seventeenth through the nineteenth centuries, the divine Pekingese of the Manchu queens had their own human wet nurses.

Moved by their dogs' openness, big-heartedness, and liberal-ism, the early Macedonians and Etruscans naturally became egalitarians. They founded progressive governments not just for the favored few, but representing the warp-and-woof of society. Because the "noble dog" was a "lover of learning" and "a beast worthy of wonder," Plato recommended that it be the guardian of his ideal Republic. (The philosopher surely kept abreast of current canine news, too: in 400 B.C., a watchdog at the Temple of Aphrodite, according to Plutarch, captured an art thief after chasing him twenty miles.)

In 390 Plato's friend Xenophon wrote *Cynegeticus,* the first and very popular treatise on Greek hounds. In fact, so well loved were canines by writers and academics of the day that Diogenes of Sinope, that great thinker who lived in a bathtub, took the nickname "Kyon." Kyon meant dog. Based on his nickname, Diogenes founded one of the greatest ancient schools of philosophy: the Cynics, AKA, the Dog Thinkers.

As for ordinary Greeks, they weren't so much interested in the minds of dogs as in their more practical abilities in hunting and sports. Great hunters and sports fans, the Greeks were partial to the sporting group, especially early retrievers. The Romans, on the other hand, were partial to the working group, especially shepherds (for herding stock), hounds (for tracking runaway slaves), and mastiffs (for Christian control).

But what of cats during the Golden Age? Unfortunately they received less than the regal treatment of the Pyramid Period. In Greece, the mouse was sacred to Apollo, so the favorite feline pastime was pooh-poohed there. In Rome, though the goddess of liberty had a feline at her feet, and legion banners bore the feline, the cat's retiring life-style did nothing to popularize it. So the emperors put the group to work in the Colosseum.

But the milestone pet dates of the early Golden Retriever Age do not just involve our two favorite species—as we see now, there were also historic developments with cocks and bulls, a heifer, a woodpecker, a tortoise and eagle, a unicorn, and twenty thousand Carthaginian war elephants. . . .

Dateline	**Milestone**

1200 (B.C.) Argos, Odysseus' dog, recognizes him when, after twenty years, the hero returns from the Trojan War disguised as a beggar. Argos wags his tail, then dies.

1000 First bullfights in Greece and Crete featuring Dionysian and Minoan matador/priests.

776 At the first Olympic Games in Olympia, Greek sprinter Milo is devoured by wolves after he carries a heifer through the Olympic stadium, then eats her in one sitting. (See "The Thrill of Victory, the Agony of No Treat," page 78.)

760 Homer writes *The Iliad* and *The Odyssey,* the first Greek literature to include dogs.

753 Romulus and Remus found Rome after being suckled by a she-wolf and fed by a woodpecker.

700 Pomeranians, pugs, and Pekingese are brought to the West by Phoenician dog traders.

600 Egyptians ban the export of cats.

Phoenicians run a black cat market, fencing Egyptian *maus* to Romans, Gauls, Celts.

550 Aesop writes his fables: "The Boy Who Cried Wolf," "The Dog and the Shadow," "The Dog in the Manger," "Belling the Cat," and "The Cat-Maiden."

500 Carthaginian adventurer Hanno describes the gorilla after sailing to Africa.

490 Greek naval admiral Themistocles introduces Persian cockfighting to Athenian sports fans.

480 The dog of Xanthippus (Pericles' father) swims alongside his galley all the way from Athens to Salamis, where the Greeks defeat the Persians in the most decisive sea battle of the Persian War.[2]

---

[2] Later, Xanthippus buries his faithful dog on a hillside called Cynossema (Dog's Grave).

456   Playwright Aeschylus is killed by a tortoise dropped on his head by an eagle.

450   Greek historians Herodotus, Ktesias, and Megasthenes record sightings of animal people, especially "dog-headed men," in the Far East and Ethiopia.

405   Greek historian Ctesias reports sighting the Monokeros—the unicorn. His description: "White body, purple head, blue eyes. Single horn, one cubit in length: red at tip, black in middle, white below."[3]

403   Playwright Aristophanes writes *Wasps*, in which Labes, a mongrel, is tried for stealing cheese.

325   Alexander the Great meets Diogenes, the Cynic, and asks him if he can do him a favor. The Dog's reply: "Yes. You can move out of my sunshine."

324   Alexander, his horse Bucephalus, and his Indian hound, Peritas, conquer the world. Alexander names an entire city after his dog. (See "Profiles in Currage: Alexander's Peritas," page 61.)

   While conquering the world, Alexander captures many animals and sends them back to his former tutor, Aristotle, at work on the world's first zoology text, *Historia Animalium*.

228   First Punic War: Carthaginian general Hamilcar Barca and his army are trampled to death by wild bulls stampeded by the Romans at Ilici.

216   Second Punic War: Carthaginian general Hannibal stampedes the Romans with twenty thousand elephants at Cannae.

---

[3] Authorities later speculated that what Ctesias saw was an Indian rhinoceros.

PNN EYEWITNESS EXTRA!
SOTER, SAVIOR OF CORINTH

456 B.C.—CORINTH.

When the ancient Mediterranean city was invaded one night, fifty watchdogs fought off the attackers. All died but one, who ran to wake up the soldiers, who then mustered and successfully repelled the invaders. The hero, Soter, was given a pension and a silver collar with this inscription:

> *To Soter, defender and savior of Corinth, placed under the protection of his friends.*

Profiles in Currage
ALEXANDER'S PERITAS
336–323 B.C.

The activity of dogs in human warfare dates back to the earliest ages.

The Babylonians and Assyrians drafted mastiffs, which they called "Biters of the enemy." The Persian kings Xerxes and Artaxerxes deployed against the Greeks and Egyptians armies of fearsome Indian hounds descended, according to historian Pollux, from those of Actaeon.

Herodotus wrote that the Persian king Tritantaechmes, in addition to his eight hundred stallions, sixteen thousand brood mares, and countless war horses, marched with a standing dog army so huge that it took four towns to feed them when they bivouacked.

Philostratus says that when Alexander the Great's general, Ptolemy II, became monarch of Egypt, his triumphal parade included twenty-four hundred mastiffs.

Finally, Pliny the Elder tells us that the king of the Garamants was rescued from prison by an elite canine SWAT team that included his two hundred finest recruits.

As we will soon see, dogs were a decisive factor in future military engagements from medieval dynastic struggles, to the conquest of the New World, to our modern wars. In World War I, seven thousand Allied dogs were killed in action. In World War II, eight dogs, three horses, thirty-one pigeons, and one cat received the highest Allied animal decoration: the Dickin Medal for Valor. Can there be any question, then, about pet participation in the very first world war of history?

In the cases of many ancient kings and conquerors, very little reliable information about their dogs survives. So the pet historian must piece together the few available tidbits, then rely on sober conjecture. On that basis we try now plausibly to reconstruct the story of Alexander the Great and his Indian hound, Peritas.

Alexander may have been given Peritas as a puppy by his tutor, Aristotle, who certainly had good connections with Phoenician dog traders. The young prince probably called the puppy the Greek equivalent of "Perrie."

When Alexander turned twenty in 336 B.C., his father, Philip of Macedon, was assassinated by Theban guerrillas. We know that for sure. But what exactly happened right afterward is sketchy. According to unconfirmed but reliable sources, Peritas vanished, and his young owner posted signs around Macedonia.

Lost Dog!!!
"Perrie"
Big, Black, One White Sock (left rear).
Very Friendly.
Reward for Return or Info!
Call Alexander the Great
Macedon 8-1212

When he had no calls, he set out looking. He finally tracked down Peritas in Thebes, where the hound had (here again, no surviving documents discourage the educated guess) arrested Philip of Macedon's murderers. Alexander crushed the town, renamed it after his best friend, and appropriated the country.

Soon his pet was off again. This time the young monarch tracked him down in Persia, subdued more towns, took booty, and appropriated that country as well.

In this manner, history's greatest military team conquered the known world in less than a decade.

Alexander died of fever in 323 B.C. after a night of drunken revelry in Babylon. His remains, and probably Peritas's, too, were pickled in a vat of honey, a common Eastern burial technique.

OTHER FAMOUS FURRY FIGHTERS

Just as Alexander the Great was an inspiration to military men from Caesar to Napoleon, Rommel to Schwarzkopf, so Peritas was the same to future dauntless pawsoldiers.

- In 1504, Conquistador Vasco Núñez de Balboa took Panama with his legendary war dog, Leoncico (Little Lion). So terrified were the Indians of Leoncico that they threw down their weapons and fled at the very sight of him. After the New World conquest, the mastiff was promoted to the rank of lieutenant and drew a crossbowman's pay. (See "Profiles in Currage: Balboa's Leoncico," page 145.)
- In 1560 Queen Elizabeth I put down an Irish rebellion with the help of eight thousand mastiffs in spike collars and full suits of chain mail.
- Airedale Jack, a black-and-tan stray, fought with the Allies in World War I and died carrying a message that saved the Sherwood Foresters battalion from decimation. Jack was decorated posthumously.

• Rin Tin Tin was rescued as a puppy from an abandoned dugout in France by American airman Lee Duncan. Between 1923 and his death in 1932, the German shepherd starred in over forty movies that made millions and rescued his studio, Warner Brothers, from bankruptcy.

• Judy, an English pointer, was the mascot of a British gunboat patrolling the Yangtze River during the World War II Malay-Singapore campaign. Later she was taken as a POW with RAF commander Frank Williams. When she, Williams, and others escaped, their boat was torpedoed and Judy helped save her drowning comrades.

• Rob, War Dog #471/322, a black-and-white mongrel, served with the Special Air Service in Italy and North Africa during World War II. He made more than twenty parachute jumps behind enemy lines. On retirement in 1945, Rob was presented with the Dickin Medal for Valor.

• In 1978, a stray, Rats, wandered into the English army barracks in Ulster and was drafted. Rats fought valiantly in foot and air patrols against IRA terrorists. Later the hero was decorated and retired to an undisclosed location near Kent to protect him from IRA assassins.

Nor were all war heroes pooches, as we see from a few concluding cases:

• Cher Ami, a homing pigeon with the U.S. Expeditionary Forces, served in the French infantry in World War I. He delivered his last SOS under heavy German artillery fire. The bird sustained eye and chest wounds and his leg was blown off, but he brought home his message and saved his battalion. Cher Ami was decorated with France's highest award for gallantry: the Croix de Guerre.

• When Albert Marrs enlisted in the South African army in World War I, his pet baboon, Jackie, became a regimental mascot. Jackie was later wounded in action, his leg had to be amputated, and he was promoted to the rank of corporal. In 1919 the baboon rode a captured German tank in the lord mayor of London's Victory Parade.

FIVE-STAR FIDO

Stubby, a bullterrier, became the highest-ranking dog in the history of the U.S. Army. His master, Corporal Conroy, smuggled him into France with the WWI Expeditionary Forces.

Soon Stubby was in the thick of it, fighting valiantly. He caught a German spy by the seat of his pants, refusing to let go. He warned his brigade of incoming shells in the trenches, hurling himself to the ground, paws over his head. And, though many times gassed and wounded, he fought on.

After the war the terrier shook hands with President Wilson, was photographed with General Pershing, and was promoted to sergeant, outranking his master.

Later, when Corporal Conroy tried to check Stubby into New York's Hotel Majestic, the desk clerk didn't realize with whom he was dealing.

"The Majestic does not permit guests to bring in dogs," he said.

The corporal's reply: "This is no dog. This is a war hero!"

KAMIKAZE CATS
Then and Now

Though canines made fearsome and tireless soldiers throughout the Pyramid Period and Golden Age, felines as a species seemed to be conscientious objectors.

In the annals of early military history there are only two examples of the species effectively contributing to a war effort: in 595 B.C. when the Persians routed the Egyptians by nailing cats to their shields; and in the sixteenth century of the Christian era, when Holy Roman Emperor Charles V dispatched against his enemies toms with poison bottles strapped to their backs. We find an illustration of these kamikaze cats "shedding poison vapours abroad" in Christopher Hapsburg's 1535 report to the military Council of One-and-Twenty at Strasbourg. Hapsburg concluded his battle-cat report with this caveat to the Holy Roman chiefs of staff: "This process ought not to be directed against Christians."

But the experiment must have been less than a complete success since cats went undrafted for the next four hundred years and missed many glorious struggles.

Finally they were called to duty again. The date: 1967. Venue: Vietnam.

The U.S. Army, hoping that feline night vision could be exploited strategically in Southeast Asia, undertook a top secret experiment with "seeing-eye cats." Infantrymen were harnessed to toms and set loose in the jungle after dark.

Here now some actual excerpts from the army's *Unconventional Warfare Report* on the historic experiment:

> *The animals led the troops racing through thick brush in pursuit of mice and birds.*

> *Troops had to force the cats to follow the direction of the patrol; the practice often led to the animals stalking and attacking the dangling pack straps of the soldier marching in front of the animal.*

If the weather was inclement or even threatening inclemency, the cats were never anywhere to be found.

Often when the troops were forced to take cover, the animals took the opportunity to sharpen their claws on the boots of the troops, regardless of the seriousness of the situation.

A number of the troops traded their animals to Vietnamese women for their favors. When questioned about this, the troops claimed that their animals ran away.

THE LATE GOLDEN RETRIEVER AGE

Issa's purer by far than kiss of ring-dove,
Issa's more of a tease than all the maidens,
Issa's worth all the pearls of India . . .
And if in the night she finds that Nature's calling,
Never a spot she'd leave on master's bedspread,
so modest and chaste a little lap dog is she.

MARTIAL, A.D. 90

The poet's words clearly show that the Roman Empire was in decline before the first century of the Christian era. The sporting dog was already being overtaken in popularity by the lapper.[4] But as we will soon see, this was one of the lesser excesses of the age.

One very famous canine in imperial Rome was Zippico the Poodle. Zippico worked for the Theater of Marcellus and, according to Plutarch, tickled Emperor Vespasian with his poison trick.[5] His master would feed Zippico a potion, and the poodle

---

[4] For more on the decadent influence of the fufu, see "Hail the Royal Fufu!," page 127.

[5] At this time in Rome poisoning was very popular with the imperial family: "Everyone has a taster, and the taster has his dog," as the adage went.

would begin to shiver, shake, and stagger—then he collapsed. A moment later, though, he suddenly came to and performed pirouettes around the delighted Vespasian.

The Roman on the street was particularly moved by spectacles of canine devotion and heroism. The historian Pliny tells us about the hubbub when a beheaded man's body was thrown into the Tiber and his pet tried to save it:

> *The dog swam after, and made all the means he could to bear it up afloat that it should not sink: and to the sight of this spectacle and fidelity of the poor dog to his master, people ran forth by heaps out of the city to the river's edge.*

Now some other highlights of the Late Golden Age:

Dateline	**Milestone**
45 (B.C.)	Cleopatra gives Caesar a giraffe when he visits Egypt. He brings the giraffe to Rome.[6] Starts a zoo at the Circus Maximus.
43	Flamingo tongues become the favorite delicacy in Rome. (Formerly Romans were vegetarian.)
25	The poet Virgil turns his country estate into a tax-exempt burial ground by holding a funeral for a dead fly, complete with pallbearers and eulogies. The cost of the ceremony: $100,000.
5	Jesus is born in a Bethlehem stable. According to Italian legend, Mary's cat has kittens at the same time.
40 (A.D.)	Emperor Caligula appoints his racehorse, Incinatus, consul.
60	Pliny discusses werewolves in his thirty-seven-volume *Historia Naturalis*. The creatures are also discussed by Herodotus and Dionysius the Carthusian. (See "The Fur Side: Werewolves," page 104.)

---

[6] For more on royal giraffes, see "The Last Royal Giraffe," page 182.

63   Emperor Nero—a pyromaniac, minor violinist, and matricide—wears the skins of leopards and jaguars to state banquets and dresses his horses in gilded togas.

64   Nero sets Rome on fire, reportedly fiddles during the blaze, then accuses Christians of arson and feeds them to his big cats.[7]

79   Pliny dies in Pompeii during the eruption of Mt. Vesuvius while collecting further pet stories for his *Historia Naturalis*. (Nineteen hundred years later the famous Pompeii art exhibit goes on international tour. It features the *Cave Canem*—Beware of Dog! —mural.)

80   The Roman Colosseum opens. Five thousand elephants, elk, hyenas, hippos, giraffes, lions, and tigers are killed in the first hundred days. (See "PNN's Monday Nite Super Bowl: The Thrill of Victory, the Agony of No Treat," page 78.)

300   Emperor Diocletian abdicates the throne, moves to the Dalmatian coast with his pets where he builds a nine-acre palace and finds peace growing cabbages.

523   Last recorded animal games are held in the Colosseum.

ANIMAL DIVINATION
The Seven Pet Sciences

The ancients believed that the activities of their pets in dreams, no less than waking life, were prophetic. This superstition went beyond black cats and rabbits' feet. In the Near East a popular talisman against demons was a

---

[7] Soon afterward Nero crucifies Peter upside down (at Peter's request) for snubbing his court magician, Simon Magnus, and pestering Romans door to door on Sundays.

card bearing the names of the Seven Sleepers—good Muslim boys who fell asleep in a cave while in hiding from the wicked emperor Decius—plus the dog Katmir, who guarded them for their 309-year snooze. In Rome the charm that guaranteed good luck and protection from the evil eye was a fish-shaped stone phallus inscribed with the words *Hic Habit Felicitas,*[8] which a family hanged from the front gate.

Kings went ahead with coronations, legislation, and civic programs only in the presence of favorable signs. Generals attacked, retreated, and held fast according to the same principles. The average citizen did not leave the house without consulting the sky and the disposition of his pets.

Most ancient sciences were divinatory. Scientific centers were widespread: Cumae, Delphi, Egypt, Erythrea, Hellespont, Libya, Persia, Phrygia, Samia, Tiber. Experts at the centers were excitable premenstrual women with familiars. Many sciences were practiced, but the seven most important involved animals —especially dogs, cats, and livestock—and often the sacrifice of them:[9]

1. Extispicy: Prophesy based on animal entrails, especially intestines, liver, and spleen.[10]

2. Kephalonomancy: Prophesy based on the color and vein pattern of the boiled head of an ass.

3. Scapulomancy: Prophesy based on the cracks in the shoulder bones of sheep.

4. Alectromancy: Prophesy based on the movements of a black hen in a circle.

5. Ornithomancy: Prophesy based on the song and flight of birds.

---

[8] "Happiness dwells here."

[9] Animal sacrifice was the norm in the ancient world. It continues today. In 1992 the Supreme Court rendered a milestone decision in the case of *Church of Lukumi Babalu Aye* vs. *City of Hialeah, Florida.* It overturned a ban on Lukumi Babalu Aye animal sacrifice. The church practiced *santeria,* a four-thousand-year-old ritual involving the dismemberment of chickens, pigeons, doves, ducks, goats, sheep, and turtles.

[10] Examples: Black intestines twisted to the right = increase in family. To left = loss of money. Torn recently = discord. Torn long ago = renewed harmony.

6. Ololygmancy: Prophesy based on the howling of dogs.

7. Onieromancy: Prophesy based on pet dreams.

Onieromancy was especially important. Generally speaking, if you dreamed about a dog, this portended friendship and faithful love; if you dreamed about a cat, treason and deceit. But there were many exceptions to the rule, depending on the exact type of the canine or feline dreamed of, its color, its activity. Here is a brief index:[11]

DOG DREAM

Dog, gray or black =	misfortune
Dog, white =	victory
Dog, yellow =	ruin
Dog, red =	discord or war
Dog, mad =	enmity
Dog, barking =	good omen
Dog, howling =	bad omen
Fox , dead =	triumph over cunning
Wolf =	suffering, adversity
Bitch =	joy, satisfaction

CAT DREAM

Cat, walking alone =	journey by water
Cat, mewing =	petty slanders
Cat, scratching =	deceit or rain
Cat, purring =	hypocrisy of a relative
Cat, angry =	quarrels
Cat, dead =	danger escaped
Tiger =	very bad news
Jaguar =	very, very bad news
Lion =	powerful adversary

[11] Sources: Artemidorus, Thylbus, Desormes, and Basile. And Professor Enigma.

Meaning of Other Pet Dreams

Ant =	activity, health
Bat =	torment, peril
Bear =	awkward friend
Bee (stinging) =	bother, check
Bee (dead) =	loss of money
Camel =	hard work
Cock =	early success
Turkey Cock =	serious mistakes
Duck =	anonymous letter
Flies =	teasing
Frog =	indiscretion
Goose =	insincere compliments
Hen (one, pecking) =	ruin
Hens (several) =	scandal, gossip
Horse (white) =	wealth, success
Horse (gray or piebald) =	unquiet life
Oysters =	easy and sure profit
Mule =	business difficulties
Rat =	hidden enemies
Snail =	slander
Snake =	vendettas and deceit
Spider =	lawsuit, betrayal
Worms =	little worries

The importance of these ancient sciences cannot be underestimated since few ancient rulers or generals ignored their warnings. For this reason, animals had a major hand in the course of the first four millennia of human history, from the smallest events to the very greatest.

> • After finding Peritas in Thebes, Alexander the Great
> reportedly dreamed of oysters (easy and sure profit),
> a cock (early success), and a dead fox (great triumph).
> So, he decided to press on.

Only a few ancients were ahead of their time and took all this for what it was: chicken feathers.

• On the night before the Ides, Caesar dreamed of a turkey cock (serious mistakes), geese (insincere compliments), and one hen, pecking (ruin). The next morning, shrugging it off and ignoring his wife Calpurnia's raving, he went to the Senate carrying only his rabbit's foot, lucky bean, and *Hic Habit Felicitas* phallus. He was, according to Plutarch, stabbed twenty-three times by the Republicans and once in the groin by Brutus.

PNN UPDATE

FAMOUS LATER PET PROGNOSTICATORS

We have no evidence of how Caesar's dog or cat was behaving on that fateful morning. But we do know that his successors, the Augustan emperors, began to watch their pets even more closely in the next four hundred years during the rash of imperial poisonings, stabbings, and strangulations.

Animal divination by no means died out with the fall of pagan Rome. The tradition was carried on throughout Europe and the Americas by many remarkable clairvoyant pets.

• Marocco, an Elizabethan horse, performed telepathic feats with dice for Shakespeare, Ben Jonson, Sir Walter Raleigh, and many other gentlemen of the age.
• Lady, a mare from Richmond, Virginia, predicted Harry Truman's victory in 1948, located missing persons, and was studied by parapsychologists J. B. and Louisa Rhine, who pitched a tent outside her famous red stable. The mare first gained national recognition in 1927 when she predicted that Dempsey would KO Starkey in the early rounds of their heavyweight fight.
• Jeane Dixon's Mike the Magicat, rumored to be the psychic's deep-throat in Washington, materialized on

the White House grounds twice during the Truman administration. The first time, Mike was sent back to his mistress by presidential limousine. On the second occasion, Ms. Dixon was called and told to pick the cat up herself.

• Chris the Wonder Dog, a beagle mix, owned by Mr. G. N. Wood of Warwick, Rhode Island, could subtract, multiply, divide, and do roots. He predicted weather and winners of the Triple Crown. He scored 100 percent on a Zener Card telepathy test administered by Duke University parapsychologists Dr. J. Gaither Pratt and Dr. Remi J. Cadorer.

• Rolf, a stray dog adopted by a German attorney Jutzler Kindermann, did arithmetic, square roots, and predicted the Mannheim earthquake of 1917.

• Redsey, an Irish setter, refused to go fishing with his master before the infamous hurricane of 1938. His master stayed home. Six hundred others were killed.

• Missie the Psychic Dog of Denver, a Boston terrier, could tell how many coins were in a purse or beans in a bag. Nine months before the 1966 World Series, the bitch predicted not only the winner, but the scores of each game. Also able to tell time, in the end Missie moved the hands on her toy clock to eight o'clock and pointed this out to her mistress. At exactly eight that evening, the Psychic Dog of Denver choked to death on her dinner.

• After the 1991 San Francisco earthquake, researchers at the San Francisco Zoo asked for reports of any strange inmate activity beforehand. Nancy Schofield, zoo staffer, said Pachy, a twelve-year-old orange-and-black house cat who lived in the elephant house, kept clear of the building on October 16 and 17. When carried in, she dashed back out.

OREGON'S BOB, THE WEATHER CAT

Continuing the ancient tradition of divination, Bob, a sixteen-pound gray tom, is a meteorologist for KATU-TV, Portland, Oregon, Channel Two. The weather cat's attire for his forecasts: sunglasses and sailor suit for sunshine; earmuffs and scarf if he's predicting snow. On Christmas he dresses as Santa, on St. Patrick's Day as a leprechaun. When the Bolshoi ballet was in town, Bob donned a tutu and dancing slippers.

Recently, when a tidal wave warning was on the wire, KATU, not wanting to seem light-hearted, pulled Bob from his usual Friday night slot. The station was flooded with calls.

According to David Apple, the feline's coanchor at the weather desk, "By seven o'clock the switchboard was jammed. One lady said, 'I just want you to know you ruined my evening because I invited six couples over for a Bob party!' "

Bob has a line of bumper stickers, buttons, and greeting cards. To date he has received four thousand letters and several marriage proposals.

Says Paul Linnman, KATU anchorman, "You really have to keep your ego in check when you realize a cat is getting more mail than you."

ALL THE PRESIDENTS' PETS - II
THE PAMPERED

As we have seen, pets of antiquity were pampered, if not worshiped. Tyrants seemed to have an especially soft spot for their most faithful subjects. Emperor Caligula provided his race-horse, Incinatus, with an ivory stall, a marble bed, and a golden drinking goblet and allowed him to host his own orgies. On the nights before his races at the Circus Maximus, Romans were under strict orders to keep quiet lest they disturb the stallion's sleep. Emperor Nero provided all former royal racehorses with a retirement package that included a generous oat allowance. Sixty years later, Emperor Hadrian held a state funeral for a pal-ace guard dog as a reward for a lifetime of exemplary service.

But what of our presidents two millennia later by way of contrast?

If he's the presidential dog, he will be treated like a king, won't he?

NEWLY ELECTED RICHARD NIXON, OF KING TIMAHOE, HIS IRISH SETTER

The Washington Children's Museum commissioned a royal doghouse for the Reagans' King Charles spaniel, Rex. Its de-signer, Theo Hayes, great-great-grandson of President Ruther-ford Hayes (himself a master of five dogs, four cats, four canaries, a mockingbird, and a goat), described Rex's accom-modations: "White clapboard with a cedar shingle roof. I didn't do it feminine or prissy. It's not as if I was [sic] doing it for a French poodle or a Chihuahua. There are draperies of red fabric . . . and on the wall are pictures of Ron and Nancy in acrylic frames."

When the British burned Washington during the War of 1812, the First Lady, Dolley Madison, escaped the White House with our nation's two most valuable articles: the Declaration of Inde-pendence and her pet parrot. The bird was taken to safe asylum at the Octagonal House, the French ambassador's residence, and remained there until the British were expelled from the capital.

While he was being impeached, Andrew Johnson confessed to his private secretary, William Moore, that he had been feeding mice under the table at the White House. "The little fellows gave me their confidence," he told Moore, "so I gave them their basket and poured some water into a bowl on the hearth for them."

Warren Harding threw a White House birthday party for his Airedale, Laddie Boy. The guests: congressional dogs. The menu: Milk-Bone layer cake.

One evening, Will Rogers was invited to the White House for dinner with Calvin and Grace Coolidge. He later had this to say about the experience:

"Well, they was feeding the dogs so much that at one time it looked to me like the dogs was getting more than I was. The butler was so slow in bringing one course that I come pretty near getting down on my all fours and barking to see if business wouldn't pick up with me."

President Coolidge also had a favorite cat, Tiger. In 1928, the tom slipped out of the White House and disappeared in Washington on romantic business. The Secret Service couldn't find him anywhere. At wits' end, the president turned to the airwaves and desperately appealed to Americans to help him find the First Feline. He had him back the next day.

All the Johnsons had the same initials, including LBJ's dog, Little Beagle Johnson. "It's cheaper if we all have the same monogram," explained the president. He grew very attached to LBJ, Jr., and later, when Jr. died, LBJ had him cremated and kept his ashes on top of the refrigerator.

Little Beagle was replaced by Yuki, and the president soon became very attached to this little dog also. When his daughter Luci was married, he insisted Yuki be included in the photograph of the wedding party. "We can't have a family portrait without him," he declared. But the First Lady, Lady Bird, put her foot down, calling in Yuki's handler.

"Mr. Bryant, get the dog out of here right now. He will not be photographed!"

PNN MONDAY NITE SUPER BOWL

The Thrill of Victory, The Agony of No Treat

Two things only the masses anxiously desire—bread and circuses.

JUVENAL, A.D. 80, ROMAN SATIRIST WHO WAS LATER EXILED FOR PANNING EMPEROR DOMITIAN'S FAVORITE CIRCUS ACT

The Romans were great sports fans. And animals were the stars in their two most popular spectacles: chariot racing at the Circus Maximus, and gladiatorial games in the Colosseum featuring personae non grata and large carnivores.

The Colosseum was the home of history's first bowl games. In hosting these bowls, the Romans, a most practical people, were killing three birds with one stone:

1. They were gainfully employing wild animals for the first time, big cats in particular.

2. Rather than overcrowding their prisons, they were handling shoplifters, POWs, illegal aliens, and people who were simply annoying in a way that sent a strong message to the riffraff.

3. They were providing the honest citizen a place to unwind on the weekend.

The first bowl action took place in 274 B.C. in a makeshift amphitheater. It featured a sprinkling of stray mastiffs, scrub bulls from Capua, and a ragtag assortment of bread thieves and AWOL Carthaginians from the Punic involvement.

Two hundred years later the franchise had greatly improved. Quality athletes were being imported from as far away as North Africa, pro spring training camps were widespread,[12] and leagues had a full summer and fall roster.

The main Roman Colosseum, or Big Bowl, was started by Emperor Vespasian (the fan of Zippico the Poodle) and finished by his son Titus in A.D. 80. Four stories high, 617 feet long, 512 feet wide, with a capacity for 45,000 fans,[13] the structure featured blood gutters, twenty lion gates, marble festival seating, and senatorial boxes.

At the Colosseum gala opening, Emperor Titus provided, according to historian Suetonius, "a most lavish gladiatorial show . . . and a wild beast hunt, 5,000 beasts of different sorts dying in a single day." Special professional beast killers, called the Bestiarii, were employed. The emperor and crowd demanded that the Bestiarii dispatch their prey *crudeliter*—with the right degree of cruelty.

After premiere week, the sack rate at the Colosseum wound down to five hundred or one thousand bulls, bears, lions, tigers, elephants, hyenas, hippos, giraffes, and so forth per day and about twice as many shoplifters, POWs, illegal aliens, and annoying people. (At an average of 1,000 pounds per beast, and 150 pounds per person, this came to 650,000 pounds of flesh processed daily.)

The franchise was a resounding success.

Shortly after the completion of the Big Bowl, however, an outfit arrived from the Eastern conference that didn't seem to

---

[12] In spite of some contract disputes, pros were by and large content, especially after Commissioner Crassus ended the Great Players' Strike of 72 by crucifying six thousand, plus the ringleader, a net-and-javelin man by the name of Spartacus.

[13] The Colosseum was later expanded to hold one hundred thousand, making it the largest amphitheater in the world until the construction of the Yale Bowl in 1914. (See "Mascots: Yale Handsome Dan Dynasty," page 86.)

want to play ball. Instead of grabbing the gusto, they knelt down, folded their hands, and gazed heavenward. Which was irritating to sports fans, not to mention the big cats.

BEAR TALK
Yesterday and Today

T he sports philosophy of the Bestiarii and the lions, tigers, and bears who met in the original Big Bowl was later summed up by Notre Dame coach Knute Rockne: "Show me a good loser, and I'll show you a loser."

In this light, it is interesting to note the parallels between the words of ancient and modern Bears, Lions, Saints, and a few commentators.

> *What pleasure can it give a civilized man to see a feeble human creature torn by a powerful wild beast?*
>
> **CICERO, 60 B.C.**

> *Butkus was unbelievable. I love to see—and listen—to him play. On the sound track of the Bears films, Butkus—when he's going after somebody—sounds like a lion chewing on a big hunk of meat.*
>
> **DOUG PLANK, A.D. 1972, CHICAGO BEARS DEFENSIVE BACK, ON FORMER BEARS LINEBACKER DICK BUTKUS**

> *So Laureolus, hanging on no unreal cross, gave up his vitals defenseless to a Caledonian bear. His mangled limbs lived, though the parts dripped gore.*
>
> **MARTIAL, *EPIGRAMS*, A.D. 80, OF ARENA FATE OF A STEALER (BUT NOT FROM PITTSBURGH)**

> *I won't mention the name of this particular team we were playing, but at half-time we came in, pulled off our socks, and began putting iodine on the teeth*

marks in our legs. Coach Bob Zuppke said, "I'll tell you one thing, if we ever play this team again, it'll be on a Friday."

RED GRANGE, NOTRE DAME (THE FOOTBALL TEAM)
GREAT, QUOTED IN *SPORTS ILLUSTRATED*,
DECEMBER 8, 1958

I am as the grain of the field, and must be ground by the teeth of the lions, that I may become fit for His table.

ST. IGNATIUS, FIRST CHRISTIAN MARTYR OF ARENA,
BEFORE BEING THROWN TO THE LIONS, A.D. 110[14]

When he goes on a safari, the lions roll up their windows.

MONTE CLARK, FORMER DETROIT LIONS COACH, ON
RUNNING BACK LARRY CSONKA

King Nebuchadnezzar to Daniel: "Daniel, has your God whom you serve continually been able to save you from the lions?"
Daniel to Nebuchadnezzar: "Long live the king! My God sent His angel to shut the lions' mouths!"

DANIEL, 6:21–22

I'm not mean at all. I just try to protect myself.

MIKE DITKA, FORMER COWBOY TIGHT END AND COACH
FOR THE BEARS

He plunged his hunter's spear also in a headlong-rushing bear, the king of beasts beneath the cope of Arctic skies; and he laid low a lion, magnificent, of bulk unknown before, one worthy of Hercules' might;

---

[14]Among others whom the lions later made fit for the Lord's table: Saint Prisca, Saint Martina, Saint Potitus, Saint Eleutheria, Saint Maximus, Saint Vitus, Saint Crescentina, Saint Modesta, and the New York Giants during the 1935 NFL Championship game.

and with a far-dealt wound stretched in death a rush-ing pard [panther].

MARTIAL, *EPIGRAMS*, OF CARPOPHORUS, A STAR BESTIARI

I'm for the upperdog. I was for the underdog because I was one. Now I see the pressures that are on the upperdog. When you get to be an upperdog, you know the scratching and the clawing and the grabbing that everybody underneath does.

BART STARR, FROM *QUARTERBACKS HAVE ALL THE FUN*, BY DICK SCHAPP

There! You see, Your Worship, a child might play with Tommy now. Come and pet him!

ANDROCLES TO THE ROMAN EMPEROR, AFTER THE EMPEROR HAS CALLED HIM A "DAMNED FILTHY LITTLE DOG OF A GREEK TAILOR" FOR MAKING FRIENDS WITH THE LION TOMMY IN THE ARENA (FROM *ANDROCLES AND THE LION*, GEORGE BERNARD SHAW, 1912)

PNN HARD COPY!
MAN-EATERS

With virtually all other wildlife, there's no question who's on top of the food chain. But when you're face to face with a bear, it's not so clear-cut. It makes you reassess your place in the universe.

BRUCE BATTEN, 1993, ASSISTANT DIRECTOR U.S. WILDLIFE SERVICE, ALASKA

Man-eaters have been common down through the years, not just in the Golden Ages of the Colosseum.

In 774, several centuries after the close of the Roman arena, creatures that reportedly looked like wolves but had horse ears devoured scores of men, women, and children in Abdin Rock, a Persian town. Between 1447 and 1450, villages outside Paris were terrorized by a pack of marauding vulpines led by a man-eater called Courtaud. Courtaud and his pack massacred hundreds until they were at last ambushed by farmers in front of Notre Dame Cathedral and dispatched with sickles and axes. Three hundred years later, young women from Languedoc, France, were ravaged by the Wild Beast of Gevaudan, a hyena/tiger mix. The *St. James Chronicle* reported that the beast was killed by a Monsieur Beauterme on September 20, 1765, and that its body was sent to King Louis XV at Versailles, himself an avid sportsman.

Today, man-eaters are becoming troublingly common. In the last decade there has been a dramatic increase in attacks. Colorado game officials called the 1993 camping season "the summer of the bears from hell." In 1992 the number of "DPL"— "defense of life and property"—bear shootings in Alaska reached 102 (not counting the estimated 200 to 400 unreported cases), almost double the previous annual average. Western state wildlife experts report that mountain lion maulings are ten times more frequent now than between 1909 and 1932. Nor is this just an American problem. During a four-month period in 1988 in the Sundarban forest of southwestern Bangladesh, an unprecedented sixty-five people were eaten by tigers.

But, after all, this is the wild. What about news from the city, the suburbs, and today's lions' dens?

- On May 6, 1993, Alfred Rias, a young man in fatigues, climbed into the lions' den at the Bronx Zoo. Zookeepers managed to distract two 350-pound African lions and coax Rias back out. The modern Bestiari emerged with only superficial wounds. NYPD took him downtown for routine questioning and a drug test.
- Not so fortunate was eleven-year-old Juan Perez, who was mauled to death by polar bears in 1987 after sneaking into their cage and swimming in their pool at Prospect Park Zoo in Brooklyn, New York.

• In the same year a show leopard bit dancer Juliet Prowse during rehearsal for the TV special "Circus of the Stars." Suffering only a minor injury, Prowse returned hours later to pet the leopard. In a related show business mishap a short time later, an African lion posing with model Shannon Audley clamped its jaws on her head. Audley sustained minor lacerations.

• Less fortunate was Ms. Darcy Staver, thirty-three, of Lake Louise, Alaska. On July 7, 1992, an eleven-year-old black bear broke into her cabin and chased her onto the roof. The 175-pound assailant climbed a tree beside the cabin, flushed Ms. Staver off the roof, ran her down, and terminated her.

• In 1986 the Indian government introduced twenty-five thousand Varanasi carnivorous turtles into the Ganges. The turtles are part of the Ganga Action Plan to clean up India's holy river, which has become badly polluted with the thousands of bodies thrown into it annually. Indra Prakash Yadav, deputy range officer for the Ganga turtle breeding farm, reports that the reptiles—three feet long, forty to fifty pounds as adults—have done a good job. "It's been smooth sailing. We don't see many dead bodies in the river anymore." [15]

MASCOTS
The Hall of Fame

Now the days of the Colosseum have returned. Though pets are no longer players, teams are named after species, and a real member is on the sidelines with cheerleaders.

Now and then, in spite of precautions, there is a déjà-vu to

[15] French wildlife authorities are reportedly less pleased by their current man-eating turtle situation. In 1993 French newspapers were running such headlines

the Golden Age of the arena. In 1980, just before game time, students from Tulane University sneaked onto the LSU campus and unlocked mascot Mike the Tiger's cage. Moments later LSU's professor of vet medicine, Sheldon Bivin, bagged the big cat in Bernie Moore Stadium with a tranquilizer gun.

"I was a bit scared," Bivin confessed afterward, having experienced the same rush the Bestiarii had with their javelins and bows. "There is no doubt Mike would have killed anyone he came upon."

Modern mascots, as we know, are usually bengals, bears, wolves, or other such creatures as were popular in the Roman arena.[16] But not always.

There are the Richmond U Spiders; the Henry College Wasps; the Scottsdale Artichokes; the UC Santa Cruz Banana Slugs. The UC Irvine mascot is the anteater. Their cheer when the giant myrmecophaga lumbers out onto the field before kick-off:

"Give 'em the tongue! Zot! Zot! Zot!"

Here now a brief catalog of the legendary modern mascots of the gridiron:

CAM THE RAM V
COLORADO STATE UNIVERSITY

CSU had seven straight seasons in the cellar during the reign of Cam the Ram. Deciding that the goat was hexed, the team proposed raffling Cam's head. Before the sentence was carried out, the goat allegedly died of natural causes. His epitaph reads as follows:

---

as MUTANT TURTLE TERROR THREATENS RIVIERA BEACHES! During the early 1990s teenage mutant Ninja turtle craze, an estimated three hundred thousand to one million *Chrysemys scripta elegans,* or red-eared slider turtles, were imported to French pet shops from the United States. Parents and kids got tired of them and took them out to the beach. Now bathers are being attacked.

[16] Of the approximately 250 teams in NCAA College Football Schools today there are thirty-one cat teams (Lions, Tigers, Wildcats . . .); fifteen dog (Bulldogs, Huskies, Terriers); fourteen bird (Eagles, Falcons, Gobblers); eight hoofer (Rams, Bisons, Broncos); and seven bear (Grizzlies, Goldens, Bearkats).

Here lies Cam the Ram
His soul should go to heaven,
He's lived through seven years of hell.

UGA THE WISE, BULLDOG
UNIVERSITY OF GEORGIA

Boasting a career record of 77-27-4, UGA IV—AKA "the Wise" —was UG's winningest mascot and treated accordingly. Before opening kick-off, the bulldog was pulled to the fifty in a Roman red chariot, then retired to an air-conditioned booth beside his team's bench.

Civic-minded, UGA was the 1984 chairdog for the American Cancer Society's Great American Smoke-Out. He did volunteer work for the March of Dimes, the Humane Society, and many Bulldog Clubs. And attired in white collar and black bow tie, he chaperoned Herschel Walker to the 1982 Heisman Memorial Trophy banquet.

One of the more memorable highlights of UGA's career came before the game with UG's great rival, South Carolina. The bulldog jumped from his red chariot, proceeded to SC's end zone, and relieved himself during the National Anthem.[17]

HANDSOME DAN DYNASTY, BULLDOGS
YALE UNIVERSITY

The Handsome Dan dynasty at Yale is now celebrating its 103rd anniversary. Like Caesar himself, the Great Dan I presides over the trophy room, stuffed. However, the reign of his successor, Dan II, was marred by scandal: before the 1934 Harvard-Yale clash, he was kidnapped[18] by Harvard students and photo-

---

[17] The bulldog has been equally confrontational with UG's other great rival in the southern conference, Mississippi State. Before meeting UG in 1991, Miss's football coach made his team watch a bull castration as a "motivational" experience.

[18] Other kidnapped mascots of the time knew greater indignities, especially in the southwestern conference. After a particularly stunning defeat to Texas A&M, Bevo, University of Texas's longhorn steer, was abducted by the Aggies and branded with the losing score. Some reports had it that he was barbecued.

graphed licking burger grease off the boots of John Harvard's statue.

The last great Dan, Dan XIII, who recently retired, made everyone forget those bad days. He was penpals with Millie Bush, had lunch with alumnus George, and in the summer he vacationed on the Jersey shore. During the season, Handsome was all work. He red-dogged Princeton cheerleaders and was once booted from a Harvard game for attacking a mounted policeman.

Dan's tricks were nothing to sniff at either: he could stand on his hind legs and jump through a Hula-Hoop. Last but not least, he rolled over and played dead when asked if he would rather go to Harvard.

BILLY THE GOAT
U.S. NAVAL ACADEMY

Navy's Billy dynasty, now celebrating its centenary, has seen some rough times also. The trouble started in 1899 when Billy I, AKA Cid the Kid, was kicked by Army's mule. According to one witness, the West Point mascot "hoisted that astonished goat toward the Navy stands to the delight of the yelling, laughing crowd." Cid the Kid reportedly died of shame not long afterward.

Fifty years later the Billy dynasty was rocked by the three "Great Goat Capers":

- Great Goat Caper of '52: Billy was kidnapped by U of Maryland frat boys and photographed by *The Washington Post*'s Bob Burchette, who, following an anonymous tip, tracked the goat to a garage in Glen Burnie.
- Great Goat Caper of '53: Army cadet commandos infiltrated Billy's abode, chloroformed the goat, and spirited him across the Severn River to a getaway car.
- Great Goat Caper of '72: This time Billy XVIII and King Puck, his understudy, were deep undercover at a dairy farm in Gambrills, Maryland. Army's strike team,

led by head cheerleader, Bob Sansone, was led to the secret location by the Point's homecoming queen, Gina Johannsen. Sansone said he located Billy's stall "by smell." Over the next forty-one days, he dragged the goat from one safe house to the next. Finally the Corps of Cadets ran a full-page ad in both *The New York Times* and *The Washington Post*. The ad featured a photo of the hostage and, above it, this message:

HEY, NAVY! DO YOU KNOW WHERE YOUR "KID" IS TODAY?
And under the photo:
THE CORPS DOES.

P.S. The current Billy—the XXVI—is kept under even tighter security. And, so that his scent will never again give him away to kidnappers, Navy's goat is regularly doused with dog cologne.

"The smell is very close to Chanel No. 5," says Billy's personal beautician, Terry Packard.

SCHOTTZIE 02

In the Golden Age, if the commander in chief himself, the Roman emperor, couldn't be present for a season opener, a homecoming general was called upon.

The tradition survives today. When General H. Norman Schwarzkopf returned from Desert Storm in 1991, he was asked by Marge Schott, owner of the Cincinnati Reds, to throw out the first ball at Riverfront Stadium. He wrote a note, declining, but he sent his best to Schott's St. Bernard, Schottzie 02, the Reds' mascot. "Give my regards to Schottzie," wrote the general, a pet lover and the owner of a Labrador retriever. He signed the note "Schwarzie."

On March 21, 1993, *The New York Times* reported that Schottzie had been banned from baseball along with her owner. No single reason for the ban was given, but certain Cincinnati Reds did object to stepping in Schottzie's business on the field. Her owner bristled, "I get chewing gum on my shoes! They should be happy I don't have a horse, right?"

Following their dismissal, Marge Schott married Schottzie to the mayor of Cincinnati's Groucho. A full ceremony was held. The bride wore a lace veil. Her maid of honor (Schott) and Groucho's best man (the mayor) said "I do" for the couple.[19]

Other than spending time with her new husband, the ex-mascot of the Cincinnati Reds appeared in TV ads for her mistress's local car dealerships.

"We'll bow-wow you with our great deals," guaranteed Schott, standing next to Schottzie 02 (who wore a Reds cap). "These are the doggonedest deals in town!"

MODERN PET ATHLETES
Record Holders

The other very popular Roman pet arena was the circus. If the Colosseum was the adult, R-rated amphitheater featuring the ancient equivalent of *Satyricon* meets *Cujo* —live, then circuses were the G alternative, the *Ben Hur* meets *Jurassic Park,* where the Roman could bring the kids.

Each major emperor built his own circus: Caesar had his Circus Maximus, Caligula his Circus Gai, Domitian his Circus Agonalis. Attendance was even better than that at presidential libraries now. The main attractions here were chariot races and animal shows. Occasionally there was extra excitement: in 60 B.C. twenty elephants stampeded into the stands, and Consul Pompey had to send in a garrison of barbarian gladiators to dispatch them.

---

[19] When the couple returned to the majors in late 1993, the Reds threw a surprise homecoming party. The owner was showered with red roses while being serenaded with a lively rendition of "Hello Dolly"; the mascot was given a bone. The walls of the Cincinnati office were spangled with greetings such as "Welcome Back Mrs. Schott!!!" and "A Paws-I-Tively Big Welcome Back Schottzie!"

For more pet weddings, see "Love in the Time of Collara," page 267.

Today, racetracks and circuses are widespread, providing opportunity for many modern pet performers and athletes. Shows and events are diversifying, and we now have an all new sporting group. Here are a few recent dog stars:

- Bob Curtis's Ballyregan Bob is the fastest greyhound in history. Now in retirement and living on cornflakes and Kit Kat bars, Bob earns $1,000 a time covering bitches.
- Alex Stein's Ashley Whippet is billed as "the Babe Ruth of Frisbee dogs." Stein's training secret? Since puppyhood, Ashley was fed all his meals in a Frisbee.
- Brutus, a St. Bernard, holds the world record in deadweight hauling—5,220 pounds.
- Lee LeCaptain's King Arthur, AKA Artie, billed as "the World's Most Intelligent Dog," is a champion log roller and deepwater diver: the seven-year-old Lab dives to twenty feet and can hold his breath three minutes.
- Robin Marien's shelty, Rocky, a surfer, hangs twenty in the pipe and was a recent California Grand Hotdogging champ.

Not all modern pet champs, however, are canines. *Sports Illustrated* ("Faces in the Crowd," January 7, 1993) recently honored the following track and field record holders from circuses, "olympiks," and frog-jumping jubilees around the nation.

Athlete:	Hammy Faye Bacon. Pig, 8-month-old.
Hails from:	Picnic, Florida. Robinson's Pig Racing Farm.
Event:	150-yard dash.
Record:	17.5 MPH: 420 wins in 630 starts.
Treat:	Oreo cookie for each victory.

Athlete:	Get Up. Frog, 7-year-old.
Hails from:	Sacramento, California.
Event:	Broad jump.
Record:	19 feet 11 inches

Title:	Broad Jump/Triple Hop Grand Champ of Calaveras County—Jumping Frog Jubilee.
Treat:	A kiss from his jockey, Bob Yost.

Athlete:	Slick Willie. Mallard drake, 9-month-old.
Hails from:	Bosque Farms, New Mexico.
Event:	Waddle sprint.
Record:	.90 of a second (6-foot course).
Treat:	A pat from his trainer, Robert Duck.

Athlete:	Batley. White domestic gobbler, 10-month-old.
Hails from:	Sharon, Connecticut.
Event:	Turkey Triathlon: Dash/High Jump/Slalom.
Record:	Dash (50 foot)—15.2 seconds.
	High jump—3½ inches.
	Slalom (50-foot course, 8 gates)—finishes third behind turkey triathletes Kris Kringle and Zsa Zsa.
Title:	Triple medalist at Live Turkey Olympiks, New Preston, Connecticut.

THE LAST HERCULES

The dens of the amphitheatre disgorged at once a hundred lions; a hundred darts from the unerring hand of Commodus laid them dead. . . . Neither the huge bulk of the elephant nor the scaly hide of the rhinoceros could defend them from his stroke. Ethiopia and India yielded their most extraordinary productions; and several animals were slain in the amphitheatre, which had been seen only in the representations of art, or perhaps of fancy.

EDWARD GIBBON, *THE DECLINE AND FALL OF THE ROMAN EMPIRE,* **1788**

The reign of Commodus marked the beginning of the end of the Golden Age, at least as far as the pet historian is concerned.

Lucius Aelius Aurelius Commodus came to the throne in A.D.

180 as a nineteen-year-old. Taking his divine status as emperor very seriously, he dedicated himself to one agenda: proving himself the son of Hercules, the legendary animal slayer.

According to his historian, Dion Cassius, the young tyrant regularly went one-on-one with lions. He opened the fourteen-day spring Ludi (Games) of 190 by shooting a hundred bears from the railing of the imperial box, plus some elephants, tigers, and hippos. Then, after lunch, he went mano a mano with gladiators (whose noses and ears he reportedly collected as trophies).

A certain Greek wrestler by the name of Narcissus did pets a favor in A.D. 192 when he strangled Commodus in the baths.

Two hundred years later, Emperor Theodosius converted to Christianity and, striking at the heart of pagan excess, outlawed bowl action. But by that time half the league was extinct—the hippos of Nubia, lions of Mesopotamia, the tigers of Hyrcania. In short, the Ludi weren't like they used to be. And the Golden Age was hearing its swan song.

III.
THE
DARK
AGES

God give to me by Your grace what You give to dogs by nature.

Mechtilda de Magdeburg, thirteenth-century hermitess

Qui me amat, amet et canem meum.
("Love me, love my dog.")

St. Bernard, A.D. 1150, "Sermo Primus"

THE DARK, DARK DAYS

After the Huns, Goths, and Vandals got through pillaging Rome, there was a brief lull in cultural activity. Humanity didn't exactly know what to do next civilizationwise. The Pyramid Period and Golden Ages were hard acts to follow, and every Elks, Lions, and Shriners group seemed to be waiting for their neighbor to start something new and interesting. After a few decades of suspense, the Church, seeing no other volunteers, took the papal bull by the horns.

The history and religious roots of the early Roman Church are of course beyond the humble scope of a pet history. Suffice it to say here that its doctrine, as we know, was based on Dogma and Catechism.

The three architects of doctrine—Peter the fisherman; Paul the tent maker; and St. Augustine the former Colosseum fan, womanizer, and pear thief—each did a good deal of traveling and did not have time for pets. Still, each made an important contribution to dogma on such issues as fidelity, obedience, damnation, and grace.

But what, after all, did this have to do with pets?

Where in pagan times some had been worshiped as incarnations of gods, in the Dark Ages they were believed to be servants of the Devil himself (popularly represented as a goat—the former Greek god of nature, Pan).

Of all the seven pet epochs, the Dark Age was the most fantastic, because it was the most superstitious. Many of its events were stranger than fiction, as we see from this first dateline—The Dark, Dark Days:

Dateline	Milestone
420 (A.D.)	St. Augustine develops a theology of werewolves. (Later, St. Bonaventura and St. Thomas Aquinas elaborate.) (See "The Fur Side: Werewolves," page 104.)
550	St. Patrick changes Vereticus, king of Wales, into a werewolf.
565	First sighting of the Loch Ness monster by Abbot St. Columba. His description: *"A fearsome beast: like a huge frog, but not a frog."*
613	Frankish queen Brunhilde, age eighty, is dragged to her death behind wild horses stampeded by her crazy nephew, Clotaire I of Neustria.
800	Charlemagne, son of Pepin the Short and Bertha Big Foot, is crowned Holy Roman Emperor. His first official act: He outlaws cathouses.
856	French historian Bertin reports a Black Dog attack on the Trier Church. (See "The Further Side: Black Dogs, Green Dogs, and Magical Moddey Dhooes," page 107.)
940	Pope John XII turns the Basilica of St. John Lateran into a cathouse. Later he is beaten to death by an irate parishioner while sampling the services.
943	Hatto II, archbishop of Mainz, Germany, is eaten alive by mice.
1300	Publication of *William of Palerne,* a popular Gothic thriller: the queen of Spain, a witch, turns her son, the prince, into a werewolf, and the spell is broken by hero William of Palerne.
1350	Half the human population of Europe is wiped out by the Black Plague. The continent is overrun by Asian black rats infected with Asian fleas.

1400   Cats are nearly extinct because of pet inquisitions. (See "The Great Pet Inquisitions," page 98.)

1420   Holy Roman Emperor Sigismund convokes a council of theologians on the alarming epidemic of werewolves.

1431   Joan of Arc and her familiar are burned as witches at Rouen.

1484   Pope Innocent VIII officially calls for the execution of all witches' familiars, thus beginning the Cat Reign of Terror.

1522   With the blessing of Pope Leo X, bulls are sacrificed in the old Roman Colosseum to appease devils during a renewed outbreak of the Black Plague.

Catt, catt, God send thee a blak shott,
I am in a cattis likeness just now,
But I sal be in a womanis liknes ewin now.
Catt, catt, God send thee a blak shott!

**CHANT OF A MEDIEVAL WITCH WHO
TURNED HERSELF INTO A CAT IN FRONT
OF HER INQUISITORS**

THE GREAT PET INQUISITIONS

*The familiars of Witches do most ordinarily appear in
the shape of Cats, which is an argument that this beast
is dangerous to soul and body.*

EDWARD TOPSEL, *NATURAL HISTORY* (1658)

*Avaunt, malignant enchanters!
Avaunt, ye witchcraft working rabble!*

DON QUIXOTE, TO CATS THAT LEAP ON HIS NOSE

The most incredible events of the Dark Ages relate to the
pet inquisitions.

In the year 1233, Pope Gregory IX called the first
pet purge. Cats, birds, wolves, and even insects were tried in
ecclesiastical courts as witches and heretics. Most were excom-
municated and tortured, many publicly executed.[1]

In 1310, members of the Knights Templar confessed, after
torture by agents of Pope Clement V, that they worshiped the
devil in the form of a black cat.

In 1386, a judge in Falaise, France, found a local pig guilty of
killing a little girl willfully, with forethought. The convict was
dressed in the child's jacket, conveyed to the town square,
drawn and quartered, then hanged. (The executioner was given
six sous and a pair of gloves so he wouldn't soil his hands
while dispatching his duty.)

In 1400, St. Vitus' dancing epidemic overtook Metz, Switzerland. A knight drew a sword and crucifix on a black cat. The cat
vanished, and the dancing stopped. For the next century, on
the anniversary of the exorcism, felines were flayed alive.

In 1557, Queen ("Bloody") Mary I burned cats as Protestant
heretics. Her Protestant successor and half sister, Queen Elizabeth I, burned cats as Catholic heretics.

If these events seem to stretch credibility, consider the fol-

---

[1] Among those singled out for justice: In the year 1225—eels; 1389—horses in
Dijon; 1405—oxen; 1451—rats and leeches in Bern and Lausanne.

lowing actual and fully documented cases from the official court dockets of the age:

Double Indemnity

Time: 1100
Jurisdiction: Pleyben, Briton.
Defendant: A local tomcat, seven years old.
Charge: Murdering his master.
Evidence: a) The tom's master was found in bed, his throat cut.
b) When the local sheriff arrived at the murder scene, he found the cat next to the body, about to pounce. (A local farmer, trying to frame the cat, had tied a thread to the victim's wrist, strung the end through a window, and was shaking the lifeless arm gamely.)
Verdict: Guilty. (The judge concluded that the cat had been closing in for the final kill when the sheriff arrived.)
Sentence: The tom was burned at the stake.

(Note: It was also popularly believed that if a tom wasn't killed before turning seven years old, he would indeed kill his master.)

Porklet Pardon

Time: 1457
Jurisdiction: Savigny, France.
Defendants: A sow and her "six little porklets."
Charge: "Willfully and feloniously" murdering Jean Martin, a five-year-old.
Defense: The sow was not provided with counsel.
Verdict: Guilty.
Sentence: The sow was publicly hamstrung in the town square.

(Note: Though her piglets were apprehended at the scene of the crime, splattered with little Jean's blood, the court found them innocent of aiding or abetting their mother in the foul deed. As a result they were remanded to the custody of a local lady.)

Cockadoodle-Do . . . or Don't?

Time:	1474
Jurisdiction:	Basel, Switzerland.
Defendant:	A local rooster.
Charge:	Laying a yolkless egg.
Defense:	The rooster's attorney did not deny the charges or contest the popular belief that such eggs could, with the help of witches, hatch into winged snakes. Instead, he argued that his client did not lay the egg with premeditation.
Verdict:	Guilty—Satanic Possession, first degree.
Sentence:	The rooster and his egg were burned at the stake.

(Note: Two centuries later, after much debate over the case, a heretic French biologist read a paper to the Academy of Sciences asserting that the rooster was in fact a sick hen.)

Underground Justice

Time:	1519
Jurisdiction:	Stelvio, Italy.
Defendants:	Moles.
Charge:	Killing crops.
Defense:	The moles' attorney, Hans Grienebner, argued that his clients, compensating for any damage they may have unintentionally done, ate bugs and mulched the soil.
Verdict:	Guilty.
Sentence:	Exile to the next county.

(Note: The judge promised the moles safe conduct out of town "and an additional respite of fourteen days to all those which are with young, and to such as are yet in their infancy.")

Joint Tenants

Time:	1713
Jurisdiction:	Brazil.
Defendants:	Termites.
Charge:	Eating the local Franciscan monastery—food, furniture, and holy articles.

Defense:	Counsel for the termites praised their industry. He also insisted his clients had prior claim to the land, having lived there longer than the plaintiffs.
Sentence:	The court ordered the friars to give the termites their own parcel of property.

(Note: The order was read to the termite hills by the court stenographer.)

DEAD CAT CALENDAR

The precedent-setting medieval case against cats was this: Diana, queen of the witches, had once turned into a cat, slept with Lucifer in this form, and borne him Aradia. Later the cat women Diana and Aradia taught people witchcraft and devil worship.

Throughout the Middle Ages there were regular cat incinerations in most towns and hamlets on the holy days. Some affairs were more grand than others and featured Mardi Gras revelry. Here is a calendar of the dead cat galas in France.

Time	**Place**	**Festivity**
Shrove Tuesday	Vosges, France	Burning
Lent	Ardennes	Burning, boiling, and flaying
Easter	Alsace	All of above plus Chinese fireworks.
Midsummer Gala[2]	Place de Greve, Paris	Baskets, barrels, and sacks of flaming cats.
Autumn Solstice	Ypres	Town fool climbs town tower and hurls cats into the square, kicking off the harvest season.

(The last festivity, especially popular, continued until the first part of the twentieth century.)

---

[2] This event was customarily attended by the king himself. In 1648, Louis XIV, a famous cat hater, danced around the pyres.

PNN UPDATE
THE BLESSINGS OF ST. FRANCIS

The Church has relaxed its pet policy since the Dark Ages:

• In 1987 Italian nun Sister Florence Christina, claiming God spoke to her through her parakeet, petitioned for release from her Bologna convent to preach throughout the world. The petition was granted.

• On April 9, 1989, Gary E. Maier, rector of All Saints Church in Mineola, New York, conducted a blessing of animals that was attended by more than six hundred parishioner pets and their owners.

• For nearly a decade New York's Cathedral of St. John the Divine has conducted an annual blessing of animals for the October Feast of St. Francis. Thousands of pets attend, mostly dogs and cats. But there are exceptions. In 1989 a bowl of algae was consecrated. In 1992, the Very Reverend James Parks Morton, dean of the Cathedral of St. John, blessed an orangutan.

• On October 7, 1992, *The New York Times* reported that Mary McCormick-Sakurai arranged for an animal mass in Manhattan's Madison Square Park in an effort to ease hostilities between dogs and squirrels. But a "pre-emptive blessing," apparently the work of dog owners, was made a few hours before hers.

HOLY CATS

Miraculously, felines survived medieval pet purges. Today we have no cat witches, but we do have some saints:

• In 1986 a female tiger from Burma was to be slaughtered and its organs sold as magical aphrodisiacs.

Local Buddhist priests interceded and bought the tiger for $10,000, claiming that she had become a Buddhist. They sent her to Kaohsiung Zoo to convert the other animals there.

• In 1988 a stray tabby cat wandered into a Buddhist temple in Kuala Lumpur, Malaysia, and was declared a bodhisattva.

• A Mrs. Baily adopted a marmalade kitten, Rogan, from the Cat Protection League of London. Ten years later, in 1981, Rogan became a British TV network Star Cat of the Year. Soon the tom turned to faith healing. By the laying on of paws, he cured everything from blindness to slipped disks to Key-Gaskell syndrome. Mrs. Baily began bulk-mailing Rogan's fur to sufferers throughout the world. Later, the Japanese did a documentary film about the magic cat, and cameramen and crew walked backward in his presence.

PNN EYEWITNESS EXTRA!
KATTESTOET

Since 1955 the Belgians have held the Kattestoet—the Cat Parade. Celebrated on the second Sunday of every May, the event commemorates the cat inquisition, which ran from the tenth century till 1817 in Belgium.

The parade features giant papier-mâché cat floats depicting characters such as Pietje Pek (Little Peter the Devil). Jesters fling stuffed cats into the crowd. Elaborately costumed medieval royals such as Emperor Charles V lead the procession.

THE MATAGOT

In fifteenth-century Europe there lived a rare and treasured breed of feline, the Matagot—the magic cat. It was believed that Matagots brought fame and fortune to their owners. One such enchanted creature was owned by Dick Whittington, a poor boy from Gloucestershire who grew up to become the Lord mayor and richest man in London.

THE FUR SIDE
WEREWOLVES

You may recognize the fiends by these marks: they are pale, their vision feeble, their eyes dry, tongue very dry, the flow of saliva stopped . . . and they linger about the sepulchres till morning.

**MARCELLUS SIDETES, WEREWOLF EXPERT
FROM "ON LYCANTHROPIA" (A.D. 151)**

The werewolf in its cruelty, savageness, and treachery typifies the eternal enemy of the lamb, and by the Lamb is symbolized Our Lord and Savior Jesus Christ.

**FATHER CLAUDE PRIEUR (1587),
DEMONOLOGIST/WEREWOLF EXPERT**

Tales of people who took furry form abounded during the Dark Ages, worldwide. In Greece there was the wereboar. In Abyssinia and the Egyptian Sudan, the werehyena. In Java, Borneo, and Malaya, the wereleopard and tiger. In the

Orient, the werefox, the werebadger, and even the were-dog.

But none has been more abundantly and chillingly documented than the lycanthrope—the werewolf. Their man-to-monster transformations and scourges have been discussed by the scholars and historians of every age—from Paracelsus, Herodotus, and Dionysius the Carthusian to Petronius Arbiter, Marie de France, and St. Thomas Aquinas.

The greatest name in werewolf history is St. Hubert. On Good Friday of 680, Hubert, at that time a pagan, was out hunting. Suddenly a stag appeared to him with a crucifix between his antlers.[3] His dogs would not attack. Hubert converted to Christianity, later became the bishop of Liege, and restricted his hunting to the enemies of the lamb. He reportedly kept a very large kennel of hounds specially bred for werewolf tracking and which are said to have been the forebears of dachshunds.

After St. Hubert passed away in 727, werewolves rallied, and by the fifteenth century the species was epidemic. At that time, Holy Roman Emperor Sigismund convoked a council of theologians in Frankfurt to discuss the problem. Packs of the creatures were regularly invading towns on All Saints' Day, St. John's Day, and Good Friday. Scores were tried and executed. The most famous wolf trial was that of the French wildmen, Pierre Burgout and Michel Verdun, who were delivered to the flames in December 1521.

The scourge continued through the seventeenth century and climaxed in 1685 with the celebrated case of the weremayor of Ansbach, Germany. A voracious wolf, who was soon positively identified as the hamlet's deceased mayor, ate many local women and children before he was finally ambushed and gunned down. The townspeople of Ansbach cut off the wolf's muzzle and strapped to its head a wig, a beard, and a mask of

[3] St. Eustace was said to have had much the same experience several hundred years later, though his stag's rack bore Christ himself. (The buck was painted by Il Pisanello in 1450.)

the former mayor. Then they lashed the politician to the blades of a windmill. Later they installed his pelt in the town hall as a sober reminder to all of the reality of bloodsuckers.[4]

Throughout the Dark Ages clerics and demonologists—Bishop Binsfeld, Bartolomeo Spina, and St. Bonaventura, among many others—vigorously debated the lycanthrope question. Meanwhile pragmatists tried to devise a cure. Here was the most popular werewolf antidote of the age:

- Strike the creature three blows on the forehead with a knife.
- Abstract three drops of blood.
- Salute him with the Sign of the Cross.
- Shift his belt buckle to the ninth hole.
- Fling in his face a boiling broth of herbs, toads, and fungus.

If this did not work, the fiend was impaled on an aspen spike or shot with a bullet blessed in a chapel dedicated to St. Hubert. (Since in certain locales such chapels were few and far between, experts later decided that a silver bullet would suffice in emergencies.)

---

[4] Though werewolves are apparently less common today, there is some evidence that their numbers are increasing, like those of vampires. (According to the Vampire Research Center, the current world vampire population stands at 810, the majority—550—residing in the United States.) In addition to the many Wildman and Iron John camps cropping up nowadays, lupine retreats, designed for the man who wants to unleash the animal inside, are becoming popular and priced for volume. Wolf Haven in Tenino, Washington, for instance, offers a one-night howl-in for $6.

THE FURTHER SIDE

BLACK DOGS, GREEN DOGS, AND MAGICAL MODDEY DHOOES YESTERDAY AND TODAY

This mischief thus wrought, he flew with wonderful force to no little feare of the assembly, out of the church in a hideous and hellish likeness.

ABRAHAM FLEMING, REPORTING IN *A STRAUNGE AND TERRIBLE WUNDER* THE ESCAPE OF A BLACK DOG FROM THE BLYTHBURGH CHURCH ON SUNDAY, AUGUST 4, 1577, AFTER IT STRANGLED SEVERAL PARISHIONERS AND SCARED OTHERS TO DEATH

The werewolf was not the only creature that haunted the Dark Ages. Its cousin, the Black Dog, was equally common and fearsome.

The Black Dog had many AKAs: On the Isle of Man in the Irish Sea, it was known as the Moddey Dhoo or Mauthe Doog; in Wales, Gwyllgi or Dog of Darkness; in Scotland, the Cu Sith or Fairie Dog. Also, not all Black Dogs were black: the Cu Sith, for instance, was usually green; others were reportedly white, with red ears.

Let's look at a few documented cases:

- The Black Dog of Leeds Castle was thought to be the ghost of Henry VI's aunt, who was imprisoned there for witchcraft in the fifteenth century.
- The White Dog of Newgate Prison mysteriously appeared in the execution chamber for every beheading in the sixteenth century.
- The medieval Mauthe Dog was a ghostly black spaniel that lived in Peel Castle on the Isle of Man. No soldiers dared swear in his presence because it was said that once a drunken trooper uttered an oath, promptly lost his speech, and died three days later.

- Kludde, a goblin shape-shifter, haunted Belgium throughout the Middle Ages. He usually appeared as a werewolf or a winged black dog with a flaming head.
- One of the self-confessed witches at the Salem witch trials (1592–93) claimed that the Devil appeared to her as a brown dog. More than a century later, certain founding members of the British Freemasons reported seeing the devil in the form of a black poodle.[5]

Most modern historians dismiss these magical canines as figments of the medieval imagination. Before the reader over-hastily draws the same conclusion, here now some recent reports:

- In 1893, Essex, England, a man struck a Black Dog in the road with a stick and was instantly burned to ashes, along with his horse and buggy.
- An invisible Black Dog attacked two German shepherds belonging to French author Pierre van Pasen. Van Pasen described the incident in *Eastern Counties* magazine (1901):

They [the shepherds] were snapping and biting in all directions. I had never seen them in such a mortal panic. The battle with the invisible foe lasted less than two minutes. Then one of my dogs yelped as if he were in the death-throes, fell on the floor and died.

- In 1916, Buckinghamshire, England, the headless body of a Black Dog was photographed by Arthur Springer, a retired Scotland Yard inspector.
- In 1953, Reverend Dr. Donald Omand exorcised the Black Dog of Kettleness, North Yorkshire.

Scores of other Black Dog reports have been made in the last century. Among the more common eyewitness descriptions of the creatures:

---

[5] Black Dogs were not restricted to the Old World. The Mayans feared Zote, a winged dog who lived in the House of Bats and sucked blood of the damned.

- HEAD: Sometimes two-headed. Sometimes no head at all.
- EYES: "Red." "Glowing." "As big as saucers."
- BREATH: "Noxious odor." Strikes the face "in hot blasts."
- VOICE: Usually disappears with "a diabolical peal of laughter."

NAUGHTIES AND NASTIES

In spite of these persuasive Black Dog accounts, most pooches of the Middle Ages and later were—like our own now—not in league with the Devil but inclined to get a little touch of the dickens in them occasionally.

History abounds with stories of naughty dogs. Among one of the more famous mischief makers of old was a hound called Boy belonging to Sir Rupert, a confederate of King Charles I. Boy reportedly had some very rude habits, at least as far as the Puritans were concerned. Oliver Cromwell's men piked Boy and Sir Rupert at the Battle of Marston Moor and were delighted.

Here now, a few other notable naughty dogs from days gone by....

In Shakespeare's *Two Gentlemen of Verona,* Launce, complaining of all the trouble his mongrel, Crab, has gotten him into, tells of the time Crab broke wind under the duke's table, causing a hubbub among the company:

> *"Out with the dog!" says one: "What cur is that?" says another: "Whip him out," says the third; "Hang him up," says the duke. I, having been acquainted with the smell before, knew it was Crab, and goes me to the fellow that whips the dogs: "Friend," quoth I, "you mean to whip the dog?" "Ay, marry, do I," quoth he. "You do him the more wrong," quoth I: "'twas I did*

the thing you wot of." He makes me no more ado, but
whips me out of the chamber. How many masters
would do this for his servant?

Launce goes on to tell all the other times he has taken stripes
for his dog:

Nay, I'll be sworn, I have sat in the stocks for puddings
he hath stolen, otherwise he had been executed; I have
stood on the pillory for geese he hath killed, otherwise
he had suffered for't.

Then he proceeds to scold Crab for his worst bit of mischief:

Nay, I remember the trick you served me when I took
my leave of Madam Silvia: did not I bid thee do as I
do? when didst thou see me heave up my leg, and
make water against a gentlewoman's farthingale?
Didst thou ever see me do such a trick?!

A few centuries later, a country parson, Reverend James Wood-
forde, kept a diary record of his pooches' misdeeds.

10 August 1786. One of my Greyhounds (by name
Jigg) go in and ate the whole Charter, with a Cold
Tongue, etc. Sister Pounsett & Nancy mortally vexed
by it.

11 April 1794. One of my Greyhounds, young Fly, got
to Betty Cary's this morning and ran away with a
Shoulder of Mutton undressed & eat it all up. They
made great lamentation and work about it.

1 August 1796. My Dog Ranger killed Knight's favour-
ite Cat!

• • •

Our best friends weren't any less mischievous a hundred years later. Novelist Thomas Hardy had a wire-haired terrier who bit the postman three times and John Galsworthy once. He was also in the habit of jumping on the dining room table and snatching food from guests' forks. According to Hardy's friend J. M. Barrie, creator of *Peter Pan,* the terrier loved the radio, too, and refused to miss his favorite program. Barrie relates how one afternoon the dog accompanied him and Hardy to a local stage production of *Tess:*

> *The dog behaved beautifully until the time came when he knew the wireless would be putting on* The Children's Hour. *It was his favorite item. He howled for it so that even Tess's champion had to desert her and hurry home.*

ALL THE PRESIDENTS' PETS—III
CRAPPERS, SCRAPPERS, AND SNAPPERS

Mr. West, can you come down right away, we have a terrible problem in the Diplomatic Room!

MAMIE EISENHOWER, TO WHITE HOUSE USHER J. B. WEST, AFTER THE FIRST WEIMARANER, HEIDI, HAD AN ACCIDENT ON THE NEW RUG

Historically, the most common naughtiness among First Dogs has involved the White House carpets. Most of the culprits have been Democrats:

• The tradition began with FDR's Duchess: she not only refused to be White Housebroken, she went back to the same spot over and over. Jimmy Carter's Grits also objected to taking his business to the South Lawn. The Kennedys' Welsh terrier, Charlie, once relieved himself on Jackie's leg. LBJ's collie, Blanco, christened an Alexander Calder sculpture on loan to the White House from the Museum of Modern Art.

• There is no record of the Bushes' Millie expressing her feelings for a Mapplethorpe. But she did do a personal hygiene demo for Sam Donaldson during his live ABC interview with the First Lady in the Yellow Oval Room. Donaldson tried unsuccessfully to intervene. "Millie, stop that. We're on national television, Millie!"

• Her predecessor, the Reagans' Lucky, also had a mind of his own. When obedience school didn't improve his manners, he was banished from Washington. Leaving on leash with the president, the First Dog performed his last official act on the runway, in front of Air Force One, and for the cameras.

• Snapping and scrapping were also far from unheard of at the White House. FDR's German shepherd, Meg, bit newspaperwoman Bess Furman on the nose.

• LBJ's Blanco snarled at Lassie and had to be given tranquilizers when the star visited the White House.

• Though President Nixon's dogs didn't bite anyone, his Irish setter, King Timahoe, chewed the carpet in the Oval Office during Watergate.

THE SEMIDARK DAYS

Things during the Dark Ages weren't all bad. In spite of the inquisitions, the plagues, and the feudal wars, some good things were happening, too, shedding a little light on everybody, including pets:

Dateline	**Milestone**
550 (A.D.)	St. Patrick and Pope Gregory Magro breed cats.
560	St. Anthony becomes the patron saint of dogs and cats.

632   Mounted on his winged charger, Alborak, Muhammad reportedly flies to paradise with his dog, Katmir, and his cat, Meuzza.

814   Construction of the first Doges' Palace in Venice.

874   Norwegian colonists bring the Norsk Buhund dog to Iceland.

920   Arab writer Ibn al-Marzubán completes *Fadl al-Kilab (The Book of the Superiority of Dogs over Those Who Wear Clothes).*

936   Magna Cata signed by Howell the Good. (See "The Magna Cata," page 117.)

1010   Ichijo, the sixty-sixth emperor of Japan (986–1011) exiles a dog for chasing his cat, Myobo No Omoto (Lady-in-Waiting), and he imprisons the dog's owner.

1080   First official bullfight, or *corrida,* is staged in Avila, Spain, to honor the marriage of Infante Sancho de Estrada. (Twenty-six years later, another bullfight is staged in honor of the coronation of King Alfonso.)

1174   The first official horse race is run in England under Henry II.

1140   Henry the Lion, son of Henry the Proud of the House of Wolf, rules Bavaria.

1210   St. Francis of Assisi founds the Franciscan order. He preaches to the birds and bees and manages to avoid being institutionalized.

1210   Genghis Khan, according to Marco Polo, hunts with five thousand hounds.

1210   Reynard the Fox outwits Isengrim the wolf, King Noble the lion, Bruin the bear, and Tibert the cat.

1255   German scientist Albertus Magnus writes *On Animals,* based on his dissections of local pets.

1284   The Pied Piper exterminates the rats of Hamelin. Rumor has it that he employs feline assistants.

1300   First European cocker spaniels are glowingly described by Gaston Phebus.

1399   Math, King Richard II's favorite greyhound, escapes when his master is imprisoned. He attaches himself to Henry of Lancaster.

1400   While in the Pevensey Castle pen, Richard translates the greatest hound book of the day, *Livre de Chasse* by French count Gaston de Foix.

LATE GREAT DATES OF THE MKC

(Medieval Kennel Club)

525   *Celts breed the Welsh corgi.*

943   *Howell Dda, prince of Deheubarth (Wales), and Bleggwrdd, archdeacon of Llandaff, divides dogs into two classes:*

   • *"Dogs of High Value": tracker, greyhound, spaniel, bloodhound, covert hound, harrier.*

   • *"Dogs of Lower Rank," or "Curs": mastiff, shepherd's dog, house dog.*

1016   *Danish Canute the Great issues a decree to break the legs of any nonnoble dog poaching in the royal hunting preserve.*

1066   *William the Conqueror introduces bloodhounds to England after defeating Harold at Hastings. He passes a law making purebreds the sole property of "gentlemen."*

Profiles in Currage
DOGS OF DERRING-DO

The pet inquisition notwithstanding, the good dogs and cats of the Dark Ages far outnumbered the bad and even the slightly naughty. Some were no doubt great heroes, though unsung by troubadours who valued their career, much less their head.

But we do know that in the sixth century, King Arthur was followed by his great hound Cavall; and his colleague, Sir Tristram, by the gallant Hodain (AKA Leon). Other knights of the Round Table surely also traveled with doughty dogs who assisted them on chivalrous and holy missions: the slaying of dragons; the rescuing of damsels in distress; and maybe even the tracking of the Holy Grail itself. (The pet historian can only imagine what part dogs may have played in the Guinevere-Launcelot scandal and others.)

In any case, as years wore on and incidents of unsung dog heroism mounted, someone finally had to break the silence.

Who?

The duke of York himself, Edmund de Langley, from his fourteenth-century opus, *Of ye Manners and Condicions of Hounds:*

> *An hounde is trewe to his lord or his maystere, and of good love and vrey (truth). An hound is of greet undirstondying and of great knowyinge, a hounde is of greet strength and greete bounte, an hounde is a wise beast and kynde....*

On that note, now a few heroic tales of dog strength, wisdom, and kindness in the later Age of Chivalry....

Sir Peers Leigh of Lyme Hall, vassal of Edward II, duke of York, was wounded in the Battle of Agincourt on October 25, 1415. His mastiff bitch, though she was pregnant at the time, held guard over the fallen knight as the battle raged around her. She and Peers were carried back to Paris, where Peers died. The bitch saw her master's body safely home, then she had her puppies. They were the first of the Lyme Hall strain of mastiffs.

On a dark night in 1572, Julian Romero, general to King Philip of Spain, sneaked his men into the camp of William of Orange, leader of the Dutch revolt against Philip. William and his soldiers were fast asleep. The only creature in camp with his wits about him was the Dutchman's dog. Sir Roger Williams tells us what happened next in his 1618 account, *Actions of the Low Countries:*

> *William's dogge, hearing a great noyse, fell to scratching and crying, and withall leapt upon the prince's face, awaking him.... Ever since, untill the prince's dying day, he kept one of that dog's race; so did many of his friends and followers. The dogs were white little hounds with crooked noses called camuses.*

Sir Henry Lee never paid much attention to his dog, Bevis. But one night Bevis crawled under his bed and refused to come out. Later, after midnight, a servant crept into the room and tried to rob and murder Sir Henry. Bevis jumped out from under the bed and seized the rascal by the throat, and he confessed all. In 1592, Sir Henry commissioned artist Marcus Gheeraerts to paint his portrait with Bevis. He inscribed the painting with a tribute to his best friend, which ended

> *Only my dog, whereof I made no store*
> *I find more love, than them I trusted more.*

PNN EYEWITNESS EXTRA!
DOUGHTY DRAGON MASTERS MACAIRE

1371—MONTARGIS, FRANCE.

Audbrey de Mondidier was allegedly murdered by Richard de Macaire outside the castle of Montargis. Mondidier's dog Dragon tracked down Macaire, implicating him in the foul deed.

King Charles V, "the Wise," ordered a trial by combat between man and dog. Dragon prevailed, downing the villain in seconds. Macaire confessed and was duly relieved of his head.

THE MAGNA CATA

Welsh king Howell the Good enacted the first British feline law in 936: Anyone who killed, stole, or mistreated a cat was fined one sheep, plus her lambs.

Profiles in Purrage
ST. FRANCIS' BEST FRIENDS

As we have seen, at many times during the Dark Ages, and in all too many places, things were not good for cats. Or for cat lovers. Few God-fearing Christians, especially women, dared admit to consorting with the species for fear of being arrested on charges of sorcery.

In the year 1189 things turned around slightly for felines when Richard I took the English throne and proclaimed himself "the Lion-Heart." This might have been taken for reckless bravado had the king not led the Third Crusade and, under the feline standard, taken the city of Acre.

Twenty years later, bravely risking the suspicion of inquisitors, St. Francis talked openly to cats. According to Italian legend, the saint was indebted to them. The devil once sent mice to disrupt his prayers by nibbling his toes; just as he was about to lose concentration, cats jumped out of his sleeve and gobbled up all the mice but two. And since that day, so the legend goes, felines continue to sit in front of holes in the wall, waiting for St. Francis' tormentors to reappear.

Throughout the Middle Ages, cats did a good deal of ratting elsewhere, especially during the many Black Plague epidemics. The Plague bacteria (*Yersnia pestis*) was carried by the Oriental rat flea (*Xenoipsylla cheopsis*), which in the 1340s emigrated from China to the Crimea to Sicily on Asian black rats (*Rattus rattus*), who themselves were aboard Genoan trading ships.

During the great Black Plague, 1347–51, fifteen million people, half the population of Europe, was wiped out. An untold number of cats, dogs, and other domestic animals, equally susceptible to infection, also perished.[6] The Plague death toll would have been far higher had it not been for the heroism of felines. They worked very hard throughout the rest of the Middle Ages in pest control, and we may well have them to thank for our survival.

Even so, superstitions die hard. In Britain it was believed that if a woman ate food over which a tomcat had jumped and ejaculated, she would bear kittens. In 1654 a Scottish housewife, claiming to be pregnant with kittens, went to court seeking an abortion. Cats were generally associated with fallen women even outside of Europe. Until only a century ago in Turkey, adulteresses were tied in sacks with live cats and cast into the sea.[7]

---

[6] Many were also killed for medicine. A dead pig, goat, or puppy by the bedside was commonly prescribed as a Plague antidote by bleeders and barbers of the time. (See "Dark Age Pet Panaceas," page 119.)

[7] Since the very earliest times cats were also hurled into the rivers of Malaya and Sumatra. But this had nothing to do with witchcraft or easy women: it was a

CURRENT CAT AND RAT STATS

• *Today the British government employs a force of more than ten thousand cats to keep official buildings rodent free.*

• *In 1961 a Borneo rat epidemic was curbed when scores of stray Singapore cats were rounded up, airlifted, and parachuted into the infested countryside.*

• *The greatest mouser in recent history was Towser. At his retirement in 1984, age twenty-four, he had killed 28,899 mice in Glenturret distillery near Crieff, Tayside, England.*

DARK AGE PET PANACEAS

The Dark Age was a germy time. Before Louis Pasteur, barbers, who moonlighted as doctors and vets, hadn't yet made the connection between dirt and germs. They attributed everything to *foul vapors.*

Foul vapors, they thought, came from an imbalance of the humors. Every body had four humors: blood, phlegm, choler (yellow bile), and melancholer (black bile). Each humor made for a mood, and each mood was represented by an animal:

HUMOR	MOOD	ANIMAL
Blood	Sanguine	Rabbit
Phlegm	Phlegmatic	Ox
Choler	Choleric	Cat
Melancholer	Melancholy	Elk

means of making rain. Historically, felines have been rainmakers. The procedure hasn't always involved immersion, though. In Celebres, Africa, the cat is strapped onto a chair, carried around the fields, and dowsed with water.

According to medieval medical science, the four had to be in proper proportion in the system for health: equal parts rabbit, ox, cat, and elk.

If not, the body's humors started secreting foul vapors.

If this happened, the first thing to do was get bled. You could bleed yourself at home with your own leeches, or you could go to the barber and kill two birds with one stone: get a haircut while getting bled.

If you weren't in a better humor after the barber appointment, you went to the pharmacist. In medieval Europe, the blood of a white dog was prescribed for madness; whereas the blood of a black dog was prescribed to ease the pain of childbirth. If you had the bloody flux, dog kidney broth was the antidote (the kidney had to be from a male; broth from bitches was thought to be fatal).

In medieval Asia, the blood of black dogs was used to exorcise demons. In Japan black cats were prescribed for stomach spasms, melancholia, and epilepsy. Throughout the East, it was also customary to put a cat in the room of a dying person since it was believed that one of its tail hairs had the power to revive (the trick was finding exactly which one). Pet remedies also applied to matters of procreation. According to the Chinese historian Ssu-ma, these preparations for impotency were popular during the reign of Emperor Chou-hsin:

- *The Hunting Lion:* Bear paws, rhino horn, and distilled human urine.
- *Celestial Thunder:* one hundred peacock tongues with chili powder and the sperm of pubescent boys.
- *Three-Day Glory:* Soy beans with one ox penis, a dash of ginseng, and a dollop of dried human placenta.

Medieval medical practices in the West were more advanced, particularly those that related to the Bubonic Plague. Pet preventive and therapeutic measures taken throughout Europe for three centuries were these:

• All swallows were killed as disease carriers.
• Other birds were captured, released in sickrooms to absorb foul vapors, then killed.
• The sick were made to drink and wash in bat urine.
• Pigs (whose smell was believed curative) were tethered to the patient's bedside.
• Dried toads were placed over Plague boils.
• The entrails of a young pigeon or newborn puppy were applied to the patient's forehead as compresses.[8]

For any conditions relating to the eyes, cat medicines were the cure if administered carefully, according to directions:

• For sty or swollen eyelid: Pluck the tail hair of a black cat on the first night of the full moon. Place tail hair on affected area till inflammation subsides.
• For blindness: Blow the ashes of a cremated black cat's head into the eyes of the patient three times a day until sight returns.
• For the power to see demons (according to the Jewish Talmud): Burn the placenta from the first litter of a black cat who herself is from a first litter. Work the placenta ashes into a fine powder and rub thoroughly into the eyes.

LIGHT AT THE END OF THE TUNNEL

As we have seen, the Dark Ages for pets had its very dark side, its semidark, and its not-so-dark. Those who made the greatest contribution to the brighter side were the saints, all great pet lovers. They provided the light at the end of the tunnel that led to the Renaissance.

---

[8] A form of the practice persists today in certain areas of Jamaica, Haiti, and the Dominican Republic. Hairless puppies, called "fever dogs," are placed on patients to draw out fever.

The first in the group was St. Jerome. In 375, still a pagan, he had a vision in Turkey and converted. Then he went out to the wilderness and lived with animals for a while just as Moses, Elijah, John the Baptist, Christ, Muhammad, and everybody else had. Then he came back to become the Father of the Church. A lion walked into his study one day, Jerome pulled a splinter out of its paw, and after that he regularly posed with cats for official portraits. The first translator of the Bible was also the subject of this popular nursery rhyme:

> *If I lost my little cat, I should be sad without it,*
> *I should ask St. Jerome what to do about it,*
> *I should ask St. Jerome just because of that*
> *He's the only Saint I know that kept a pussy-cat.*

But, in fact, there were others. Many others. St. Yves, St. Gertrude of Nivelles, and St. Agatha (AKA St. Gato—or *"cat"*) became official puss patrons. St. Patrick energetically bred felines, as did Pope Gregory Magro, the Celtic monks, and the ascetic Carthusians.[9]

The canonized canine situation was similar. St. Bernard was crazy about dogs. So were St. Francis, Mechtilda de Magdeburg, and many others. Later in the Middle Ages, fraternal orders began breeding watchdogs. In the fourteenth century the artist Andrea da Firenze painted a famous fresco depicting Dominicans guarding the gates of heaven with their holy mastiffs. The piece was entitled *Dominicanni*—the "Dogs of God."

Accordingly, when Pope Urban II called the First Crusade in 1095, many soldiers reportedly brought their best friends with them for protection and simply for good Christian company.

All this led the way to the pet Renaissance.

But before proceeding with that glorious period, a few

---

[9] Like their pets, the monks wore hair shirts, did not speak, and ate only one meal a day.

words from writers and thinkers of future ages who, like medieval saints, praised the soul of pets, dogs in particular. . . .

Doggerel

THE RELIGIOUS ROVER

You think dogs will not be in heaven?
I tell you, they will be there long before any of us.

ROBERT LOUIS STEVENSON

The dog is a religious animal. In his savage state he worships the moon and the lights that float upon the waters. These are his gods to whom he appeals at night with long-drawn howls.

ANATOLE FRANCE, "THE COMING OF RIQUET"

My father was a St. Bernard, my mother was a Collie, but I am a Presbyterian.

MARK TWAIN, "AILEEN MAVOURNEEN"

As I lay on the floor in the dark, empty room, Tuppins, my puppy, licked at the tears running down my face. "Oh, Tuppins," I sobbed, "why has God forsaken me?"

TAMMY FAYE BAKKER, AFTER THE FALL OF THE PTL

You will find that the woman who is really kind to dogs is always the one who has failed to inspire sympathy in men.

MAX BEERBOHM, *ZULEIKA DOBSON*, 1911

continued

So many get reformed through religion. I got reformed through dogs. I underwent menopause without taking even an aspirin, because I was so busy whelping puppies.

LINA BASQUETTE

To err is human, to forgive canine.

ANONYMOUS

IV.
THE
RENAISSANCE

I speak Spanish to God, Italian to women, French to men, and German to my horse.

**Holy Roman Emperor Charles V,
son of Philip the Handsome and Joanna the Mad, 1519**

Ha traitor! Ha villain!

**King Henry VIII's words to his horse, Barbaristo,
when he rode badly**

Holla, holla, so boy, there boy!

King Henry VIII's words to Barbaristo when he rode well

A horse! A horse! My kingdom for a horse!

William Shakespeare, *Richard III*, 1594

HAIL THE ROYAL FUFU!

T he Renaissance was a time of unequaled privilege and splendor for a select group of pets who, by divine right, presided over vast kingdoms with their masters.

If the sporting group had ruled the Golden Ages, and the working group the Dark Ages, the Renaissance was the time of the toy, the companion—the royal fufu.

The world powers of the age were distinguished by what kind of lap dog their kings and queens preferred.[1]

- The Chinese: Siamese, Pekingese, and imperial ch'in people.
- The English: terrier people.
- The Spanish, Italians, and Germans: low fufu people.
- The French: high fufu people.

The pinnacle of pet privilege was reached in Europe during the reigns of Henry III and Louis XIV. Henry—who wore rouge, lipstick, ermine-trimmed gowns, and heels (though on Sundays he went to church barefoot while whipping himself) —kept two thousand lap dogs. They slept in velvet-cushioned apartments next to his bedchamber, he took them for walks in crimson silk baskets that seated thirty, and he often carried his favorite papillon in a ribboned basket that dangled from his neck. In 1576, the French monarch spent 100,000 gold crowns for new fufus. Though Henry loved dogs, he suffered the dread

---

[1] Only the Russians, stubbornly resistant to decadent Continental influences, refused to give in to the fufu craze, sticking to their wolfhounds.

affliction of the age: ailurophobia—fear of cats. When confronted by a feline he regularly swooned. During his reign he executed thirty thousand cats.

Henry's great-great-great-second-nephew, Louis XIV, also an ailurophobiac, kept scores of toy poodles, Chien Gris de St. Louis hounds, and trufflers—terriers specially trained to dig up the popular delicacy of the day. He spent 200,000 gold francs for the construction of the royal kennels at Versailles; like his cousin Charles I of Lorraine, he reserved seventy forests and eight hundred royal parks for the training of his more than 1,000 hounds; and he regularly truffled his terriers in La Muette park, accompanied by his brother le duc d'Orlean, AKA Monsieur, a transvestite and also a dog lover.

Though Louis had hundreds of retainers, he was said to have fed his dogs personally to the end. This often occurred under the dining room table in the Hall of Mirrors, much to the chagrin of his wife, Maria Thérèse, and his mistresses, Mademoiselle de la Valliere, Madame de Montespan, et al.[2]

Canines were by no means the only pampered pets of the French Renaissance. Louis's predecessor, Cardinal Richelieu, kept thirteen cats and fed them breast-of-chicken pâté twice a day. He commissioned portraits of his favorite, Perruque, from both Van Dyck and Rubens. When the cleric died in 1642 he provided for his cats handsomely in his will, but they were rounded up and burned by the Swiss Guard.

Two hundred years later, Pope Leo XII reportedly attended enclaves, conclaves, and diets with his cat, Micetto. At Leo's death the papal puss was adopted by the French ambassador to Rome, vicomte de Chateaubriand, before the Swiss could get to him. Later, after his demise by natural causes, Micetto was stuffed and installed in a French château.

During the brave new age of the Renaissance, dogs, cats, horses, and even an elephant or two made great strides forward not only socially and politically, but in the world of art, in the

---

[2] Since Louis's average dinner consisted of four plates of soup, one whole pheasant, two slices of ham, salad, mutton with garlic, pastry, fruit, hard-boiled eggs, and ice cream—many of his dogs had a weight problem, as he did (at his death in 1715 the monarch reportedly tipped the scales at 280 pounds).

fledgling sciences, and in that wonderful new adventure of the time—the discovery and exploration of the New World. True, pet persecution was not yet entirely a thing of the past, but things were definitely looking up for most species:

Dateline	**Milestone**
1309 (A.D.)	Doges' Grand Palace built in Venice.
1490	Lorenzo de Medici the Magnificent sings the praises of his papillons, Bolognese, and Continental spaniels, which his family has raised since 1380.
1490	Leonardo da Vinci paints *Lady with a Weasel* and *Virgin with a Cat*. (See "Mad Cat Painters," page 164 and "The Late Great Dog Gallery," page 150.)
1496	Columbus's men export syphilis to Europe, contracted from New World sheep. (See "Forbidden Fruit," page 162.)
1499	Chinese scientist Wan Hu tests history's first rocket, strapping his cat to a chair equipped with forty-seven gunpowder charges. Hu guinea-pigs himself the following year and joins his pet above. (For more recent launches, see "Space Cadet Pets," page 297.)
1510	First recorded Cesarean operation performed by Swiss pig gelder Jakob Nufer.
1513	Pope Leone I's prize elephant, Annone, dances for SRO crowds every Sunday in Vatican City. (See "The Pope's Hoofer," page 141.)
1519	Conquistador Hernán Cortés discovers the great Aztec Zoo of Mexico, staffed by three hundred animal keepers.
1524	Turkeys from South America are eaten for the first time in the English court.
1525	Sheeps' hearts are nailed to church doors as love spells.

1530 Cardinal Wolsey—who takes his cats to church services and state dinners—is arrested for treason by Henry VIII.

1536 Anne Boleyn and her wolfhound familiar, Urian, are beheaded by Henry VIII for witchcraft and adultery.[3]

1540 Ten-year-old Ivan the Terrible hurls puppies off the walls of the Kremlin.

1558 At her coronation, Elizabeth I popularizes herself with the Protestant constituency by burning live cats inside a wicker dummy of the pope.

1587 Mary Queen of Scots is beheaded by her half sister, Elizabeth I. Afterward her lap dog creeps out from under her gown, but, according to an eyewitness, *"would not departe from the dead corpse."*

1588 The English crush the Spanish Armada. Manx ratters jump off Spanish ships, clamber ashore, and colonize Britain.

1590 The weimaraner is bred by Grand Duke Karl August of Weimar to tear the testicles off a stag in a single bite.

1598 First cat show in Winchester, England, at St. Giles Fair.

1600 Elizabeth I imprisons Henry Wriothesley, third earl of Southampton, in the Tower. The earl's black-and-white cat crawls down the Tower chimney to join him. Later, after his release by James I, Sir Henry has his portrait painted with the faithful cat.

1600 Shakespeare writes of the cat demon Grimalkin in *Macbeth;* King Lear's loyal dog, Sweetheart; and in *Two Gentlemen of Verona* Launce's Crab, who steals

---

[3] A year later, on the anniversary of her execution (May 19), the ghost of Anne appears in the form of a hare at the Tower of London. It has continued to do so every year to this very day.

puddings, breaks wind at the duke's table, and re-lieves himself on Madam Silvia's leg.

1647   Louis XIV, age nine, recovering from smallpox, asks for his new English pony to be brought into his room.[4]

1690   Shogun Tsunayoshi, AKA the Dog Shogun, adopts one hundred thousand canines and almost bank-rupts Japan feeding them.

THE FIRST DOGGIE BAG

In 1676, Louis XIV reportedly asked for a doggie bag when presented with a meal prepared by Prince de Conde's celebrated chef, Le Grand Valtel. Valtel was so mortified, he committed suicide.

SACRED PEKINGESE

For two thousand years the imperial families of China kept sacred Pekingese. The dogs were provided with their own wet nurses, each had a eunuch to protect it from assassins, and many were provided with their own palaces complete with servants. Imperial Peking-ese were kept in this fashion until the fall of Li Hsui, last of the Manchu queens, in 1911.

---

[4] Nearly three centuries later, President Teddy Roosevelt's son Archie, recovering from the flu, is visited by his pony, Algonquin, whom his brothers, Kermit and Quentin, sneak up to his room in the White House elevator.

PET BUTLERS, ORGANISTS, AND SAVANTS

In the old days before the advent of TV, people spent more time with their animals, teaching them tricks. Pet tricksters, performers, and prodigies abounded in the Renaissance.

In his popular nineteenth-century text *Animal Biography,* Reverend William Bingley mentions that the Medici family had a dog that waited on tables, changed plates, and served wine without a spill. He was also an excellent hunter and dancer, and when his master mounted his horse the pooch held out the stirrup with his teeth. Reverend Bingley also mentions a dog from Saxony who could speak thirty words and call intelligibly for tea, coffee, and chocolate.

When King Philip II of Spain visited his father in Brussels, 1549, an animal parade was staged in his honor. The procession was headed by a huge bull with a devil between its horns, from which shot fireworks. Behind was a boy sewed in a bearskin, mounted on a prancing horse. Bringing up the rear was a chariot driven by a bear playing a "cat organ"— a box containing twenty cats, the tail of each tied to levers that the bear pulled to produce an "infernal gallemaufry o' din." Philip II, usually sour-tempered, was said to have chuckled.

Fifty years later Marocco the horse was touring England, delighting crowds with a song-and-dance routine.

Sir John Harrington, soldier, poet, and godson of Queen Elizabeth I, had a dog, Bungey, who performed many services for him, including delivering his letters to Greenwich from London, a distance of one hundred miles. Sir John was inclined to boast about Bungey, but one day it backfired on him. The dog was kidnapped by some "idle pastimers" and spirited to the residence of the Spanish ambassador. When Sir John heard of Bungey's whereabouts and went to claim him, he ran into trouble. He mentioned it in a letter to Prince Henry, heir to the throne.

*The household would not listen to any claim or chal-
lenge, till I rested my suite on the dogge's own proofes,
and made him perform such feates before the nobles
assembled, as put it past doubt that I was his master. I
did send him to the hall in the time of dinner, and
made him bring thence a pheasant out of a dish, which
created much mirthe; but much more, when he returned at my commandment and put it again in the
same cover. Herewith the company was well content
to allow me my claim.*

Sir John recounts more of his dog's feats, then concludes his
letter to Prince Henry:

*I doubt not but your Highness would love my Dogge
for not one hath more diligence to please, or less pay
for pleasing than him I write of; for verily a bone
would contente my servante, when some expecte
greater matters. . . .*

Doggerel

SMARTS

*What the English noticed about their dogs, they attrib-
uted to their kings.*

**DONALD MCCAIG,
EMINENT DOGS, DANGEROUS MEN**

*The world was conquered through the understanding
of dogs; the world exists through the understanding of
dogs.*

FRIEDRICH NIETZSCHE

continued

All knowledge, the totality of all questions and all answers, is contained in the dog.

**FRANZ KAFKA,
"INVESTIGATIONS OF A DOG"**

Ah! you should keep dogs—fine animals—sagacious creatures!"

CHARLES DICKENS, *THE PICKWICK PAPERS*

He may be a dog, but don't tell me he doesn't have a real grip on life.

**KENDALL HAILEY, "THE DAY I BECAME
AN AUTODIDACT"**

Talking with intelligent dogs.

**REV. MONTAGUE SUMMERS, BRITISH
SCHOLAR, WHEN ASKED HIS
FAVORITE HOBBY**

If Jofi sniffed somewhat haughtily around the legs of a caller and then stalked off with a touch of ostentation, there was at once a strong impression that there was something wrong with that caller's character.

**MARTIN FREUD, OF HIS FATHER
SIGMUND'S FAVORITE CHOW, WHO
ATTENDED HIM AT ALL HIS
PSYCHOANALYSIS SESSIONS**

PET SPORTS OF THE KINGS

P et tricks and pet sports went hand in hand in the Renaissance no less than in the ancient ages. They were the most popular amusements. Kings and queens were very active sportspeople. Here now, portraits of three great monarchs and what they loved best.

HENRY VIII
HORSEMAN

His courtiers described Henry VIII as a "pretty" tennis player, an expert "hustler of stones" (bowler of duck pins), and a "doughty" jouster and wrestler. But his favorite sport was the equestrian, and while on horseback he was said to look "like St. George in person." The king practiced "Italianate" riding, using only a wand, his calves (which were also said to be "pretty"), and his magnificent voice.

"Holla, holla, so boy, there boy!" he called to his mount in encouragement.

But when it refused a jump or misstepped: "Ha traitor! Ha villain!"

He taught his horses to "seek his cherishing" rather than to "fear his spurs." He reportedly exhausted many mounts in an afternoon, slaloming barriers, rearing them up, and performing "goat leaps."

The monarch's great romantic loves were said to have been Jane Seymour and Catherine Parr. But other reports have them as Canicida and Barbaristo, his Arabians. In any case, there is no report of his ever beheading a horse.

ELIZABETH I
BEAR BAITRESS

Tomorrow, Her Majesty hath commanded the bears, the bull, and the ape to be baited in the Tiltyard. Upon Wednesday she will have solemn dancing.

SOCIAL SECRETARY OF ELIZABETH I, 1600

Henry's daughter by the beheaded Anne Boleyn also loved riding. Her best horses were Pool and Black Wilford. As for other sports, though the queen objected to cockfighting as "masculine," she had a particular weakness for bearbaiting—the practice of setting canines on chained bears.[5] She kept a pit at Paris Garden on the south bank of the Thames, and her favorite personal bears were Sackerson, Great Ned, and Harry Hunks. The queen's heavyweights were maintained by her master of the bears.

The average Monday night baiting started with the apes, moved on to the bulls, and climaxed with Sackerson, Great Ned, and Harry Hunks. Elizabethan bear bouts were customarily three-rounders.

> *Round 1:* Dwarfs were sent out to warm Bruno up with prods and pikes.

> *Round 2:* Three of the queen's Lyme mastiffs were sent out by her master of the mastiffs. (In the case of lions, four were unleashed.)

> *Round 3:* Sackerson, Great Ned, and Harry Hunks now warmed up; a Catholic, an Irishman, or a friend of the queen's late sister, Mary, was sent out.

Many conversions took place at Elizabeth's Monday Nite Bear Bowl. Sackerson, Great Ned, and Harry Hunks were said to have been fiercely evangelical Protestants.

LOUIS XVI
"DRIVE-UP GUNNER"

Louis confessed in his diary that a day in which he did not kill game was a "blank day" for him.

---

[5] Organized royal British bearbaiting dates back to the reign of Henry II in 1154. (Henry and future monarchs also kept fighting leopards, tigers, lions, and elephants.) Royal polar bears were reportedly taken on leash to the Thames to catch their own fish. Thousands of bears—blacks, browns, polars—perished in the pits. In the eighteenth century, according to J. A. Brooks's *Ghosts of London*

The fifteen Louises who had preceded him—Louis II (AKA "the Stammerer"), Louis d'Outremer ("from Overseas"), Louis VI ("the Fat"), Louis X ("the Quarrelsome"), and the others—had also been ardent sportsmen. Louis XIII, so preoccupied with hunting that he turned France over to Richelieu, was said to have dispatched as many as six wolves in a single day. His son, Louis XIV, reportedly shot sparrows and chickadees in the Tuileries with his blunderbuss as a boy.

As for Louis XVI, his favorite activity was "drive-up gunning" —a hunting technique in which hounds drive game past the sportsmen. The king was drive-up gunning at Versailles when the French mob arrived in 1789 and asked him if he, Marie, and the dogs cared to join them downtown.

PNN EYEWITNESS EXTRA!

OX AND BEAR BLAST

1772—VIENNA.

King Charles III himself attended this eleven-event gala at the Great Amphitheatre presented by the Imperial License Board.

The first event featured "a wild Hungarian ox" with fire under his tail and firecrackers fastened to his ears and horns. After exploding, the beast was mauled by dogs.

In the final event a "furious and hungry bear," starved for eight days, devoured a young bull.

Wolves were caged in the wings in case the bull overpowered the bear. They were not needed.

(1982), there were numerous ghost bear sightings in the paved yard across from the Jewel House at the Tower of London complex, where the royal menagerie was kept until the reign of William IV in 1830.

LATE GREAT HAIRS
TO THE THRONE

B reeding in the Middle Ages was known gamely as "sporting." As in any age, sporting was perhaps the most popular of all sports in medieval times for all species and groups—people and pets, royals and commoners, alike. And there were certainly good reasons for this: sporting was a bracing coed, intramural activity, usually nobody got killed (on the contrary), and though it was based on scoring, nobody really kept a tally.

As a result of a good deal of in-line and out-line sporting, many new pet breeds were born in the Renaissance. But, since national kennel clubs and cat fancy societies were still a thing of the future, the pet historian has no exhaustive genealogical records.

The first information is provided to us by a Swedish scientist, Linnaeus (AKA Carl von Linne), in his 1753 text *Species Plantarum,* which became the basis for modern botanical and zoological classification. The historic volume included the first catalog of Old World dogs, many of them observed in the royal courts of Europe. The majority are no longer with us. But Linnaeus's descriptions give us some idea of the kind of sporting that must have been going on in the old days.

A few examples from *Species Plantarum* (translated from the Latin):

> • *Bastard Pug Dog*
> Has small, half pendulous ears, and thick flattish nose.
> (Resembles the bulldog but is much smaller and entirely wants his savage ferocity.)
> • *Artois Dog of Buffon*
> Produced between the pug dog and the bastard pug dog.
> • *Alicant Dog of Buffon*
> Produced between the pug dog and the spaniel.

- *Naked Dog*
Has no hair on the body.
- *Shock Dog*
About the size of a squirrel, having very long, soft, silky hair all over the body.
- *Fat Alco*
About the size of a squirrel, but prodigiously fat.... The female has six conspicuous paps.
- *Techichi*
Is like the small dogs of Europe but has a wild melancholy air.

The Techichi is of particular interest to the pet historian because it was originally a New World dog bred by the Aztec kings and later eaten to extinction by the Spanish conquistadors (see "Wild and Woolly Age: Cur à la Carte," page 193). The Mexican historian Manuel Orozco y Berra confirms Linnaeus's characterization, repeating that the Techichi was indeed a "wildly melancholy" creature. It was first discovered by Columbus, who reported that it was barkless, ran in packs, climbed trees, and was "delicious." In his *Decades of the Newe World or West Indies* (1515), Richard Eden says this of the explorers' discovery:

> ... *yet found they there dogges of marvelous deformed shape, and such as could not barke. This kynd of dogges, they eate as we do goats.*

As a final note, and by way of putting Linnaeus's *Species Plantarum* dog breed descriptions in context, we should close with his scientific description of canines generally, as a species:

> *The dog is the enemy of all beggars, and often attacks strangers without any provocation; will lick wounds, and by doing so relieves ulcers and the gout; is often infected with gonorrhea; grows sick at the approach of storms; howls at certain notes in music, and sometimes urinates on hearing them.*

THE GIFT THAT
KEEPS ON GIVING

Since the Pyramid Period, emperors, presidents, prime ministers, and VIPs have been giving each other pets— everything from puppies, kittens, and horses to goldfish, giraffes, and elephants. In this way hostilities were smoothed over, friendships made, alliances sealed. Pet gift exchange reached its heyday in the sixteenth and seventeenth centuries.

- In the year 680, Chinese emperor Tien Wu Ti sent to Japan Pekingese puppies, which were enthusiastically received by Shogun Tenmu.
- After visiting the royal Japanese court of Daimio of Hirado in 1614, Portuguese sea captain Saris sent his host "a mastife, a watter spaniell, and a fine Greyhound."
- Richard Cooke, chief factor for the Japan of East India Company, gave his clients "a great black dogg." In return, Cooke received rare goldfish.
- Nothing pleased the ordinarily implacable King Henry VIII more than a gift horse. In 1514 the marquis of Mantoa's horse breeder, Giovanni Ratto, presented the monarch with three of his finest brood mares. In 1520 Edward Guildford gave him what was to become his favorite bay, Byard Hays.
- King Charles I also accepted complimentary horses. By 1648 he had 139 stallions and 37 brood mares.
- As we shall see, Conquistador Juan Ponce de León gave his colleague Balboa the legendary war dog Leoncico. And Muhammad Ali Pasha presented Charles X with a giraffe.

The tradition of pet giving has continued through the Victorian era and to the present day in the highest circles. The last empress of China gave Victoria a Pekingese. President Franklin Pierce gave Jefferson Davis, the head of the Confederacy, a

Japanese ch'in. The commander of the Nazi SS, Martin Bormann, gave Hitler his favorite German shepherd, Blondie.

THE POPE'S HOOFER

In 1513 the king of Portugal gave Pope Leone I seventy animals, including Annone, a dancing Indian elephant.

Annone became the pontiff's favorite pet; he lived in Vatican City and every Sunday danced for large crowds, accompanied by Leone's master of chambers, Giovanni Battista Branconio.

Later, after Annone died of angina, Pope Leone commissioned Raphael to paint the elephant's life-size portrait.

ALL THE PRESIDENTS' PETS—IV
MORE GIFTS

Having observed a few months ago in an American newspaper that you were fond of cats, I have taken the liberty of forwarding to you one of the finest specimens of Siamese cats that I have been able to procure in this country: Miss Pussy. . . .

DAVID SICKELS, U.S. CONSUL TO SIAM, IN A LETTER TO MRS. LUCY RUTHERFORD HAYES, 1878

(The proper, prohibitionist First Lady, otherwise known as "Lemonade Lucy," accepted the cat but renamed it "Siam.")

U.S. presidents and members of the First Family have also received many gift pets. French general Lafayette gave George

Washington five hounds and James Monroe two sheepdogs. The empress of China sent Theodore Roosevelt's daughter, Alice, a black Pekingese. Postmaster General Bob Hannigan presented Margaret Truman with Mike, an Irish setter. White House photographer David Kennerly brought Gerald Ford Liberty, a golden retriever. President Auyb Khan of Pakistan graced Jackie Kennedy with Sarda, a bay gelding. Ulysses Grant's favorite mount, Cincinnatus, was donated to him by the citizens of Cincinnati.

While these gift horses and many others were gratefully accepted by presidents and turned out well, other pet presents were less than problem-free. . . .

GEORGE WASHINGTON'S JACKASS

The king of Spain gave our first president a prize jackass in 1787. Washington decided to breed him to his best mare at Mount Vernon and create a line of "supermules." But when he put the Spanish donkey into the mare's stall and pulled out his Arabian stud, Magnolio, there was a problem. He mentioned it in his diary:

"His most Catholic Majesty surely could not proceed with more deliberation and majestic solemnity to the act of procreation."

Though Washington didn't want to look a gift horse in the mouth, he thought the donkey might be gay.

But in the end the jack came through when the Mount Vernon stable hands got creative. They brought the experienced Magnolio back in to warm the mare up; then, using the old bait-and-switch, quickly reintroduced "His most Catholic Majesty."

MARTIN VAN BUREN'S TIGERS

Kabul al Said, sultan of Oman, gave Martin Van Buren a pair of tiger cubs. The president and Congress argued over whom they belonged to. Congress won, confiscated the cubs, and sent them to the Washington Zoo.

JAMES BUCHANAN'S ELEPHANTS

The King of Siam gave James Buchanan a herd of elephants. Avoiding a showdown with Congress, he donated them to the zoo.

JFK'S CIA DOG

Premier Khrushchev gave Caroline Kennedy Pushinka, a daughter of the Samoyed bitch Strelka, who had recently been shot up on *Sputnik*. The CIA confiscated the puppy and sent it to Walter Reed Hospital to check for bugs.[6]

LBJ'S FBI DOG

FBI director J. Edgar Hoover gave LBJ a little dog whom the president named Edgar. One day Johnson's other dog, Blanco, a white collie, bit Edgar on the nose so badly that he had to have stitches.

RICHARD NIXON'S CHECKERS

After receiving the black-and-white cocker spaniel puppy from a Texas oilman, the future president had to go on TV and explain that it was not a political donation and, come what may, he intended to keep it.

---

[6] Pushinka was found to be clean. Later the Cold War thawed when she had puppies with the Kennedys' Welsh terrier, Charlie, a nephew of Asta, the famous sleuth dog of *The Thin Man*.

THE CURRAGEOUS
CONQUISTADORS

Old World canines played an especially important part in the expansion of empires during the Renaissance: thousands of them participated in the conquest of the New World:

- The conquistadors took the Americas with the help of mastiff war dogs. According to Bartolome de las Casas in his *Historia de las Indias,* these dogs were trained to "bite out the bellies" of the Indians and were the conquistadors' "most fearsome weapon of all."[7]
- For their training, dog soldiers were baited with mannequins dressed as Indians and smeared with their blood. The canines entered battle in spike collars and arrowproof chain mail.
- Columbus was the first to beach canine troops in 1492. They were particularly useful to him against the Jamaican and Arawak Indians on his second voyage. Columbus's favorite companion on his fourth voyage in 1504 was an Irish wolfhound.
- Francisco Coronado used war dogs on the Pueblo Indians. However, he insisted that they didn't bite anyone.
- In 1540 Coronado sent Melchor Diaz to explore the far west. Diaz was the first European to set foot in California but died shortly afterward in a fluke accident. One of the expedition's greyhounds attacked a sheep, and Diaz threw a spear at him; the spear ricocheted off a rock and drove into Diaz's groin.

---

[7] Indian dogs, on the other hand, were mongrels called *chonos*. The Spanish described them as "yellow hound dogs." The Tiano Indians, among others, raised *chonos* for meat. The Aztecs kept "Xoloitzcuintle" dogs, which were named after the god Xoloti and regularly sacrificed to him.

Other conquistadors also came to bad ends. Christopher Columbus died penniless in a Spanish boarding house, reportedly suffering from a social disease contracted from Arawak sheep. Columbus's first mate, Juan Ponce de León, was eaten by Indians outside Miami while searching for the Fountain of Youth. Francisco Pizarro, the former pig farmer, was fragged by his men in Peru.

PNN HARD COPY!
DOG SHOW À LA CONQUISTADOR

1570—CARACAS, SOUTH AMERICA.

A local Indian chief, Tamanaco, organized a rebellion against the Spaniards. The Spaniards arrested the troublemaker, built a stadium, and placed the chief inside with their dog Amigo, whom they had neglected to feed for several days.

They also invited other local Indian chiefs to the first AKC-sanctioned show in the untamed land. It didn't last long.

Amigo KO'ed Tamanaco in the first round, tearing off his head.

The other chiefs decided to drop the rebellion.

Profile in Currage
BALBOA'S LEONCICO

Leoncico (Little Lion) was the most celebrated of the conquistador war dogs. Sired by Juan Ponce de León's own prize stud, Becerillo, Leoncico was born in 1504, in Hispaniola, West Indies. Ponce de León was putting down an Indian uprising at that time with a valiant young colleague and countryman, Vasco

Núñez de Balboa, and, as a token of appreciation, gave him pick of Becerillo's litter.

Balboa trained his puppy with Indian mannequins, and the Little Lion took to K-9 work enthusiastically.

At this time Balboa was having some problems with local creditors; also, he had a bit of a wanderlust and had been hearing tales about South America. So he and Leoncico stowed away in an empty grain cask on a ship bound for that land. When they were discovered by the captain, they narrowly escaped being thrown overboard when Balboa demonstrated his swordsmanship and Leoncico his own mettle.

The ship landed in Cartagena, Colombia, where there was a brief engagement with inhospitable Indians. So it continued on to San Sebastian. Here it struck a reef. Everyone on board drowned—including horses, pigs, goats, and chickens—except Balboa and Leoncico.

An enterprising young man, Balboa mustered a small force of unemployed Spaniards and began reducing the native population around San Sebastian with their matchlock harquebuses and dogs. Leoncico proved particularly valorous in the effort. Indians fled him on sight. By the end of the campaign, Leoncico was drawing the salary of a crossbowman, and Balboa decorated him with a gold collar.

The conquistador spent the next years expanding his real estate portfolio in Colombia. Many stories were told about his dog during this time. According to one account, he won a wager with his captain when he bet that Leoncico, by sheer intuition, could tell the difference between a good Indian and a bad one and a Spaniard from both. According to another story, an old woman came into camp one day and Leoncico greeted her in his customary fashion. "Sir dog," she pleaded under his jaws, "have mercy on me. I only came to beg for food and mercy for my people." Leoncico urinated on her. Balboa's men, short of meat for their dogs, asked permission to let them have the old woman. But Balboa refused.

"If Leoncico had mercy on her," he said, "I can do no less."

In the fall of 1513 the pair set out for Peru. Bringing up the rear were Francisco Pizarro and his dogs, plus 150 other soldiers and theirs. Many soldiers contracted yellow fever in the swamps. By the time the expedition reached the Pacific—the first to do so—Leoncico was fighting almost single-handedly. His salary was raised from a crossbowman's to a lieutenant's.

A short time later, the great dog was poisoned. Grief-stricken, Balboa carried him into the jungle and buried him. He suspected Leoncico's murderer to be Viceroy Pedrarias Davila, his rival for the conquest of Peru.

Soon Davila framed Balboa for stealing ships, and Balboa was beheaded on charges of treason.

Love in the Time of Collara—1

CLIPPED[8] DOGS AND ENGLISHWOMEN

These dogs are little, pretty, proper, and fine, and sought for to satisfy the delicateness of dainty dames, and wanton women's wills . . . to trifle away the treasure of time . . . and to content their corrupted concupiscences with vain disport.

**JOHN CAIUS, "OF THE DELICATE, NEAT AND PRETTY KIND
OF DOGS CALLED THE SPANIEL GENTLE OR THE
'COMFORTER,' " FROM *A TREATISE OF ENGLISH DOGGES*
(1556)**

Englishwomen and their dogs have been kissing and carrying on for many years. The alarming trend began in the Renaissance. We see the gentleman's point of view on the situation from John Caius's dour remarks above.

But where snubbed Elizabethan academics got snappy, rejected poets tended to get tearful. Consider a poem Sir Philip

---

[8] Elizabethan English, meaning "cuddled."

Sidney wrote in 1580 to his mistress, who had been ignoring him in favor of another:

> *Dear, why make you more of a dog than me?*
> *If he do love, I burn, I burn in love . . .*
> *Bidden perhaps he fetcheth thee a glove,*
> *But I unbid, fetch even my soul to thee.*
> *Yet while I languish, him that bosom clips,*
> *That lap doth lap, nay lets in spite of spite,*
> *This sour-breathed mate taste of those sugared lips.*

English ladies ignored such entreaties for more than three hundred years. Dog clipping, kissing and carrying on were still going strong well into the nineteenth century. The trend climaxed in the reign of Victoria. The virgin queen kept collies, Pekingese, Pomeranians, dachshunds, greyhounds, and a Tibetan mastiff. Her first love was Dash, a miniature spaniel.

"I dressed <u>dear sweet little Dash</u>[9] for the second time after dinner in a scarlet jacket and blue trousers," she said in her diary on April 23, 1833.

Then six years later, January 9, another important entry: "I sent for Dashy, who Lord Melbourne accused of having crooked legs, which I won't allow! We put him on the table and he was very much petted by Lord M. We gave him tea and Lord M said, 'I wonder if lapping is a pleasant sensation'—for that is a thing we had never felt."

In the early 1850s Mary Russell Mitford gave a spaniel, Flush, to Victorian poet Elizabeth Barrett Browning. Browning wrote to Mitford regularly, telling her how they were getting on:

"If you were but to see him eat partridge from a silver fork. . . . Of course, he has given up his ice creams for the season, and his favorite substitute seems to be coffee—coffee, understand, not poured into the saucer, but taken out of my little coffee cup. . . . He sees that I drink out of the cup and not out of the saucer; and in spite of his nose, he will do the same. My dear pretty little Flushie!"

[9] The underline is Victoria's.

Soon Ms. Browning was teaching her spaniel to talk. She was impressed by his progress. "My Flush clearly understands articulate language.... 'Dinner,' 'cakes,' 'milk,' 'go downstairs,' 'go out' ... 'go and kiss [the maid] Miss Barrett.' "

After that, she taught her dog numbers and the alphabet. "I have begun arithmetic with Flushie—and am trying to teach him his letters ... with a 'Kiss A, Flush—and now kiss B.' ... But I am afraid he has no very pronounced love for literature."

Near the end of the eighteenth century, Horace Walpole, the fourth earl of Orford, reported an amusing visit to the house of a lady. "I must celebrate the sense of Fidelle, Mrs. Damer's terrier," he said. "Without making the slightest gesture, her mistress only said to her, 'Now, Fidelle, you may here jump on any chair you please'; she instantly jumped on the settee; and so she did in every room for two days."

The Victorian novelist George Eliot, daughter of a fire-and-brimstone Protestant, never married and was considered by many rather cold and strait-laced. Toward the end of her life she wrote to a friend about a new arrival in her house whom she took right to bed:

"Pug is come!—come to fill up the void left by false and narrow-hearted friends.... He is snoring by my side at this moment."[10]

---

[10] For more, see "The Fur Side: Great People Who Went to Bed with their Dogs," page 159; and "The Further Side: Forbidden Fruit," page 162.

THE LATE GREAT
DOG GALLERY

*I would rather see the portrait of a dog that I know,
than all the allegorical paintings they can show me in
the world.*

SAMUEL JOHNSON

*Imagine you are dead. After many years in exile, you
are permitted to cast a single glance earthward. You
see a lamppost and an old dog lifting its leg against
it. You are so moved that you cannot help sobbing.*

PAUL KLEE

The Renaissance was a time of great flowering in art—
not only human art, but pet art. Fifteenth- and sixteenth-
century frescoes and canvases throughout Europe, from
Florence to Spain to the Netherlands, reflected and epitomized
the new splendor, worldliness, and optimism of the day. No
longer were palace walls covered only with crucifixions and
final judgments. Now, between them, were nature scenes—
sun-splashed woods with stags and steeds, frolicking satyrs, and
rosy-cheeked Cupids; or courtly portraits of princes, ladies-in-
waiting, minstrels, jesters, and hounds.

Renaissance masters devoted hours to pet studies. Albrecht
Dürer specialized in rabbits, ducks, and guinea hen; Hierony-
mous Bosch—birds, pigs, and goats; Michelangelo—white
chargers and Garden snakes; Raphael—lambs, Ezekiel's lions,
and Galatea's dolphin. And the greatest master of all, Leonardo
da Vinci, did everything. He especially liked cats. "Even the
smallest feline is a masterpiece," he said.[11]

Some of the most moving Renaissance masterpieces were of
dogs. Here now, by way of concluding the age and illustrating
its spirit, a small gallery. . . .

---

[11] For more on feline art, see "Mad Cat Painters," page 164.

ADORATION OF THE MAGI, TITIAN (1477–1576)
CLEVELAND MUSEUM OF ART

Nativity scene with kneeling magicians, retainers on horseback, and in the foreground a small white dog lifting his leg on the farmhouse post.

SAINT EUSTACE AND THE STAG, IL PISANELLO (C. 1450)
NATIONAL GALLERY, LONDON

Seven dogs and St. Eustace, on horseback, stare at a trophy stag whose rack bears Christ on the cross.

ANOLFINI MARRIAGE, JAN VAN EYCK (C.1422)
(NATIONAL GALLERY, LONDON)

In their bedroom together, Mr. Anolfini makes the sign of the cross, Mrs. A., pregnant (or retaining water), holds her belly; at their feet, the couple's terrier poses, tail erect.

KNIGHT AND HOUND PURSUING A WOMAN,
BOTTICELLI (C. 1482) THE PRADO, MADRID

A hound, flanked by a knight on a charger, engages the naked buttock of a fleeing woman.

WOMAN WITH A DOG, RUBENS (1577–1640)

The artist's buxom wife (Helen Fourment) is having her hair done, topless; to her right stands a black man, holding out her mail; at her feet, teeth bared, stands her spaniel.

DWARF AND DOG,[12] BY KAREL VAN MANDER III (C. 1650) STATENS MUSEUM FOR KUNST, COPENHAGEN

A bearded dwarf in striped pantaloons and slippers with bows stands in front of a palace under storm clouds. In one hand he holds the foil at his belt, in the other the collar of a muscular mastiff. The dwarf smiles pleasantly; head cocked, one eye wide and fixed, the mastiff stares into the foreground as if the painter or his assistant—out of the picture—were making faces or saying "Cheese!"

Dog art, inspired by such Renaissance masterpieces, came to full blossom in the Victorian era. For Queen Victoria's seventeenth birthday in 1836, her mother, the duchess of Kent, gave her a Sir Edwin Henry Landseer portrait of her spaniel, Dash. Canine portraiture became an overnight sensation, and the greatest artists of the genre—Landseer, Stubbs, and Jean Baptiste Oudry—became celebrities.

In 1989 Landseer's *Neptune,* a painting of a Victorian Newfoundland, fetched $577,500 at a Sotheby's auction and became the *Sunflowers* of dog portraiture. And so it is—the legacy of Renaissance pet art.

---

[12] According to Leslie Fiedler's scholarly work, *Freaks* (1978), dwarfs were popular in royal courts from the earliest ages and were often painted with dogs. The tradition began with the Egyptian noble Ti. Ti had a painting in his sepulcher of his dwarf jester holding a greyhound on a leash. (Future royals especially known for the dwarfs in their service ranged from Roman emperor Augustus, to sixth-century Chinese emperor Wu-Ti, Russian czar Peter the Great, and King Charles I of Great Britain. The last two monarchs in particular were also famous dog lovers and patrons of the arts.) Among other dwarf-and-dog canvases of the later Renaissance: *Dwarf and Child with Dog* by Jan Fyt, *Dwarf and Dog* by Karel van Mander III, and *The Dwarf and Dog of Cardinal de Granvelle* by Anthonis Mor.

V.
RUFFURMATION AND ROVERLUTIONS

Be comforted, little dog, thou too in the Resurrection, shall have a little golden tail.

Martin Luther, founder of the Reformation, dog lover, Lutheran

It is quite impossible to worship the bones of a martyr without danger of rendering by mistake such reverence to the bones . . . of a dog!

John Calvin, Luther's nemesis, Calvinist (and reportedly a cat person)

THE RUFFURMATION

If it be the chief point of friendship to comply with a friend's motions and inclinations, he possesses this in an eminent degree; he lies down when I sit, and walks when I walk, which is more than many good friends can pretend to do.

ALEXANDER POPE, OF HIS DOG (1740)

B y the seventeenth century Protestant dogs and cats had come a long way from the dark days of witch's familiars, werewolves, and moddey dhooes.

As we have seen, during the Renaissance the most privileged pets were carried in crimson baskets, fed at the table, tutored in arithmetic, exchanged as royal gifts, clipped, nursed, and painted by the masters.

In the Ruffurmation pets made even greater strides forward. They were bred more energetically, and persecution was less common. There was even a heated debate among theologians as to whether dogs had a soul and went to heaven. Protestant thinkers as eminent as Martin Luther, Samuel Clarke, and Augustus Toplady insisted they did.

Cats had great friends and champions during this new age as well. They became the darlings of French society ladies such as Madame de Staël, Madame Recamier, and the duchesse de Bouilon. The English Romantic poet Robert Southey invented names for his cats equal to his esteem for them: the Most Noble the Archduke Rumpelstilzchen, Marquis Macbum, Earl Tomemange, Baron Raticide, Waowler, Skaratchi. And

Boswell (though, personally, he hated cats) said of Samuel Johnson:

> *I shall never forget the indulgence with which he treated Hodge, his cat, for whom he himself used to go out and buy oysters, lest the servants having that trouble should take a dislike to the creature.*

Dogs also had champions in the highest circles. King Charles II took his King Charles spaniels with him to all privy council meetings and whelped puppies in his bedroom. Catherine the Great consecrated an entire cemetery in memory of her dear hound Zemire.

Here now the milestone dates of this magnificent but stormy time for pets and pet lovers:

Dateline	**Milestone**
1648 (A.D.)	At the annual Paris Midsummer Cat Burning on Place de Greve, King Louis XIV lights the fire and dances around the pyre.
1650	Louis XIV, doing a royal 180, prohibits cat burning.
1651	Jan Steen paints *The Cat's Reading Lesson,* wherein three children try to teach a pussy to read. (See "Mad Cat Painters," page 164.)
1660	Charles II regains the throne from Oliver Cromwell and the pet-hating Puritans. He reopens alehouses, legalizes cockfighting and mixed dancing, and begins openly raising King Charles toy spaniels.
1670	The mad Queen Christina of Sweden dresses up as a Moorish prostitute for Catholic mass and romps with her dogs.
1680	Wild boars and dodo birds are hunted to extinction in Britain.
1682	The pug is imported to Europe from China.

1687   Sir Isaac Newton develops the cat door (and, in his spare time, the laws of motion, mechanics, and optics).

1688   Scottish duke Alexander IV of Gordon develops the Gordon Setter.

1704   Queen Anne puts her official seal of approval on horse racing and raises revenue for the crown through sweepstakes, exactas, and daily doubles.

1712   Last execution of a cat for witchcraft in England.

1715   Peter the Great has city officials ride in carts drawn by cows, goats, dogs, and pigs. At dinner he serves baked cats, wolves, and ravens to annoying guests.

1750   Madame Helvetius dresses her cats in fur robes and silk costumes.[1]

1752   Opening of the first great European zoo: Imperial Menagerie at the Schonbrunn Palace in Vienna (followed in 1775 by the Royal Park, Madrid, and, eighteen years later, Jardin des Plantes, Paris).

1762   The sandwich is invented by the fourth earl of Sandwich, giving dogs something else to beg for.

1762   Catherine the Great, an animal lover, further modernizes Russia. Anyone who displeases her is banished to the anteroom and must squat there for days, mewing like a cat, clucking like a hen, and pecking his food from the floor.

1770   Louis XV searches for truffles in La Muette park with truffling dogs given him by his grandfather, the king of Sardinia.

---

[1] In spite of these great strides for felines during the period, anticat fervor was again stirred up in France by Georges Louis Leclerc de Buffon, who stated in his *Histoire Naturelle* (1776): "The cat is an unfaithful domestic that we keep only out of necessity." Fifty years later, Dr. Ludwig Jerrer declared in his *Natural History for the Young,* "You know what a flattering, snuggling, but also false, spiteful, faithless animal the house cat is."

1786   Frederick the Great of Prussia dies. Is buried beside
                  his eleven greyhound bitches at Sans Souci palace.
                  (See "Celebrity Pet Profile: The Bitches of Frederick
                  the Great," page 158.)

1791   English stud book published—a *Who's Who* of the
                  top British stallions.

1796   Catherine the Great's reign ends when, attired in
                  negligee and leathers, she is crushed by a stud don-
                  key. (See "Forbidden Fruits," page 162.)

CELEBRITY PET PROFILE
THE BITCHES OF FREDERICK THE GREAT

Poet, flutist, general, statesman, animal lover—Frederick the
Great was the true embodiment of the Enlightenment.

His favorite pastime, besides hobnobbing with intellectuals
such as Voltaire, was spending quiet evenings with his whippets. The monarch's inner circle of whippets were all females.
He considered bitches smarter and more devoted than studs.
Frederick's detractors, mostly Catholics and Hungarians, called
the group—since it was rumored that he slept with them—
"his harem."

Frederick was also very fond of his horses. After one disas-
trous engagement during the War of the Austrian Succession—
which left him with no books, no flute, no snuff, no tableware,
and no dogs—he wrote of the battle and his losses to Freder-
dorf, his wounded general:

> *I was in the soup up to my ears all right. Annemarie
> is killed, Champion must be dead too—terrible! . . .
> Albert is dead too—no great loss.*

Annemarie and Champion were his horses. Albert was his
brother-in-law.

Later, during the Seven Years' War, Frederick suffered one of his most dispiriting losses when the Hungarians kidnapped his favorite whippet bitch, Biche. The monarch appealed to them for her return. At last they complied, sending her back ahead of the other Prussian POWs and in exchange for border concessions. When Frederick was reunited with Biche, he broke down in tears.

At the monarch's death in 1786, he was, at his instruction, buried beside his eleven favorite females in the shadow of Sans Souci palace. Since that time, he and the dogs have been exhumed and reburied three times.

THE FUR SIDE

GREAT PEOPLE WHO WENT TO BED WITH THEIR DOGS

Frederick wasn't the only important person to sleep with his dogs. In spite of the lack of official records in certain cases, the following self-confessed dog lovers surely did the same with theirs.

Noah, Romulus and Remus, Plato, Alexander the Great, Lorenzo the Magnificent, Henry III, Anne Boleyn, Balboa, Louis XIV, Josephine, Catherine the Great, Lewis and Clark, Daniel Boone, Geronimo, Crazy Horse, Freud, Walt Disney, Bud Weatherwax (owner/trainer of the Lassies), FDR, General Patton, and Hitler. To name a few.

Here are some other notables:

KING LOUIS XI, AKA "THE SPIDER" (1461–83)

The French monarch's bunk mate for the early part of his reign was his greyhound bitch, Chermai, whom he kept in a gold and ruby collar. Later "the Spider"—whose favorite health drink was the blood of infants—bedded a white St. Hubert hound,

Souillard. (Sleeping around, Souillard became the sire of two great lines of royal hunting dogs: The Talbots and *Les Grands Chiens Blancs du Rois,* or The Great White Dogs of the Kings.)

KING CHARLES IX (1560–74)

Charles's sack hound was Courte, a *Chien Blanc* descended from his predecessor's, "the Spider's," original line. The king also ate from the same plate as the bitch. When she died, he had her skinned and a pair of shooting gloves made from her hide.

PETER THE GREAT (1672–1725)

The Russian czar shared his bed with his wife, Catherine, and his Italian greyhound bitch Lisette. Lisette held great sway over Peter. Once a member of the court was wrongly accused of corruption, Catherine attempted to intervene for him, and the tempestuous Peter fell into a rage, forbidding her to mention the case again. Catherine wrote a petition, tied it to Lisette's collar, and signed the bitch's name. When Peter found the message, he pardoned the man.

GENERAL GEORGE CUSTER (1839–1876)

When camping in Indian territory, the commander of the Seventh Cavalry—much to the dismay of his wife, Libbie—slept with his white bulldog, Turk, and his greyhound stud, Byron. (He also kept a pack of beagles, staghounds, wolfhounds, and foxhounds, who stayed outside his tent and kept their eyes out for the Sioux.)

MANFRED VON RICHTHOFEN, AKA "THE RED BARON" (1892–1918)

The celebrated German aviator and top gun of World War I not only slept with his Great Dane, Moritz, he flew with him. The dog was in the cockpit and at the baron's side for many important aerial dog fights.

THE DUKE OF WINDSOR (1894–1972)

Edward VIII's favorite bedmate was Cora, a cairn terrier. When, in her old age, Cora could no longer jump into bed because of arthritis, the duke had steps built for her.

THE DUCHESS OF WINDSOR (1896–1986)

At the age of seventy-six, after the death of her husband, Edward, the duchess began to sleep with her two pugs—Gin-Sing and Black Diamond. "It is flattering to know," she said, "that there are creatures who still want to share my bed."

WINSTON CHURCHILL (1874–1965)

The prime minister shared his quarters with his poodles, Rufus One and Rufus Two, his cat, Mr. Cat, and his parakeet, Toby (with whom he also shared breakfast in bed).

DORIS DAY (1924–   )

The actress and animal rights activist sleeps with many dogs, among them El Tigre de Sassafrass, a gray poodle whom Ms. Day adopted from a shelter. Shy at first, El Tigre spent most of his time under the actress's bed; now, after much TLC, he reportedly spends most of his time on the bed.

THE FURTHER SIDE
FORBIDDEN FRUIT

*On June 6, 1662, at New Haven, there was a most unparalleled wretch, one Potter by name, about 60 years of age, executed for damnable Beastialities [sic].
. . . The man's wife had seen him confounding himself with a bitch 10 years before; and he had excused himself as well as he could, but conjured her to keep it a secret.*

COTTON MATHER, PURITAN CLERGYMAN, SON OF INCREASE MATHER, GRAND INQUISITOR AT THE SALEM WITCH TRIALS

In the seventeenth and eighteenth centuries, before the advent of dating services and when the world was still quite rural, otherwise upright men sometimes found themselves overpowered by unholy temptations in barnyards and stables. Capital punishment did little to put a damper on the activity. As late as 1940, a French farmer and three cows were burned at the stake for unnatural acts. Here are some older, historic cases, including the one above noted by Cotton Mather:

• 1606, France. Guillaume Guyard and a certain bitch of his acquaintance were sentenced to be hanged and burned. But the couple managed to run away together before execution. The court confiscated Monsieur Guyard's property to pay for the trial and, to satisfy the mob, hanged a portrait of him from the gallows.
• 1662, New Haven, CT. After Mr. Potter's wife caught him in congress with their pet, he apparently said it wouldn't happen again, and by way of showing his good faith and firm resolve, he hanged the hussy. This apparently appeased the missus, because she didn't mention her husband's extracurriculars for a decade. During this time, however, it seems that Potter fell off

the wagon a time or two. Finally, the wretch found himself on the gallows in front of half of New Haven —and next to him, in shackles, two sows, three sheep, two heifers, and a cow.

(Note: Rev. Mather stated that his parishioner was a regular churchgoer known for his "zeal in reforming the sins of other people.")

• 1750, Vanvres, France. Jacque Ferron was caught compromising a she-ass and duly sentenced to swing. Though a sodomist's partner was customarily dispatched with him, Ferron's she-ass was granted an eleventh-hour pardon when the townspeople of Vanvres put together a petition that attested to the she-ass's irreproachable character. "In all her habits of life . . . [she is] a most honest creature," it stated.

Today, such unnatural unions are no longer capital offenses, but misdemeanors. Strangely, the decriminalization has cut down on volume. Also, the sprinkling of cases are handled quietly, tastefully, and without the carney atmosphere that once surrounded them in the days before CNN (and PNN) and "A Current Affair." Consider the following recent example involving a California auto mechanic:

PNN HARD COPY!
WHAT'S LOVE GOT TO DO WITH IT?

JANUARY 23, 1990—PLEASANTON, CA.

On a quiet California evening, David Vincent Delarosa, twenty-eight, mechanic, entered a sheep barn in Livermore (a bedroom community of San Francisco) carrying three items: an orange nylon rope, a hypodermic needle, and a jar of Vaseline.

No granola, flowers, or tickets to a Michael Bolton concert.

Since Delarosa's last visit to the barn, its owner—having

reportedly suspected that for months someone had been socializing secretly with his ewes after dark—had installed an
alarm on the door.

Hearing the alarm that January night, the owner promptly
phoned the Pleasanton police.

According to an article in the *Sacramento Bee* ("Denial in
Sheep Case," January 31, 1990), when the deputies arrived in
the barn moments later, Delarosa was found "sitting near a
young ewe with a jar of Vaseline." Though he had her tied up
with the orange nylon rope, he denied any misconduct.

Delarosa was charged with misdemeanor on three counts:
trespassing, possessing a hypodermic needle, and molesting a
sheep.

The mechanic pleaded innocent on the third count. In so
doing, according to the newspaper report, he "waived his right
to a speedy trial."

MAD CAT PAINTERS

*CHESHIRE CAT: We're all mad here, I'm mad. You're
mad.*
ALICE: How do you know I'm mad?
*CHESHIRE CAT: You must be. Or you wouldn't have
come here.*

LEWIS CARROLL, *ALICE'S ADVENTURES IN WONDERLAND*
(1865)

*For he is good to think on, if a man would express
himself neatly.*

**CHRISTOPHER SMART (1722–1771) FROM "JUBILATE
AGNO," A POETIC TRIBUTE TO HIS CAT, JEOFFREY—
WRITTEN FROM A LUNATIC ASYLUM**

Felines have been a favorite subject of artists throughout
history. Cat portraiture became particularly popular in
the eighteenth and nineteenth centuries, both in the East
and in the West. Though most of the painters depicting cats

throughout this period were stable enough, others had their quirks.

- Chu Ta (1625–1705), a descendant of the Ming dynasty, took a spill one day. Afterward, he took a vow of silence, became a Buddhist monk, and painted nothing but cats for the rest of his life.
- Swiss painter Gottfried Mind (1768–1814) was called the "Cat Raphael," a title given him by Madame Vigee-Lebrun, court painter for Marie Antoinette. Mind was a hunchback and an eccentric who painted only the cats of the French aristocracy.
- Kuniyoshi (1893–1953), also reputed to be quirky, painted cats in kimonos, Samurai outfits, and No and Kabuki masks. Among his masterpieces: *The Cat Family at Home, The Cat-witch of Okabe.*
- Louis Wain (1880–1939) began his career by doing a portrait of Peter, his dying wife Emily's cat. Shortly after completing the piece, Wain complained of being harassed by spirits. The artist was declared insane in 1924 and sent to the paupers' ward of a London mental asylum, where he continued to feverishly paint cats. Later, H. G. Wells, Prime Minister Ramsay MacDonald (whose trousers FDR's German shepherd, Major, tore off in 1933), and other admirers of his work had Wain transferred to a private facility.

PNN UPDATE
PET PAINTING TODAY

Obviously she has talent.

**MARIA BAKER, SACRAMENTO ZOO DIRECTOR, OF
ELEPHANT ARTIST, WINKY**

It can't be art, not if it's done by an elephant!

**DONALD HERBERHOLZ, ART PROFESSOR, CALIFORNIA
STATE UNIVERSITY, SACRAMENTO**

When I was first approached, I was completely dubious. But when I saw Ruby's work, I was sold immediately.

**RUDY TURK, RETIRED DIRECTOR OF ARIZONA STATE
UNIVERSITY ART MUSEUM, OF ELEPHANT ARTIST RUBY**

Today pet painting has kept stride with the most avant-garde art movements. The reason? The cutting-edge practitioners are no longer people—normal, quirky, or just plain nuts—but pets themselves.

Here are a few of the greats:

RUBY
SOUTHWESTERN LANDSCAPE ARTIST

With the help of an assistant who hands her brushes dipped in the color of her choice, the Phoenix Zoo's Ruby, an 8,500-pound elephant, produces sweeping landscapes and evocative free-forms. Her canvases fetch as much as $3,500. She has made over $400,000 in her four-year career and has generously donated the entire sum to endangered animal funds.

CONGO
ABSTRACT EXPRESSIONIST

Congo, the chimp star of Desmond Morris's *Zoo-Time,* was the most celebrated Abstract Expressionist of his time. Salvador

Dalí rated his work higher than that of Jackson Pollock. Joan Miró bought one of his canvases. Picasso expressed admiration.

Finally, a young talent from California whom collectors already have their eye on:

BUD D. HOLLY
PAWNTILLIST

Bud D. Holly, a black-and-gray tiger-striped tabby, is the "artist in residence" at Sharon Flood's Village Art Gallery in Mendocino. He works with paws and watercolors. In 1992 he had a one-cat show. Twenty of his works sold, fetching $15 to $150 apiece. Lately a certain "lightness" has crept into his palette. Ms. Flood says it has been that way "ever since he was fixed."

WILLIAM WEGMAN

Weimaraner Conceptualist

In 1992 the Whitney Museum of New York held a William Wegman retrospective. A Conceptualist, Wegman works in weimaraners. His first weimaraner was Man Ray; his second, Man Ray's daughter, Fay Ray; his third, Fay's daughter, Bettina.

Wegman has dusted his subjects with flour, decorated them with Christmas ornaments, and dressed them in various outfits. Man Ray often wore slacks and roller skates. The bitches regularly modeled colonial dresses, nipples exposed.

When asked about his decision to turn to dog art, Wegman said, "As soon as I got funny, I killed any majestic intentions in my work."

MUSICAL HAIRS

Last evening I took him to hear Luisa de Sodre play and sing. Pomero was deeply affected, and lay close to the pedal on her gown, singing in a great variety of tones, not always in time. It is unfortunate that he always will take a part where there is music, for he sings even worse than I do.

**WALTER SAVAGE LANDOR, POET, OF HIS WHITE
POMERANIAN, c. 1820**

P et music became particularly popular during the Ruffurmation and Roverlutionary Period. The great operas, concertos, and folk compositions of the day inspired future work.

VERDI'S "LITTLE COLLEAGUE"

Giuseppe Verdi (1813–1901), composer of such masterpieces as La Traviata, Aida, *and* Requiem, *had a Maltese spaniel, Lulu. The maestro carried Lulu everywhere under his coat and consulted her on his compositions. After Lulu's death, Verdi complained he could no longer write opera without his "little colleague." He buried her just outside his bedroom window.*

Here now, the milestone musical dates from the sixteenth century to the present day:

Dateline	**Milestone**
1500 (A.D.)	Invention of the cat organ (see page 170).
1600	Traveling animal bands, featuring cat vocalists and monkey or owl conductors, tour Europe.
1650	Artist David Teniers paints *The Cat Concert*. Cats sing a libretto, accompanied by a chimp on a French horn.
1700	*La Musique des Chats*—a woodcut depicting a maestro balancing cats on his head and shoulders while others play viola, bass, and mandoline, and sing "miaou."
1735	Alessandro Scarlatti composes "The Cat's Fugue," imitating a cat running over piano keys. (Later, in 1921, Zez Confrey follows up with his jazz classic, "Kitten on the Keys."[2])
1936	Prokofiev composes *Peter and the Wolf*: the cat is a woodwind, the wolf a bassoon, the bird a piccolo.
1945	Ella Fitzgerald, the jazz cats, and the hep cats popularize scat singing.
1956	The King goes platinum with "Hound Dog."
1958	Animal trainer Jacques Bisset stages *The Cat's Opera* in London.
1962	Arnold Ziffel, a Chester White pig, plays piano in "Green Acres" with Eva Gabor.
1963	Pet pop groups dominate the charts: Animals, Monkees, Beatles, Byrds, Cricketts, Turtles, Three Dog Night, Steppenwolf. Later: Eagles, Stray Cats, Pet Shop Boys, Temple of the Dog, Poi Dog Pondering, Tattooed Love Dogs.

[2] Other important cat compositions: 1840—Chopin, "Cat Valse"; 1940—Stravinsky, "Lullabies of the Cat"; 1945—Aaron Copland, "The Cat and the Mouse."

1965   Singing Dogs go platinum with "Jingle Bells." (For other pets hits, see "Pet Rock Platinum and Gold," page 284.)

1970   Burt the Duck, of Animal Behavior Enterprises, plays Chopin. Andy the Poodle stars in the Broadway musical *42nd Street*. A few years later, scores of pooches show up to try out for the role of Sandy in *Annie*.

1980   Pet writer Jilly Cooper's dog, Barbara, eats Mozart's Prague Symphony (then chases it with Cooper's ratting cap and her husband's sneakers).

1982   *Cats* debuts on Broadway.

1987   Louisa, a pig who works for a German narcotics squad, retires from duty: as a farewell present, the sow is taken by fellow officers to the Hanover Opera to hear its Christmas rendering of *Oh, Louisa!*

1989   A Floridian mynah bird, Simon, records Fats Domino's classic "Blueberry Hill." (See "Woofers and Tweeters," page 180.)

THE CAT ORGAN

The cat organ was a popular seventeenth-century music box. A tom or queen was sealed inside a small wooden box with holes on the top and one in back through which the cat's tail was strung. The instrument was played by yanking, twisting, or pinching the tail, each manipulation producing a different note from the top holes and in some cases arpeggios.[3]

In 1650, a Dominican, Father Kirchner, devised a "barbarous variation" of the instrument whereby keys drove barbs into the tailbone.

An illustration of the cat organ appears in Gaspard Schott's Magia Universalis *(1657).*

PNN CAT ORGAN UPDATE!

Felines never forget an insult. According to an August 12, 1989, New York Times *article, stray cats invaded the Steinway piano factory in Queens and used hand-crafted $50,000 pianos as litter boxes and scratching posts. Company officials said that a nearby illegal dump was the source of the problem. But one has to wonder.*

---

[3] The instrument was said to have sounded like a combination of Robert Plant ("Dazed and Confused" period), Little Richard ("Tootie Fruitie"), and Janis Joplin ("Ball and Chain")—at least if the cat was in heat.

CATERWAUL
Dead Cat Jokes of the Maestros

The late great composers loved a good dead cat joke as much as the next guy.

Giacomo Meyerbeer (1791–1864), the father of French grand opera, related the following story about Brahms. He said it had come to him from Wagner himself. . . .

Antonin Dvorak once gave Brahms a Bohemian Sparrow Slaying Bow (a *Slugj Hym Inye Nech*). Brahms often shot cats with this bow from his apartment window in Vienna.

Meyerbeer described Brahms's procedure as he had heard it from Wagner:

> *After spearing the poor brutes, he reeled them into his room after the manner of a trout fisher. Then—so Wagner averred—he eagerly listened to the expiring groans of his victims and carefully jotted down in his notebook their antemortem remarks. Wagner declared that he worked up these piteous utterances into his chamber music, but then Wagner had never liked Brahms.*

The French poet Baudelaire provides an epilogue to this story:

> *I love Wagner, but the music I prefer is that of a cat hung by its tail outside of a window, trying to stick to the panes of glass with its claws. There is an odd grating on the glass which I find at the same time strange, irritating, and singularly harmonious.*

In fact, the ironic Baudelaire secretly loved cats and hated Wagner.

CELEBRITY PET PROFILE
WAGNER'S OPERA DOGS

Brooding. Tragic. Tempestuous. Such words have been used to describe the operas of Richard Wagner. What was at the root of such emotion?

Wagner had many dogs. The life and untimely demise of each affected the composer deeply.

Musicologists divide the career of the great German composer and dog lover into the standard periods: *Tannhäuser* period, *Tristan und Isolde* period, *Parsifal* period, and so on.

The pet historian uses others. . . .

THE PEPS PERIOD
(1841–55)

Wagner and his wife, Minna, moved to Dresden in 1841. Childless, they decided to get a puppy.

"We are forced to make do with dogs since there is still absolutely no prospect of human progeny," complained the composer in a letter to friends. "We've just got another one, only six weeks old: a funny little animal called Peps or Striezel because he looks like one of the dogs from the Striezel bread market."

Peps, an English toy spaniel, sat on a leather stool next to the maestro when he composed *Rienzi,* his tragic French opera,[4] and, later, *Tannhäuser.*

When Prussian troops invaded Dresden, Wagner and Minna fled to Zurich with Peps, Papo (a gray parrot), and Nette (Minna's illegitimate daughter). In Switzerland the spaniel saw Wagner through the composition of *Das Rheingold,* then fell gravely ill. The composer rowed across Lake Lucerne to the veterinarian for medicine. Peps died shortly afterward.

"He slept that last night as usual in his basket at my bedside," said Wagner, "his invariable habit being to wake me with his paws in the morning. . . ."

Wagner buried Peps in his landlady's garden (now a tourist attraction).

THE FIPS PERIOD
(1856–61)

The maestro adopted Fips, another English toy, while working on *Siegfried.* He left Fips with Minna briefly to have an affair with Mathilde Wesendonck. He rendezvoused with them in Paris and regularly walked Fips on the Bois de Boulogne.

The spaniel was poisoned in the spring of 1861, a blow not only to Wagner personally, but to his marriage. "The sudden death of this lively and lovable animal acted as the final rift in a childless union which had long become impossible," he recorded in his diary.

After Fips's death, Wagner went to his "beaver's nest" in Wiesbaden. Dogless here, he played with his landlord's bullterrier, Leo, while scoring his masterpiece, *Die Meistersinger.* The composition was interrupted when Leo bit the maestro so badly that he was unable to play the piano for several weeks.

---

[4] Hitler says his rise to power began after viewing a performance of this opera in Linz, 1906. (For further information, see "Hitler's Fuchsl and Blondie," page 245.)

THE POHL PERIOD
(1863–66)

In 1864 Wagner and Pohl, a hound given him by his landlord, fled their creditors in Austria and retired to the hunting lodge of Ludwig II, the mad eighteen-year-old king of Bavaria. Here, Wagner scored *Parsifal*. During this time Pohl shared his master's attentions with Franz Liszt's daughter, Cosima, a married woman.

After *Parsifal,* composer and dog moved to "the Artichokes," an estate in Geneva. Leaving Pohl behind there with a cough, Wagner traveled to Lyon and Marseilles. In his absence, Pohl died in Geneva, as did his estranged wife, Minna, in Dresden. After returning from France, Wagner exhumed his beloved hound, put a necklace on him, and buried him in a casket, with a marble headstone. He never visited his wife's grave.

THE RUSS PERIOD
(1866–75)

In 1866 the composer was back in Geneva, cohabiting with Liszt's daughter, Cosima, her fox terrier, Koss, and her three illegitimate children. The housemaid, Vreneli Weidmann, gave him a black Newfoundland, Russumuck, whom he called "Russ."

The Wagner household included many other pets, too: sheep; chickens; cats; two golden pheasants, Wotan and Fricka; and two horses, Fritz and Grane, gifts from King Ludwig II.

During this period, the composer spent afternoons with Friedrich Nietzsche, who was working on his Superman theory then and who firmly believed that "the world exists through the understanding of dogs." Also, the father of existentialism was desperately infatuated with Cosima.

In 1874 Wagner, Cosima, and the dogs moved into Villa Wahnfried (meaning "Freedom from Illusion")—another present from Ludwig. Russ died here. Wagner buried the faithful Newfoundland beside his own tomb, with the epitaph "Here Lies and Watches Wagner's Russ."

. . .

In the final years of his life, the maestro was active with the Geneva SPCA. Committed to the cause, he wrote a society colleague, Ernst von Weber: "We must begin by drawing people's attention to animals and reminding them of the Brahman's great saying, 'Tat twam asi!' " ("That is you!")

Wagner suffered a fatal heart attack in 1883 and was buried beside Russ. His surviving dog, King Marke, also a Newfoundland, reportedly howled with grief and died a few days later. Marke's epitaph:

"Here Rests Wahnfried's Guardian and Friend, the Good, Beautiful Marke."

THE GLORIOUS ROVERLUTIONS
American and French

The more I see of men, the more I admire dogs.

**MADAME ROLAND, REVOLUTIONARY
(BUT LATER GUILLOTINED FOR
SUSPECTED ROYALIST LEANINGS)**

Until the middle of the eighteenth century, pet history had been dominated by pedigrees. Their parties, their palaces, and their wars had all been exacted from the hide of the masses (or, as the pet historian knows them, the puppetariat).

Though the members of this group had no personal contact with royalty, they did bring in the newspaper in the morning or do their business on it. So front-page pictures didn't escape them: royal fufus whisking about town in golden litters, truffling in La Muette park, and so on.

At last, the puppetariat on one side of the Atlantic and the colonists on the other threw moderation to the wind, took a very long drink of water, and headed to the Bastille and the Boston Harbor for relief, bravely following their masters.

And here are the immortal dates:

Dateline	**Milestone**
1776 (A.D.)	Signer of the Declaration of Independence Ben Franklin lobbies for the turkey, not the eagle, as U.S. national symbol. He calls the eagle "a sharper, a robber, a bird of bad moral character."
1789	George Washington becomes first U.S. president. His First Dog: Cloe. (See "Our Founding Fidos," page 178.)
1789	Louis XVI seized by the mob at Versailles while "drive-up gunning" with his dogs.
1793	October 16, Marie Antoinette is guillotined. Her spaniel, Thisbe, is so distraught, she jumps into the Seine and drowns herself.
1794	Braque Dupuy hunting dogs are saved from extinction by heroic gamekeeper Jacque Dupuy.
1796	Napoleon Bonaparte—a hemorrhoid sufferer and ailurophobiac—takes Paris, establishes martial rule, and uses strays as watchdogs around sensitive military installations. (See "Napoleon's Lesson in Nature," page 177.) Josephine's toy spaniel attacks Napoleon in bed.[5]
1797	John Adams succeeds George Washington. Among his first executive acts: building the presidential stables, where he keeps his favorite filly, Cleopatra.

[5] This annoyed Napoleon. Though a passionate lover, he was said to have suffered from feelings of inadequacy due to the size of his penis. (After his death, the Corsican's gland was removed and given to his father confessor. The penis went through many hands and in 1977 was sold at auction to an American urologist for $3,800. It is said to have looked like "a sea horse" and to have measured one inch in length.)

1810   After divorcing Josephine and her toy spaniel, Napoleon marries Marie Louise, princess of Austria.[6]

1815   Wellington and his charger, Copenhagen, put Napoleon and his charger, Marengo, to flight at Waterloo.

1812   The British invade Washington, D.C. Dolley Madison escapes the White House with the Declaration of Independence and the First Parrot.

1825   President John Quincy Adams puts up General Lafayette and his pet alligator in the East Room of the White House.

[6] On his deathbed in exile on the island of St. Helena, 1821, Napoleon instructed that his heart be pickled in Bordeaux and given to "dear Marie Louise."

NAPOLEON'S LESSON IN NATURE

During the Italian campaign in 1796, Napoleon took a walk on the battlefield one night among his wounded and fallen soldiers. He was suddenly startled when a dog dashed out of the darkness as if to attack him, then retreated into the shadows, howling terribly. The general found the dog crouched over the body of a dead infantryman, licking his face. Later, Napoleon recorded in his diary what he had seen, and concluded with these words:

"No incident on any field of battle ever produced so deep an impression on me. I involuntarily stopped to contemplate the scene. This man, thought I, had friends in the camp, or in his company; and now he lies forsaken by all except his dog! What a lesson nature here presents through the medium of an animal!"

OUR FOUNDING FIDOS

There are three faithful friends—an old wife, an old dog, and ready money.

BENJAMIN FRANKLIN, *POOR RICHARD'S ALMANACK* (1757)

The father of our nation and the signers of the Declaration of Independence—Thomas Jefferson, John Adams, William Whipple, Ben Franklin, Francis Lightfoot Lee, and the others—were all great animal lovers. But the greatest of them all was certainly George Washington himself.

Our first president had a particularly soft spot for dogs. His feelings for them are clear from the names he chose for his own: Venus, Sweetlips, and Truelove. There were also the hounds given him by General Lafayette: Busy, Drunkard, Taster, Tipler, Forester, Vulcan, and Searcher. Nor should we forget Madame Moose.

When he was not seeing to affairs of state, the president was often at Mount Vernon, seeing to the needs of his pets. He recorded such matters in his diary.

> *A new coach dog has arrived for the benefit of Madame Moose; her amorous fits should therefore be attended to.*

The first First Dogs sometimes got into mischief, and the president was often amused. One day his hound Vulcan stole a prize Virginia ham from Martha's table, devouring the whole thing. Martha was beside herself with her husband no less than his dog. Instead of spanking Vulcan, the president reportedly roared with laughter.

ALL THE PRESIDENTS' PETS—V
RED, WHITE, AND BLUE BIRDS

I sincerely congratulate you on the arrival of the mockingbird. Learn all the children to venerate it as a superior being in the form of a bird.

THOMAS JEFFERSON, IN A LETTER TO
HIS DAUGHTER MARTHA

Birds have been venerated by great men and at the service of nations since the beginning of time. Following the Revolution, the eagle became the symbol of our fledgling nation, against the strenuous objection of Benjamin Franklin, who preferred the turkey. Franklin was outvoted by his colleagues Thomas Jefferson and George Washington, detractors of the gobbler.

Now a brief catalog of our nation's First Birds, no eagles or turkeys among them, but all great patriots:

- George Washington had a green parrot whom his granddaughter Nellie Custis taught to sing "Pauvre Madelon."
- Thomas Jefferson's constant companion was Dick, a mockingbird. Perched on the president's shoulder, Dick took food from his lips and provided vocal accompaniment when he played violin.
- Andrew Jackson kept his prize Tennessee fighting cocks at the White House, plus a parrot named Poll. When Jackson died and was laid to rest in Nashville, Poll attended his funeral and screamed expletives at his mourners.
- Ulysses S. Grant had a parrot given him by Mexican minister Matias Romero. Of the bird's excitable disposition, the president said: "One might have imagined him nurtured on chili peppers."
- Calvin Coolidge's wife, Grace, kept two warbling Hartz Mountain canaries, Nip and Tuck; Snowflake, a

white canary; Old Bill, a thrush; and a mynah bird that regularly perched on the First Lady's head.

• JFK had two parakeets, Bluebelle and Maybelle, and a canary, Robin. When Robin passed away, he was buried with pomp on the South Lawn by Caroline and John John.

• William McKinley kept a Mexican yellow-headed parrot, Washington Post. In addition to being very affectionate—"Oh, look at the pretty girls!" he would call to elderly matrons visiting the White House—the First Bird was also a great patriot. His master boasted:

That parrot could complete almost any ordinary song I'd hum, sing, or whistle. If I began a few bars of "Yankee Doodle" or "America," and then stopped, he would finish the song!

RAFFLES

Raffles, a mynah cock brought from Malaya by American explorer Carveth Wells, was decorated with the Lavender Heart Award of 1943 for his stirring renditions of "The Star-Spangled Banner" throughout World War II. Later the bird worked in radio and film. His annual personal appearances netted $15,000. Walt Disney threw a retirement wingding for Raffles in 1949.

WOOFERS AND TWEETERS

Though birds were quite vocal during the Revolutionary Period and in the formative days of our nation, they seem to have quieted down along with all other pets. So it is commonly believed that we don't have any real talking animals anymore. The late great days of Pluto's dog, Balaam's ass, and Thomas Jefferson's Dick are over, we think.

But, in fact, this could not be farther from the truth:

- 1936, Washington, D.C., FDR invited Golden Gloves boxer Arthur "Stubby" Stubbs and his pit bull champion, Bud, to the White House to sing. Bud (who had recently performed at the Grand Ole Opry) sang an entire set of Stephen Foster tunes; Stubby accompanied on banjo.
- 1954, England. Mattie Williams, a teacher from Newcastle, entered her budgie, Sparkie, in a budgie talking competition. Besting 2,768 competitors, Sparkie recited 531 words, 383 sentences, and 8 nursery rhymes. At his death in 1962 the bird uttered these last words to Ms. Williams: "I love you, Mama."

Ms. Williams stuffed Sparkie and donated him to the Hancock Museum in Newcastle.

- 1965, England. The Best Talking Bird Award of the National Aviary Show went to an African gray parrot, Prudle: he had a vocabulary of eight hundred words, spoke in complete sentences, and reasoned.
- 1980, Soviet Union. The Tass News Agency reported that a raven from Minsk was found flying around a local fishing hole, inspecting anglers' catches and telling them what they had hooked.
- July 13, 1983, Soviet Union. Tass reported that an elephant in the Russian zoo, Batir, was found talking to himself. He used more than twenty phrases, including "Batir is good" and "Have you watered the elephant?"
- 1986, Soviet Union. Tass reported that a parrot from Minsk, belonging to Boris Kozyrev, had flawlessly recited Shakespeare's eighth sonnet (in English) and a Pushkin poem (in Russian).
- 1986, U.S. Koko, a female gorilla under the care of Dr. Penny Patterson, learned sign language at the San

Francisco Gorilla Foundation. Her favorite phrases included "dirty toilet devil," "bad gorilla nut," and "rotten bird." Besides talking, her other favorite pastimes were photography, riding in the car, playing telephone, and tickling her cat, All Ball.

THE LAST ROYAL GIRAFFE

Returning to the Ruff and Rover Age now, it is only fitting to conclude with a pet story that includes all the ingredients of that complicated, stormy period when royalty saw its last great days.

In 1825, ten years after the fall of Napoleon, relations between Egypt and France were strained. Bernardino Drovetti, French consul-general in Cairo, hoping to improve them, persuaded the viceroy of Egypt, Muhammad Ali Pasha, to give King Charles X one of his pet giraffes.

Meanwhile, the British—whose relations with Egypt also needed a boost—put in a request for a giraffe, too. Muhammad Ali Pasha happened to have a pair on hand that had just recently come to him from a Sudanese nobleman, Muker Bey.

Sensing rivalry between the French and English—France hadn't forgotten Waterloo ten years before—Muhammad Ali had the consuls draw lots for the giraffes. Afterward the French consul, Drovetti, wrote triumphantly to his superior, Baron de Damas: "I am happy to inform Your Excellency that fate has been kind to us. Our giraffe is strong and vigorous, whereas the one destined for the King of England is sickly and will not last long!"

In fact, the English giraffe died shortly after the drawing.

Meanwhile, Drovetti arranged to ship the French giraffe—a robust female—to King Charles by a Sardinian brig, *I Due Fratelli (The Two Brothers)*. A hole was cut through the upper deck for her neck, and a tarp was strung overhead. To keep her company, Drovetti shipped with her two milk cows, two antelope, and three Sudanese natives. Finally, he draped a miniature Koran from her neck to ward off disease and evil spirits.

The giraffe arrived on the Continent safe and sound, if a little wobbly from the voyage, on October 13, 1826. She wintered in Marseilles. Early that spring a triumphal 880-kilometer, forty-one-day giraffe parade set out for Paris. The route was thronged with cheering crowds that included celebrities such as the novelist Stendhal. From Paris, the giraffe was immediately sent on to the imperial château at Saint-Cloud. Here King Charles was waiting impatiently.

When she arrived, the royal family was out en masse for the reception: Charles (in a blue sash), his son and heir, the duke of Angouleme, and the duchess of Berry. After his color guard presented arms, Charles showered his animal with rose petals. Following the gala, she was returned to Paris and installed in a heated apartment in the rotunda of the Jardin des Plantes (Zoological Gardens).

Mementos of the parade and reception became the rage in France: giraffe-printed cloth, warming irons, snuff boxes. The claviharp was renamed the "giraffe piano." Women wore towering bouffants.

The giraffe outlived Charles X, died in 1845, was stuffed and installed in the Jardin des Plantes gallery.

And, on this grand note, so ended the Revolutionary Period of pet history.

VI.
THE
WILD AND
WOOLLY AGE

*My husband was as courteous in responding to his dogs'
demonstrations, and as affectionate, as he would be to a
person.*

Elizabeth B. Custer, *Gen. Custer in Kansas and Texas* (1889)

*He was squatting behind his camp fire, gnawing some-
thing which he held between his fingers—surely a baby's
head! In a moment, my nerves recovering, I saw it was
only the boiled head of a small flat-faced dog. I "How-
How'd" a greeting and he grunted in return.*

**Moreton Frewen, British adventurer, of a dinner encounter
with Sitting Bull, shortly after the Dakota chief's victory
over Custer, c. 1878**

*Having been so long accustomed to live on the flesh of
dogs, the greater part of us have acquired a fondness for
it, and our original aversion for it overcome by reflecting
that while we subsisted on that food we were fatter,
stronger, and in general enjoyed better health than at any
period since leaving buffalo country.*

**Meriwether Lewis, leader of the Lewis and Clark
Expedition, 1804**

THE VERY WILD AND WOOLLY DAYS

The events of the Wild and Woolly Age took place in the untamed wilderness of the New World. The Indians and their pets had been residing in this land for several thousands of years, but somewhat uneventfully until Europeans arrived with theirs.

Native Americans from the Atlantic to the Pacific held animals to be sacred. The canine was a particular object of reverence. Some Great Plains tribes called the dog *kadosch,* or "son-in-law." One group called themselves the Karankawa, or the "dog-lovers." The Bella Coola of western Canada believed canines understood human speech.

By the middle of the nineteenth century Indian dogs abounded. "Each wigwam had a goodly supply," reported adventurer James F. Rusling in 1874. But he added, "They were the most incessant yelpers I ever listened to. . . . When they became noisier than usual, some passing squaw would dash at them with a stick and a shower of goddamns."

For their part, the settlers named many frontier locales after their companions. Dogtown, California, was named in honor of a local Frenchwoman's kennel. Dog Lake, Yosemite, after a sheepdog originally found there with a litter of puppies. There was also Dog River, Oregon; Dogtooth Creek, North Dakota; Dog Valley, Utah.

Soon the canine population in many frontier towns exceeded the human. In 1847, Los Angeles (human population 1,600) was so overrun by dogs, Colonel Philip St. George

Cooke ordered his soldiers to "shoot or bayonet" all strays. New Mexico also had a problem. "If Santa Fe could boast of nothing else," said resident George Rutledge Gibson, "it might lay claim to the appellation of 'biggest dog town in the Union.' . . . There is a perpetual bark from sundown to sunrise."[1]

Acting as Indian fighters, hunters, explorers, shepherds, and Gold Rush mushers, dogs were indispensable to the taming of the West. Nor should we forget the contribution of others. Until the dawn of the railroad, horses were of course the most important means of transportation. Cats did a good deal of mousing and provided companionship to scores of lonely settlers.

Though they had less than an easy time of it during this rugged period, pets were still well loved in the important circles. At the height of the Indian Wars and the career of Buffalo Bill, president Rutherford Hayes had a greyhound, Grim, who was run over by a train. And of that dog he said, "The death of Grim has made us all mourn. He was a great ornament to our house. The whole country knew him, and respected him."

Now, the other historic events of the early or Very Wild and Woolly Age:

Dateline   **Milestone**

1609 (A.D.)   While exploring Lake Champlain, French explorer Samuel de Champlain witnesses Champ, the sea monster. His description of the creature: "Serpentine, about twenty feet long, thick as a barrel and with the head of a horse."

1784   Daniel Boone explores the Appalachians and Ozarks with his dogs and the family cat, Bluegrass. Years later American artist Alonzo Chappel

---

[1] The barking problem wasn't restricted to the Wild West. Back across the Atlantic, Charles Dickens was complaining in a letter to a friend: "I am driven mad by dogs who have taken it into their accursed heads to assemble every morning in the piece of ground opposite (my study), and who have barked this morning for five hours without intermission; positively rendering it impossible for me to work!"

painted a portrait of the frontiersman with his favorite English setter.

1788   South Carolina becomes the Coyote state.[2]

1804   Lewis and Clark, Sacajawea (or Bird Woman), and Scannon (Lewis's black Newfoundland) explore the Louisiana Purchase. (See "Mange on the Range," page 190.)

1805   October 10: Lewis and Clark buy dog meat on the Snake River. (See "Cur à la Carte," page 193.)

1812   Canned food is invented by Bryan Doukin but doesn't catch on immediately with explorers.

1815   Barry, the hero St. Bernard rescue dog, is stuffed and installed in the National Museum, Bern, Switzerland.

1824   RSPCA, the Royal Society for the Prevention of Cruelty to Animals, is founded in London.

1850   Cathouses flourish in the Old West. Miss Kitty reportedly runs the franchise in Dodge City.

1852   President Millard Fillmore, a one-termer and in 1856 a candidate for the "Know-Nothing Movement," founds a Buffalo preservation society.

In the next three decades, thirteen million bison are wiped out. Buffalo Bill bags 4,862 in a single season.

1876   The Battle of Little Big Horn. Comanche, Captain Myles W. Keogh's horse, is the only survivor. (Comanche dies of colic in 1893, at thirty. He is stuffed and displayed at the University of Kansas.)

1876   A "Big Hairy Monster" (AKA BHM) is captured in Kentucky and exhibited in a traveling freak show as "the Wild Man of the Woods." (See "The Fur Side: Big Hairy Monsters," page 218.)

---

[2] Later, Louisiana became the Pelican State; Minnesota—the Gopher State; New Mexico—the Roadrunner State; Oregon—the Beaver State.

1880 Sixty-foot winged monsters with the heads of collies and the feet of frogs are spotted in various locales, from Arizona to New Jersey, by ranchers, Ojibway Indians, and other "reputable persons." (See "The Feather Side: Big Birds," page 220.)

Profiles in Currage
MANGE ON THE RANGE

The Old West had many canine heroes. Here are a few:

SCANNON
NEWFOUNDLAND OF MERIWETHER LEWIS, HEAD OF LEWIS AND CLARK EXPEDITION

Scannon rescued Lewis and several others from a charging buffalo in Montana, pushing them out of its path, then driving the bison from camp. Later, Meriwether and Bill rescued the dog from Indian kidnappers.

CUFF
NEWFOUNDLAND OF "COLONEL" P. A. SARPY, NEBRASKA TRAPPER/TRADER/MOUNTAIN MAN

When Sarpy was robbed by Omaha Indians, Cuff chased them down but was shot and killed in the effort. Sarpy went to the Omaha chiefs—dog lovers themselves—and persuaded them to banish Cuff's murderers to the Kickapoos. Then he buried Cuff and, in honor of the dog's heroism, raised a wolf tail above his grave and hired an Omaha to wail at the gravesite at regular intervals.

TOOTS
IRISH SETTER OF A FRONTIER LIEUTENANT, MEXICAN TERRITORY

His master boasted of Toots, "He has whooped every bulldog that ever attacked him, was bitten by a rattlesnake, and sprinkled by a polecat, and has as much sense as many men, and more principle." According to Dabney Herndon in *Recollections of a Virginian in the Mexican, Indian, and Civil Wars* (1894), Toots, when bitten by a rattler a second time, took himself to the vet personally, propped himself on a chair, and, teeth gritted, held out the injured paw for treatment.

FLORA
SHEEPDOG OF FRED FAUL, OROVILLE, CALIFORNIA

In 1880 Flora had a litter of puppies, then went out coyote hunting with her master, Mr. Faul. She chased a coyote into its den and, finding seven pups there, promptly began to nurse them. After Faul killed the mother, Flora adopted the orphan pups, abandoning her own.

(From *Dog Stories and Dog Lore,* Thomas W. Knox, 1887.)

DICK OF ARIZONA
MASCOT OF THE COPPER MINERS OF GLOBE, ARIZONA

According to western chronicler C. H. Buffet in his article "Dick, of Arizona" (1887), though only "8 inches high and 16 round," Dick took on shepherds and cowpokes many times his size. Whom he took on often depended on how much he'd had to drink.

"Dick's no tenderfoot," reported a Globe miner. " 'E'll drink anything, tho' 'e do make a face at whiskey. Beer is what tickles 'im."

One day after one too many, Dick took a spill down a sixty-four-foot mining shaft. His men hoisted him up in a bucket, gave him another draft, and soon he was himself again.

But the next day he fell down another shaft. This time a brew didn't snap him out of it.

At Dick's burial the next day, there was not a dry eye among the miners of Globe.

BUMMER AND LAZARUS

Bummer, part Newfoundland, and Lazarus, a Heinz 57, were old-time San Francisco strays. They became friends when Bummer rescued Lazarus from a killer dog, then nursed him back to health, feeding him scraps. Later, the two chased down runaway horses, killed rats, and performed many other heroic acts. In 1862 voters petitioned the San Francisco Board of Supervisors to exempt the pair from city leash laws.

The following year Lazarus was run over by a fire wagon. Bummer mourned. The *Daily Evening Bulletin* ran an obituary: "Two dogs with but a single bark, two tails that wagged as one."

When Bummer died in 1864, Mark Twain himself penned the epitaph, saying the Newfoundland passed away "full of years and honor and disease and fleas."

In 1992 the E Clampus Vitus Society honored the dogs with a plaque. E Clampus Vitus president Bruce Shelton said of his thirty-eight-chapter historical society, "We don't take ourselves too seriously. We do, however, take history seriously. We're interested in preserving history, recognizing those people, events, and colorful characters, like Lazarus and Bummer, that would be overlooked by mainstream historians."

FURRY FORTY-NINERS

• *In Sonora, California, a prospecting nineteenth-century pooch, while digging for a gopher, struck a nugget worth $70 (a small fortune in those days).*

• *In Idaho, another Gold Rush retriever after another gopher struck such a mother lode that his master gave him a share in the claim.*

PNN EYEWITNESS EXTRA!
GOLD RUSH MUSHERS
(FROM THE WYOMING TELESCOPE—APRIL 9, 1859)

Prospector R. S. Osborn has a light wagon, two New-foundland dogs, two greyhounds, and two pointers for the lead, and with this he expects to distance all the competition!

CUR À LA CARTE
A Tasteless Two-Courser
(with Reviews)

I. APPETIZER

The pièce de résistance was the meat . . . a fat young puppy. . . . I took from my own store a box of sardines . . . but Chino [a Hopi Indian] rejected them with horror. There's gastronomic prejudice for you. This man is sweet on dog, and rejects a sardine with abhorrence. . . . My catholic stomach takes dog and sardine with equal impartiality.

J. H. BEADLE, WESTERN ADVENTURER, GOURMET, OF DINING WITH THE HOPI IN 1865

The ancient Chinese *Book of Rites* classified canines in three categories: 1. House pets. 2. Hunters. 3. Food. The favored breed in the third group was dubbed the chow chow.[3] Until recent years, a sixth of China's food came from dogs, cats, and horses.

The Asians crossed the Bering Sea millennia ago, bringing with them their pets. When the Europeans arrived in the New World, they identified seventeen canine breeds. The Indians raised many for meat.

But not all tribes indulged. The native community was sharply divided into two factions: dog-eaters and non-dog-eaters. In the latter camp were the California Yuki, Crow, and Blackfoot, among others. In the former: the Tiano, Algonquin, Huron, Arapahoe (meaning "dog-eater"), and many more.

The Utes of Utah ate their object of worship before performing the dog dance. The Tsimshian dog-eaters of the Pacific Northwest believed their diet bestowed magical powers.

Tender and succulent, puppies were generally preferred. They were fattened with a special mixture of pemmican and dried fruit. After harvest with a tomahawk, the puppy was suspended upside down from a lodge pole, and the carcass hand-marinated with buffalo fat. Then it was skewered.

According to Randolph Keim, one of Colonel Phil Sheridan's troopers who regularly dined with the Comanche, his hosts followed the roasting with "anxious expectation."

Cat was also consumed. But this was considered a less satisfying meal.

In Yorkshire, England, 1777—lest we think pet eating was restricted to America—a shepherd reportedly ate a large black tomcat on fair day—alive. A year later, March 1, the fifth duke of Bedford bet Lord Barrymore four hundred pounds Barrymore could not find a man who would repeat the deed. His Lordship easily won the wager. His man: a laborer from Harpenden, near St. Albans.

[3] Thus giving rise to the common Western expressions: "chow mein," "chow hound," "chow down," "good chow," "Let's have some chow."

2. ENTRÉE
EXPLORER DOG EATING

> By placing side by side select parts of the two, it would be no easy task even for a good judge to tell the difference by either looks or taste, unless he were previously informed.
>
> **MOUNTAIN MAN RUFUS B. SAGE, OF PORK VERSUS DOG MEAT FROM ROCKY MOUNTAIN LIFE; OR, STARTLING SCENES AND PERILOUS ADVENTURES IN THE FAR WEST (1884)**

• Álvar Núñez Cabeza de Vaca was the first Westerner to reach what became Texas. After shipwreck in the Gulf of Mexico, he wandered eight years on foot throughout the Southwest. He was taken as a slave several times, escaped, and ate canine regularly.

• Captain Gaspar Villagra—a conquistador and a poet —was caught in a snowstorm in the Arizona high country one winter, his horse fell into a crevasse, and he had to turn to his dog for food. Just after Villagra impaled him, the dog, in his death throes, licked Villagra's hand. The conquistador lost his appetite. However, in a footnote to the story, Hubert Howe Bancroft in his *History of Arizona and New Mexico* (1884), adds the following:

In the interests of history, and to the sacrifice of sentiment, I must add that the want of a fire to cook the dog was not without influence on the poet's decision.

There was his head sticking partly out of the kettle, with a fine set of ivories, growling as it were, and the scum was frothing about the teeth. After the mirth had abated and no one had offered to dish out the dog, I appointed Pitcher [a fellow diner] master of ceremonies.

AMERICAN BEAVER TRAPPER CHARLES LARPENTEUR, OF A DINNER WITH COLLEAGUES, PREPARED BY AN INDIAN WOMAN (LARPENTEUR'S CRONIES EXCUSED THEMSELVES)

• In 1719 M. de Belisle, a French explorer, got lost in the Texas wilderness with four companions, plus his dog. After living off bugs and herbs for weeks, Belisle's men inquired if they might eat his dog. Belisle said no. One evening while Belisle was out on a nature call, the men fell on the pet with silverware, and he narrowly escaped. The men died. Belisle survived on earthworms until his best friend killed an opossum and, as a token of gratitude, brought it to him.

• Not all explorers had the forbearance of Belisle. In his account *An Excursion to California over the Great Prairie* (1851), William Kelly admits to splitting his puppy with his traveling companions in the Trinity River country. The victim's name was Sligo. Sligo had recently been given to Kelly as a Christmas present. Right after they decided on the evening's menu, Sligo dropped his ears, let out a whine, and resigned himself to his fate.

Each guest had a large wooden bowl placed before him with a quantity of dog's flesh floating in a profusion of soup or rich gravy.

FANNY KELLY, MY CAPTIVITY AMONG THE SIOUX INDIANS (1871)

• Cannibal parties were not uncommon during this period, including the Oregon-bound Peoria party of 1840, the Bidwell-Bartleson party of 1841, and others. The most notorious was of course the eighty-seven-member Donner group of 1846, trapped in a Sierra snowstorm. According to Frances Donner, one of her family's hounds ate her shoes before she, John, and the kids ate him. Later, after thirty-nine members of the party had suffered the same fate, the survivors were rescued by a Mr. Reed and his five dogs—Tyler, Barney, Trailer, Tracker, and little Cash—and returned to civilization to tell the harrowing story.

I will simply state that dog is not such bad eating; but the quantity which the Indians insist on one's consuming is discouraging in the extreme. You eat a reasonable meal to assure your host that you appreciate his hospitality, when another Indian secures you, and more dog must be eaten. This is continued till you have satisfied yourself of the flavor of various canines, and are absolutely incapable of enduring more dog.

THEODORE R. DAVIS, "A SUMMER IN THE PLAINS," FROM HARPER'S MAGAZINE (1868)

PNN UPDATE
PET EATING TODAY

• On May 25, 1988, *The New York Times* reported that Sir Paul Reeves, leader of New Zealand's Auckland Society for the Prevention of Cruelty to Animals, participated in a ceremony in which pigs were clubbed to death and eaten. The feast was held in honor of an official visit by Vanautu chiefs from the South Pacific. After the affair, Sir Paul resigned his post with the society.

• In 1989, two Cambodian refugees were arrested for cruelty to an animal after eating a puppy given to them as a pet. On March 13, the *Los Angeles Times* reported that a judge dismissed the charges when the detainees claimed that dog eating was customary in Cambodia and so assumed it was okay in America, too.

• According to various news services, Iraqi soldiers shot and ate animals at the Kuwait City Zoo in 1991. The original zoo population was 442; seven months later, it was two dozen.

POETS AND PET LOVERS

I take the liberty of confiding to your charity and humanity the precious little person of my dachshund, Max, who is the best and gentlest and most reasonable and well-mannered, as well as most beautiful small animal of his kind. . . . I shall take it kindly if he be not too often gratified with tidbits at meals. Of course what he most intensely dreams of is being taken out on walks, and the more you are able to indulge him the more he will adore you and the more all the latent beauty of his nature will come out.

HENRY JAMES, TO HIS HOUSESITTER

If 'twere not for my cat and dog, I think I could not live.

EBENEZER ELLIOTT, FROM HIS POEM "MY ONLY FRIENDS"

Where do dogs go? You ask, you unmindful people. They go about their business. Business meetings, love meetings. . . . They go, they come, they trot, they slip under carriages, urged on by fleas, passion, need, or duty. Like us, they get up early in the morning, and they seek their livelihood.

CHARLES BAUDELAIRE, FROM HIS POEM "THE PARISIAN PROWLER"

While pets endured a rugged existence on the American frontier, elsewhere during the same period many were quite well off. Especially those that belonged to the English and French Romanticists.

Alexandre Dumas (author of *The Three Musketeers, The Count of Monte Cristo,* and other classics) founded the Feline Defense League. His colleagues Charles Baudelaire, Guy de Maupassant, and Anatole France joined him in the charitable group. George Sand had breakfast from the same bowl as her cat. Colette, the "poet laureate of the cat," was so devastated by the death of "La Chatte Derniere" she vowed never to have another of the species. Byron took his four geese and his Newfoundland, Boatswain, everywhere.[4] Matthew Arnold wrote with his dachshunds, Geist, Max, and Kaiser; and Mark Twain with his tabbies, Appollinaris and Zoroaster.

Among other literary pets who collaborated with their masters and mistresses on historic work of the age:[5]

KEEPER, BULLDOG, AND TIGER, CAT
EMILY BRONTË

Tiger and Keeper played at Emily's feet while she composed *Wuthering Heights*. After the novelist's death, Keeper slept for many nights at the door of her empty bedroom, as if waiting for her return.

CATARINA, TORTOISESHELL CAT
EDGAR ALLAN POE

Catarina in fact belonged to Poe's wife, Virginia. Notwithstanding his famous "The Black Cat," the author was very fond of Catarina. While Virginia was dying of consumption on a straw bed in the couple's unheated house in Baltimore, the cat kept her warm. Said a visitor, "Her husband's greatcoat and a large tortoiseshell cat were on her bosom. The wonderful cat seemed conscious of her great usefulness."

WILLIAMINA, A WHITE CAT, AND SULTAN, A MASTIFF
CHARLES DICKENS

Originally, Dickens called his cat William—until he had kittens, at which point "he" became Williamina. Williamina was report-

---

[4] Not all of the Romantics, however, were cat lovers. Percy Shelley was said to have tied the string of a kite to a tomcat's tail during a thunderstorm.

[5] Later, many other literary pets flourished: Ernest Hemingway kept many cats, some of whom were on his desk during the composition of *For Whom the Bell Tolls, Old Man and the Sea,* and other works. T. S. Eliot consulted his own

edly a fixture in the novelist's study and would often snuff out his desk candle with a paw to distract him. As for Sultan, Dickens said, "Between him and me there was a perfect understanding." But the mastiff killed neighborhood cats and went after people, too. Finally when Sultan bit a maid's little girl, Dickens took him out to the meadow with a gun, a wheelbarrow, and a heavy heart.

EPONINE, A BLACK CAT
THÉOPHILE GAUTIER

The French novelist, poet, and coiner of the phrase "Art for art's sake," named his cat after the character in Hugo's *Les Misérables*. He set a place for Eponine at his dining table. She sat there, he said, "her paws folded on the tablecloth, her smooth forehead held up to be kissed, and like a well-bred little girl who is politely affectionate to relatives and other people."

CAMP, BULL TERRIER
SIR WALTER SCOTT

Washington Irving described a country walk with Sir Walter in 1817:

> *As we sallied forth, every dog in the establishment turned out to attend us. There was the old staghound, Maida, a noble animal; and Hamlet, the black grey-hound, a wild, thoughtless youngster;... and Finette, a beautiful setter with soft, silken hair, long pendant ears, and a mild eye, the parlour favorite.*

Scott's bullterrier, Camp, reportedly understood many words, people's names in particular. He bit the local baker once; his

---

felines while writing *Old Possum's Book of Practical Cats,* starring Macavity, Bustopher Jones, and Rum Tum Tugger. Raymond Chandler always read first drafts of his murder mysteries to his black Persian, Taki, whom he called "my secretary."

master boxed his ears for it, and afterward every time the baker's name was mentioned, Camp would hide in the corner, tail between his legs.

CHRIS, SPANIEL
JOHN GALSWORTHY

The author of *The Forsyte Saga* played cricket with Chris. The spaniel was an avid cricketer. Said Galsworthy:

> *He played in a manner highly specialized, following the ball up the moment it left the bowler's hand, and sometimes retrieving it before it reached the batsman. When remonstrated with, he would consider a little, hanging out a pink tongue and looking rather too eagerly at the ball, then canter slowly out to a sort of forward short leg.*

Chris was an especially keen fielder when one was hit out of the park:

> *And if the ball were really lost, then indeed he took over the proceedings with an intensity and vigour that destroyed many shrubs.*

(For more of Chris, see "The Further Side: Tails of the Undead—II," page 230.)

GREAT DOG POEMS
1600–1900

Sir John Harrington	"To His Wife, For Striking her Dog"
James Hogg	"An Address to his Auld Dog, Hector"
John Clare	"My Rover"
William Cowper	"Beau and the Bird"

Ebenezer Elliott	"My Only Friends"
Elizabeth Browning	"Flush or Faunus"
Rudyard Kipling	"The Power of the Dog"
Alphonse de Lamartine	"O Dog of Mine!"

THE PETLITZERS
Top Ten Pet Literature 900–1900

Down through the ages there have been two types of pet literature: works that seem to be about something else but are actually about pets; and works that seem to be about pets, then about something else, but in the end turn out to be about pets after all.

The Pet Pulitzers go to works of both types. Listed chronologically, they reflect changing attitudes toward pets—or the domesticated or tameless pet inside us all—in the last thousand years.

Some of the works were obscure or less than enthusiastically received in their day (*Moby Dick,* "The Black Cat," "The Metamorphosis" and so on); others enjoyed bright lights and critical kudos (*Beowulf, Winnie-the-Pooh, Millie's Book,* and others). But they have all withstood the test of time and distinguished themselves as classics:

BEOWULF
UNKNOWN (c. 700)

Epic tale of a wolflike Anglo-Saxon hero who goes mano a mano with Nordic monsters. Much dismemberment, decapitation, and feasting.

BESTIARY
PHILIPPE DE THAUN (c. 1200)

An illustrated omnibus of medieval beasts ranging from unicorns to dragons—posing in picnic scenes with virgins, dogs, and/or sportsmen.

"THE BLACK CAT"
EDGAR ALLAN POE (1843)

An otherwise mild-mannered man spoons out the eye of his favorite cat, Pluto, hangs him, then accidentally ax-murders his wife.

MOBY DICK
HERMAN MELVILLE (1851)

Tale of a godlike white whale and a certain one-legged very irritable sea captain who doesn't know enough to cut his losses and leave Moby alone.

"THE HOUND OF THE BASKERVILLES"
SIR ARTHUR CONAN DOYLE (1902)

A ghostly pooch stumps the famous sleuth.

"THE METAMORPHOSIS"
FRANZ KAFKA (1915)

A Prague accountant turns into a cockroach, takes a sick day, and locks himself in his room, to the growing annoyance of his family.

WINNIE-THE-POOH
A. A. MILNE (1926)

The adventures, trials, and tribulations of Pooh, Eeyore the Donkey, Tigger the Tiger, Roo the Kangaroo, and little Piglet.

PORTRAIT OF THE ARTIST AS A YOUNG DOG
DYLAN THOMAS (1940)

About the poet's winsome youth in Wales before he read Joyce and developed a drinking problem.

ANIMAL FARM
GEORGE ORWELL (1945)

A ruthless pig sets up a fascist junta on a farm, hustling the cows, chickens, and sheep with utopian rhetoric.

MILLIE'S BOOK
MILLIE BUSH (1990)

Heartwarming First Dog's account of having a litter at the White House, and life inside the Beltway.

HONORABLE MENTION

Origin of the Species (1859)—Charles Darwin

The Jungle Book (1894)—Rudyard Kipling

"The Lady with the Dog" (1898)—Anton Chekhov

Call of the Wild (1903)—Jack London

I Am a Cat (1905)—Natsume Soseki

The Wind in the Willows (1908)—Kenneth Grahame

Steppenwolf (1927)—Hermann Hesse

Of Mice and Men (1937)—John Steinbeck

Rabbit Run, Rabbit Redux, Rabbit is Rich (1960–81)—John Updike

Good Dog Carl (1991)—Alexandra Day

DOG LAW

B ack in the land of Colt .44's, desperadoes, cattle rustlers, Billy the Kid, Pat Garrett, and the James gang, pets were second-class citizens in a fledgling judicial system. A Texas judge freed a man for shooting a dog in church when the suspect cited Deuteronomy 23:18 in his defense. "Thou shalt not bring . . . the price of a dog into the house of the Lord thy God."

But as some of the following cases show, dogs and dog lovers did not always get the short end of the stick when seeking justice in the Wild West:

- 1850, California Mother Lode country. A Mexican drifter allegedly stole a watchdog. The penalty was whipping or hanging. The judge favored the latter. But a miner, Luke, pleaded for clemency, and the case was finally dismissed. When the Mexican was set free, the dog jumped up and licked his face, proving his innocence. The miners took up a collection of gold for the Mexican and gave him the pooch, too.[6]
- 1858, San Francisco. According to the *Daily Evening Bulletin,* Thomas O'Brien was charged with grand larceny for stealing the valuable purebred of James Donahue. The judge dismissed the charge, stating that under California law dogs were not property. So Donahue accused O'Brien of petty larceny—for stealing the dog's collar and muzzle. He prevailed.
- 1860, Ranger, TX. Two men claiming ownership of the same pooch took their case to the Honorable Judge McFatter. The defendant said that if he did not answer to the name he gave him—Snip—he would drop his claim since, in that case, he "wouldn't want him anyway." The dog was reportedly snoozing in court when the defendant, before Judge McFatter and

[6] From "The Days of '50," *The Pioneer* (San Jose, CA, 1878).

the jury, knelt down and called, "Here, Snip!" The pooch awakened instantly and dashed over, tail wagging. The defendant prevailed. But the plaintiff appealed, filed a bond, and retained custody of the dog.

The defendant appealed the appeal, but Snip died before a higher court could hear the case.

• 1876, MO. George Graham Vest, who later became a U.S. senator, represented the plaintiff in a dog shooting case. His closing arguments, moving many to tears, sealed the shooter's fate:

The one absolutely unselfish friend that a man can have in this selfish world, the one that never deserts him, the one that never proves ungrateful or treacherous, is his dog. He will sleep on the cold ground where the wintry winds blow and the snow drives fiercely, if only he may be near his master's side. He will kiss the hand that has no food to offer. . . . If fortune drives the master forth an outcast in the world, the faithful dog asks no higher privilege than that of accompanying him, to guard against danger, to fight his enemies.[7]

• 1879, Abilene, KS. Gambler/gunfighter "Wichita Tom" shot citizen Jack Nash's black-and-tan foxhound in cold blood. Witnesses set on Wichita Tom "Kansas style." He was saved by the sheriff and placed under protective custody. That evening, fifty Abileners stormed the jail, dragged out Wichita, took him to a railroad tressel, and dangled him there by his boots till he promised to leave town and never come back.

---

[7] From *U.S. Congressional Record,* second session of the Sixty-eighth Congress.

CALIFORNIA DOG DUTY

California was suffering from another budget crunch a century ago. Also, the canine population was booming. So a new tax was levied: $1 for a dog, $2 for each additional, $3 for a bitch. There was a public outcry. But when in Sacramento the tax was hiked 1000 percent, the Sacramento Reporter *ran an editorial:*

If you want to fight with a man, kick his dog; if you want to fight with a whole town, cart off their dogs to the pound. Seriously, the regulation of dogs may be well enough; but the prohibition of dogs is foolish, and not to be endured!

The Sacramento Board of Trustees reduced canine duty to $2.50 for dogs, $5 for bitches.

OTHER WILD AND WOOLLY CASES
Yesterday and Today

Perjured Pig

Time: 1846.
Jurisdiction: Pleternica, Slavonia.
Defendants: A local pig.
Charge: Eating the ears off a 1-year-old little girl.
Verdict: Guilty.
Sentence: Public execution.

(Note: The pig's owner was sentenced to hard labor to pay for the little girl's dowry, ensuring her of a husband later on, though she had no ears.)

The Case of the Open Aviary Door

Time: c. 1860
Jurisdiction: Paris, France.
Defendant: Mysouff the Cat, belonging to novelist Alexandre Dumas (chairman of the Feline Defense League).
Charge: Eating Dumas's entire collection of exotic birds. (The trial was held at Dumas's residence. His weekend houseguests served as jury. The defense lawyer—another Dumas friend—pleaded clemency for the accused due to "extenuating circumstances": the aviary door had been opened for Mysouff by Dumas's pet monkey.)
Verdict: Guilty.
Sentence: 5-year imprisonment in the cage of his accomplice—the monkey.

(Note: A short time later Dumas sold the monkey and cage and released Mysouff on his own recognizance.)

"A Nice Country for Justice!"

Time: 1877.
Jurisdiction: New York City.
Defendant: Jimmy Dillio, an organ grinder's monkey.
Charge: Biting an Irishwoman, Mary Shea, on the finger.
Disposition: Dismissed

(Note: Enraged by the judge's clemency with her assailant, Jimmy the Monkey, Ms. Shea, who had recently come to New York from Ireland, cried: "This is a nice country for justice!" As soon as the plaintiff was gone, Jimmy, dressed in a scarlet suit and velvet top hat, shook hands with the judge.)

Camel-Smoking Monkey

Time: 1905.
Jurisdiction: South Bend, Indiana.
Defendant: Circus chimpanzee.
Charge: Smoking in public (a misdemeanor in Indiana at that time).
Verdict: Guilty.
Sentence: Owner ordered to pay fine.

Kangaroo Court

Time:	1924.
Jurisdiction:	Chicago.
Defendant:	A local horse.
Charge:	Murder: Throwing gangster Nails Morton off his back, killing him.
Trial:	None.
Sentence:	Nails's buddies from the Dion O'Banion gang kidnapped the horse, took it to the scene of the crime in Lincoln Park, and executed it with tommy guns.

Monkeyshines on the Stand

Time:	1962.
Jurisdiction:	Paris, France.
Defendant:	Makao, a cercopithecoid monkey.
Charge:	Vandalism. Larceny. Mayhem. (The chimp broke into a nearby apartment, ate lipstick, broke household items, and stole a diamond ring from a jewelry box.)
Defense:	Makao's owner argued that the chimp could not open a jewelry box. Makao took the stand, was sworn in, and promptly opened the box when the prosecutor presented it to him.
Verdict:	Guilty.
Sentence:	Owner ordered to pay for lipstick, destroyed knickknacks, and diamond ring.

Smuggler Pigeons

Time:	1963.
Jurisdiction:	Tripoli, North Africa.
Defendants:	75 carrier pigeons.
Charge:	Grand larceny. (Working for an international smuggling cartel, the birds flew stolen currency from Europe to North Africa.)
Verdict:	Guilty.
Sentence:	Calling them "too well trained and dangerous to be let loose," the court ordered all 75 pigeons to be executed. Their employers were fined.

CAT CODE

Some of the Old West pet laws are still on the books, especially those that pertain to that most unruly species —cats.

- *Montana (Lemonine)* Cats must wear three bells to warn birds of their approach.

- *Louisiana (Morrisburg)* Cats are strictly prohibited from chasing ducks.

- *Texas (Dallas)* Cats in the street after dark must wear a headlight.

- *Mississippi (Natchez)* Cats are strictly prohibited from drinking beer.

ROOTIN', TOOTIN', AND DOG SHOOTIN'

There was a good deal of lead flying from the Mississippi to the Rio Grande, and dogs found themselves trying to dodge it almost as often as did buffalo, Indians, and cattle rustlers.

On July 15, 1789, Spanish officials in Santa Fe, New Mexico, ordered the elimination of all strays.

Pioneers on an 1845 Oregon-bound wagon train were informed: "Every dog found running about camp at large shall be shot at the discretion of the Captain." Three years earlier, the leader of another Oregon-bound train, Reverend Elijah White, a missionary, ordered that all dogs be shot to avoid a rabies plague. The order was carried out in Dog Encampment, Missouri, but after protest from dog owners the shooting was stopped and Reverend White was fired.

On December 27, 1881, a miner checked into a Los Angeles

rooming house but couldn't sleep because of the racket outside his window. He wrote a letter to the *Times:*

> *"Scarcely had my head touched the pillow when my ears were greeted with an unearthly howl. . . . In vain I covered my head with blankets and a pillow. . . . Finally, half suffocated and wholly enraged, I sprung from my bed. "City of Angels, indeed, city of devils rather," I exclaimed, and seized my forty-horse-power, double-action link-motion, centre-fire liver-searcher!*

The hapless visitor did not hit any dogs but dispatched a prize neighborhood bull. His tormenters scattered, but it wasn't long before they were back with a vengeance. He continued:

> *Only last night I had the doubtful pleasure of seeing the right sleeve of my best coat disappearing up Aliso Street, propelled by a huge dog, who in his haste to sample the quality of my broadcloth managed to take a fair portion of the muscular development of my forearm at the same time.*

Another tale of underdog triumph is related by George E. Peckham in his "Reminiscences of an Active Life" (Nevada Historical Society Papers, 1917–19). It seems that around 1870 a certain "undesirable cur" was hanging around the coach station in Virginia City, Nevada. The ticket agent tried every means to shoo him off, but to no avail. Finally he and his assistants struck on a foolproof plan: they tied a stick of dynamite to the loiterer's tail. No sooner was it secured, however, than the dog charged the clerk and his cackling cronies. They scattered, the pooch dashed into the next-door saloon, wagged the bomb off his tail, and it exploded under a potbellied stove, throwing many saloon patrons under tables if they were not already there.

Doggerel

SPOT POT SHOTS

I tried to kill that Spot once—he was no good for anything.... I stopped in a likely place, put my foot on the rope, and pulled my big Colts. And that dog sat down and looked at me. I tell you he didn't plead. He just looked.... And I want to tell you right now that it got beyond me. It was like killing a man, a conscious, brave man who looked calmly into your gun as much as to say, "Who's afraid?"

JACK LONDON, "THAT SPOT"

Don't look now, dear. I'll tell you about it afterwards.

WINSTON CHURCHILL, TO HIS POODLE, RUFUS, COVERING HIS EYES WHILE THE TWO WATCH OLIVER TWIST—THE SCENE WHERE BILL SIKES IS ABOUT TO KILL HIS DOG

Here [in California] you will find in every little village a thousand dogs who never had a master.... They had become so troublesome that an order was given to thin their ranks. The marines, with their muskets, were to be the executioners....

> *The dogs, the dogs! My gallant lads,*
> *Let each one seize his gun,*
> *And lead the battle's fiery van,*
> *Though Mars himself should run!*

WALTER COLTON, POET—MAYOR OF MONTEREY, CALIFORNIA JANUARY 11, 1847

PNN EYEWITNESS EXTRAS!
BOULDER PASSES THE SPASM— DOGS MAY BARK AGAIN! (FROM THE BOULDER DAILY CAMERA— MARCH 18, 1910)

BOULDER, CO.

A crowd gathered on 10th and Barton to watch a handsome fox terrier that was running about, nose in the air, while froth was running from the dog's mouth.

"He's mad!" yelled a St. Louis reporter.

The fox terrier stood in the center of the group with wide-opened eyes, either too mad or too frightened to move. At this juncture a policeman arrived. A dozen voices began to tell him that the dog was mad and must be shot. . . . A tall, gaunt-looking woman pushed through the crowd and started toward the dog. A dozen men yelled at her, two or three grabbed her. She picked the dog up and started out of the crowd. The policeman stopped her with: "Madam, the dog is mad. He must be shot. Look at the foam coming out of his mouth!"

"Foam?" she said contemptuously. "That's the cream puff he's been eating!"

AN IDIOT
(From the *Golden Transcript*— January 12, 1905)

SALMON RIVER, ID.

Captain Jack Tubbs, also known as the "Dynamiter," was on a prospecting tour of the Salmon River. He was followed by his favorite dog, which, like most of his species, was fond of running after sticks. Tubbs, making camp with his associates one evening, decided to use his dynamiting skills to fish. He threw a large, lit stick into the river, and the dog immediately jumped in and retrieved it. The captain broke into a frantic run through the hills to get away from the dog and was almost overtaken. The captain was saved, but not a visible hair of the dog was left to tell the tale.

THE PIANO RETRIEVER

You didn't have to throw a stick in the water to get him to go in. Of course, he would bring back a stick if you did throw one in. He would even have brought back a piano if you had thrown one in.

JAMES THURBER, "SNAPSHOT OF A DOG"

ANIMAL PEOPLE

My mother was an Ape. . . . I never knew who my father was.

**TARZAN, EDGAR RICE BURROUGHS,
FROM *TARZAN OF THE APES* (1914)**

In the 1500s, explorers reported animal people in the New World. Christopher Columbus witnessed dog-headed men (*Cynecephalus*) in the West Indies. Ferdinand Magellan encountered dog-faced people in the Andaman Islands, Burma, and Russia.

In 1573, Ambroise Paré wrote *Monstres et Prodiges,* the first definitive encyclopedia on animal people. The text included clinical descriptions and illustrations of "examples of the Wrath of God": a horse-man, a cat-child, the Birdman of Ravenna, the frog-faced boy,[8] among many others. Ulisse Aldrovandi followed Paré with his even more inclusive 1642 study *Monstrorum Historia,* which included such wonders as the goose-headed man.

Public interest in animal people peaked in the late 1800s. At this time, both in the United States and abroad, there were many traveling freak and monster shows, some affiliated with circuses. The most popular, P. T. Barnum's Greatest Show on Earth, boasted a full cast of wonders: "Koo Koo, the Bird Girl," "Priscilla, the Monkey Girl," "Lionel, the Lion-faced Man," as well as Armadillo Man, Alligator Boy, the Leopard Family, and many mermaids.

Animal people flourished especially during the Wild and Woolly Age. Here is a survey of some of the most notable cases then and now.

JOSEPH, THE LITHUANIAN BEAR-BOY

Captured by hunters in the mountains of Lithuania in 1661, he was caged and carried to Warsaw, where he was baptized and christened Joseph. He bit, clawed, snarled like a bear, and subsisted on raw flesh and grass. Though later he mastered a small vocabulary and became a gamekeeper for a Polish count, he persisted in most of his original habits.

FRAUMARK BEAR-GIRL

In 1767, hunters from Fraumark, Hungary, shot a bear in the mountains and were instantly attacked by his eighteen-year-old

---

[8] According to Paré, the frog-faced boy was conceived in 1517 when his father forced himself on his mother while she was holding a frog. The mother was sick in bed with a fever at the time, and holding a frog was a common antidote for fever with sixteenth-century French country folk.

The conception of future animal people invites comparison to the frog-boy. Joseph Merrick, the Elephant Man, who died in 1890, attributed his condition, according to his physician, Dr. Frederick Treves, to "a shock experienced by his mother shortly before his birth, when knocked down by an elephant at a circus." Another interesting case during the same period was that of Marie Bartels, the "Dog-Woman," who said that her mother, when pregnant with her, had been terrified by a "big, shaggy dog."

girlfriend. After some effort, they overpowered the Amazon, skinned her boyfriend, and transported her to the Karpfen insane asylum. Here she shunned dresses and continued to eat jerky and birch bark.

TARZAN OF THE APES
(AKA William Mildin, the Fourteenth Earl of Streatham)

In 1868, the young English nobleman, eleven years old, was the sole survivor of a shipwreck off the African coast. He was adopted by monkeys. Fifteen years later, he was captured by adventurers and returned to civilization. Edgar Rice Burroughs's *Tarzan* series was based on William Mildin. (The nonfiction Tarzan legacy continued in 1933 when an ape-boy, "Tarzancito," was captured in the jungles of El Salvador.)[9]

JO-JO THE DOG-FACED BOY (AKA FEODOR)

Jo-Jo toured Europe with a small circus at the turn of the century. "Looks like a man, barks like a dog, crawls on his belly like a snake!" cried his barker. In fact, Jo-Jo looked more like a Skye terrier. He was exhibited with his father, who resembled a poodle and was billed as "l'Homme-Chien," the Man-Dog.[10]

GRACE McDANIELS, MULE-WOMAN

She toured with American circuses during the same period as Jo-Jo and became a rival to Julia Pastrana, "the ugliest woman in the world." Said Edward G. Malone, owner of the largest collection of freak photos, "She didn't actually look like a mule, of course; more like a hippopotamus—in the face." Malone went on to say, "She was attractive to a lot of men, too, believe it or not. I can't tell you how many proposals of marriage she

---

[9] The most recent ape-boy was discovered in South Africa in 1974. His story was run in the *Johannesburg Times* two years later. The boy was studied by behaviorists B. F. Skinner and colleague Dr. Harlan Lane.

[10] Photos of the two, as well as many other animal people, can be found in the Circus World Museum, Baraboo, Wisconsin.

received before Grace finally accepted a nice-looking young fellow who was very much in love with her."

IRAQI GAZELLE-BOY

This lad grew up in the 1950s in the desert with a herd of gazelle. As an adolescent he was chased down by Iraqi soldiers. He ran at remarkable speed in soaring leaps, and his captors needed a jeep to catch him. Later, he escaped, but the Iraqis recaptured him and cut his Achilles' tendons.[11]

KARIN BELANG, INDONESIAN SNAKE-BOY

In 1987, Karin, at age two, was adopted by his brothers' pet female python, Si. Throughout Karin's infancy, Si spent most of her time coiled around his crib, baby-sitting. Today, the thirty-foot constrictor reportedly takes daily baths with the boy, swims with him in local lagoons, and slithers by his side when he goes for walks. Si leaves her adopted son's side only for brief periods to return to the jungle for meals. She is said to take goats and pigs in a single bite.

THE FUR SIDE
BIG HAIRY MONSTERS

During the Wild and Woolly Period there were many sightings of Big Hairy Monsters—BHMs, AKA Big Foot or Sasquatch. The Big Hairy Monster is of particular interest to scientists since some believe it is the missing link—the evolutionary linchpin between man and animal. Many, of course, dismiss the creature out of hand. Yet there have been over ten thousand documented sightings in the last century alone.

---

[11] Not long afterward, in 1960, another gazelle-boy was documented in the Sahara by Jean Claude Armen, the noted Basque poet. Armen studied the boy for a time—he behaved just like his adoptive family, grazing, rooting, watering —then left him as he had found him.

In Kentucky, 1876, a BHM was captured and exhibited as "the Wild Man of the Woods." A few years later, according to President Theodore Roosevelt in his book *Wilderness Hunter,* a Bigfoot killed a sportsman in Wisdom River, Idaho. On October 20, 1967, Roger Patterson took a snapshot of a fleeing BHM in Bluff Creek, California. A Yeti was photographed in the Garhwal Himalayas by Anthony Woolbridge, researcher for Central Electricity Generating Board, 1986. And in that same year the Chinese declared Hubei Province National Park a BHM reserve.[12]

Naturally reclusive, Big Hairy Monsters avoid humans. But some have made an exception in the case of bachelor loggers and menstruating women.

- In the Middle Ages, BHMs regularly carried damsels off into the woods. A scene of such an abduction appears in the fourteenth-century Taymouth *Book of Hours.*
- British Columbia, 1871. An Indian woman was kidnapped by a BHM and lived with him and his parents in a cave for a year. She later reported that he treated her "kindly."
- British Columbia, 1924. A logger, Albert Ostman, was muscled out of camp by three BHMs—an older couple and their spinster daughter. Ostman later reported:

The Old Lady was over seven feet tall . . . 500–600 pounds. She had very wide hips and a gooselike walk. She was not built for beauty or speed. Some of those Lovable brassieres and uplifts would have been a great improvement on her looks and her figure.

[12] According to *The New York Times* (June 19, 1990), the International Society of Cryptozoology, headed by Quentin Keynes (great-grandson of Charles Darwin, nephew of economist John Maynard Keynes), has done field research on the Wildmen of Shennonjia Forest in central China. The main thrust of the study: to determine scientifically if the creatures really exist or are a product of the Chinese imagination.

Ostman believed he was taken as a husband for the Old Lady's daughter. He said he escaped the BHMs before their honeymoon night.

• China, 1939. A peasant woman was spirited off by creatures locally known as "the Wildmen of Hupeh." On return, she denied having consummated her relationship with her abductors. Nine months later she gave birth to a small gorilla.

• South Lake Tahoe, CA, 1989. Erik Beckjord, forty-three, head of the National Cryptozoological Society, informed *Los Angeles Times* reporter Al Martinez that he had recently had a telepathic conversation with Bigfoot in the High Sierra. "This is going to sound weird," he told Martinez. "But I received a mental message [from Bigfoot] that said, 'We're here, but we're not here.' " (*Los Angeles Times,* September 2, 1989)

THE FEATHER SIDE
BIG BIRDS

Another creature often spotted during this untamed period was something known to Native American tribes as *piasa* ("the bird that devours men"). It was called thunderbird, mothman, owlman, and later, by New Yorkers, the Jersey devil.

On April 26, 1890, the *Tombstone Herald* of Arizona reported the shooting of a specimen by two ranchers in the Huachucas mountains. It measured sixty feet in length, with a wingspan of one hundred feet, and its torso resembled an alligator's. The ranchers took a snapshot of the creature, but unfortunately it was misplaced.

Here are some eyewitness descriptions of big birds:

> *The creature was as large as a calf; had deer horns, a horrible red eye, a tiger beard, and a face like a man's.*

JACQUES MARQUETTE, MISSIONARY EXPLORER, 1675

*He was about three and a half feet high, with a head
like a collie dog and a face like a horse. . . . My wife
and I were scared, I tell you, but I managed to open
the window and say, "Shoo!" and it turned around,*
barked *at me, and flew away.*

**NELSON EVANS, OF THE JERSEY DEVIL THAT LANDED ON
HIS ROOF JANUARY 19, 1909, SHORTLY AFTER THE
MONSTER HAD REPORTEDLY FLOWN OFF WITH
A DOG IN NEARBY CAMDEN**

It was on my lawn, flames coming from its mouth.

**MRS. J. H. WHITE, WHO SPOTTED THE CREATURE AFTER
IT, OR A LOOK-ALIKE, HAD ALLEGEDLY BEEN SHOT BY
PHONE COMPANY EMPLOYEE THEODORE D. HACKETT**

There's a bird outside as big as a B-29!

**JAMES TRARES, TWELVE-YEAR-OLD, TO HIS MOTHER
AFTER SPOTTING THE CREATURE OUTSIDE THEIR
ILLINOIS HOUSE, JANUARY 1948**

*A huge bird it was: a lot bigger than the planes you see
go by today. It didn't flap its wings. Not even once.*

**JAMES RED SKY, OJIBWAY INDIAN, OF THUNDER BAY,
ONTARIO, CANADA, 1950S**

PNN HARD COPY!

DEVIL MAKES FOR JERSEY
(FROM THE NEW YORK TIMES—
SEPTEMBER 12, 1880)

NEW YORK, NEW YORK.

At the height of at least a thousand feet a strange object was in
the act of flying toward the New Jersey coast. It was apparently
a man with bat's wings and frog's legs. . . . It wore a cruel and

determined expression. . . . It was seen by many reputable persons and they all agree that it was a man engaged in flying toward New Jersey.

THE SEMIWILD AND WOOLLY DAYS

A s the nineteenth century advanced toward the twentieth, pet history was still wild and woolly, but a little less so than before. Important moderating and civilizing influences were now at work: much pedigree dog and cat breeding was being done, the first officially sanctioned purebred shows were held, a revolutionary zoological theory was conceived, and there were important political developments for the larger quadrupeds:

Dateline	Milestone
1828 (A.D.)	The donkey becomes the standard-bearer of the Democratic party.
1844	Queen Victoria's poodle attacks P. T. Barnum and his seven-year-old, two-foot-tall dwarf, Tom Thumb, while the monarch holds audience with the famous pair. Tom beats off the royal poodle with his cane, much to the delight of Victoria and the court.
1847	General Robert E. Lee writes home from the Mexican War, asking his daughter, Mildred, to send him his cat to keep him company on the front.
1854	The elephant becomes the standard-bearer of the Republican party.
1856	Darwin explores the Galápagos on the HMS *Beagle* and conceives the idea that man is descended from apes.
1859	First official dog show: Newcastle upon Tyne, England: fifty pointers and setters.

1860   German tax collector Ludwig Dobermann breeds the first Doberman Pinscher from Great Danes, German shepherds, rottweilers, and pinschers—for protection from bandits.

1860   Louis Pasteur discovers germs, develops a rabies vaccine, and praises cats for cleanliness.

1863   Outbreak of Civil War. President of the Confederacy Jefferson Davis visits various battle sites with his dogs, Bonin and Traveler. (See "Celebrity Pet Profile: Jefferson Davis's Bonin and Traveler," page 224.)

1866   Abraham Lincoln's dog, Fido, is assassinated the year after his master. (See "All the Presidents' Pets —VI: Tragedy," page 226.)

1870   The golden retriever is developed through a cross of bloodhounds and golden-coated Russian circus dogs.

Modern Yorky is developed by English miners to kill giant gray rats in mine shafts.

1871   First official cat show opens in London's Crystal Palace, emceed by feline fancier and impresario Harrison Weir. One hundred and seventy cats enter and compete for $100 in prize money.[13]

1873   EKC, English Kennel Club, is founded in London. First English stud book compiled.

1884   AKC, American Kennel Club, is founded in New York. First American stud book compiled.

1890   Gia Long, emperor of China, dies. Grief-stricken, his war elephant retires to the hills. From that day on, he returns once a year to the emperor's grave, on the anniversary of his death.

---

[13] One of the winners is Harrison Weir's fourteen-year-old tabby, Old Lady. The judges for the Crystal Palace Show were Weir himself and Weir's brother.

1897   Harrison Weir founds the National Cat Club of England.

1903   Jack London writes *Call of the Wild, The Sea Wolf, White Fang.*

SALLIE, CIVIL WAR HEROINE

Sallie was the bulldog mascot of the Eleventh Pennsylvania Volunteers during the Civil War. She entered many battles and comforted the wounded. She was wounded herself and recovered after surgery in the field. When President Lincoln reviewed the Eleventh Penn, he tipped his hat to Sallie marching at the head of the color guard. Later the heroic bulldog fell at Gettysburg. A monument was erected there in her honor.

CELEBRITY PET PROFILE
JEFFERSON DAVIS'S BONIN AND TRAVELER

In 1854 Commodore Matthew Perry returned from his first expedition to Japan with parasols, vases, wall hangings, and many other gifts from the emperor to President Franklin Pierce. The president told his secretary of war, Jefferson Davis, to help himself to anything he liked. Davis declined.

"Well then, General," declared the president, "I have a present for you—a dog."

Davis already had many hounds and cats, even a spider monkey. Seeing him hesitate to take on anything more, Pierce added, "Oh, if it crowds your big house, you can put it in a tea saucer!"

The next day a White House messenger arrived at the Davis residence with a black-and-white Japanese ch'in in his coat pocket—Bonin.

The future president of the Confederacy grew very fond of Bonin. He especially delighted in his new pet's mischief. When his wife, Varina, complained, he would grin and offer to "build a house for myself and my dog."

Bonin was short-tempered with children and one day snapped at Davis's two-year-old, Maggie. But Maggie got him back by biting him on the nose. When Franklin Pierce visited Davis in prison some years later, after the Civil War, he brought a smile to his former colleague's face by mentioning the Bonin-Maggie nose-biting incident.

Davis's favorite dog was Traveler, a mastiff (or "Dogue de Bordeaux"). Traveler[14] had once belonged to Samuel and Sara Dorsey, former owners of the Davis estate, Beauvoir. Traveler —so named because of his worldwide travels with the Dorseys —had been Sara's bodyguard: he had saved her from a murderer in the Arabian desert and torn the throat out of a jewel thief in Paris.

When the Dorseys passed away, Davis adopted Traveler. The mastiff kept such a careful watch on his home, no doors were ever locked. Whenever a guest arrived, Davis would say to the dog, "Traveler, this is my friend," the dog would give the person an official sniff, then let him come and go at leisure for the rest of his stay. Traveler also protected the Davis children, let them ride piggyback, and often escorted their playmates safely home.

The great dog was poisoned some years later and died in his master's arms. Laying him down, Davis said, "I have indeed lost a friend."

He buried Traveler in the front yard of his estate, with an engraved headstone.

---

[14] The legendary horse of General Robert E. Lee, Davis's future commander of the Confederate army, was also called Traveler.

ALL THE PRESIDENTS' PETS—VI
TRAGEDY

Jesse has a new dog. You may have noticed that his former pets have been peculiarly unfortunate. When this dog dies every employee in the White House will be at once discharged.

ULYSSES GRANT TO WHITE HOUSE STAFF WHEN HIS SON GOT A NEWFOUNDLAND PUP, AND AFTER OTHERS OF HIS DOGS HAD DIED MYSTERIOUSLY

Other presidents also lost dear pets. Here are a few:

JOHN TYLER (1841–45)

When his favorite horse, General, died the president buried him at his estate, Sherwood Forest, with this epitaph:

Here lies the body of my good horse, the General.
For years he bore me around the circuit of my practice
and all that time he never made a blunder.
Would that his master could say the same.

—*John Tyler*

ZACHARY TAYLOR (1849–50)

When our twelfth president passed away after sixteen months in office, his favorite horse figured prominently in the funeral procession. Old Whitey followed the silk-draped hearse, riderless, the boots of his master turned backward in the stirrups.

ABRAHAM LINCOLN (1861–65)

When Lincoln went to Washington he left his dog, Fido, behind in Springfield, Illinois. Fido was killed less than a year after his master. One day he playfully jumped on a drunk lying in the street. The drunk, thinking he was being attacked, stabbed him to death.

WARREN HARDING (1921–23)

Harding's Airedale, Laddie Boy, also passed away not long after his master. The Newsboys' Association commissioned a statue of Laddie Boy by sculptor Bashka Paeff. Newsboys throughout the country donated a penny apiece, and 19,134 pennies were melted down and turned into a First Dog memorial. It was installed at the Smithsonian.

JOHN FITZGERALD KENNEDY (1961–63)

Caroline and John Jr. had a canary, Robin, whom they laid to rest in the South Lawn. Tragedy also struck the Kennedy hamsters, Billy and Debbie. Debbie gave birth to six piglets, Billy ate them. Debbie ate Billy, then passed away herself.

LYNDON BAINES JOHNSON (1963–69)

LBJ's beagle, Her, died in surgery when vets tried to remove a rock she had eaten. Two years later Him was hit by a car while chasing squirrels at the White House.

"OBITUARY"

Daisy died December 22, 1931, when she was hit by a Yellow Cab in University Place. At the moment of her death she was smelling the front of a florist's shop. . . . She never took pains to discover, conclusively, the things that might have diminished her curiosity and spoiled her taste. She died sniffing life, and enjoying it.

E. B. WHITE, FROM HIS TRIBUTE "OBITUARY"

KIBBLES 'N' OBITS

Today pet cemeteries abound worldwide from Lisbon to Portugal, Paris, Rio de Janeiro, Los Angeles, and London. In Wynard Park, ancestral home of the lords of Londonderry, lie the deceased dogs of Marchioness Frances Ann, their epitaphs penned by Lord Ravenscroft Henry Liddel. The dukes of York bury their pets at the ducal seat at Oatlands. Many royal corgis are laid to rest in the garden at Buckingham Palace.

Woburn Abbey is the home of the grandest pet monument dedicated to a past duchess's Pekingese, Che Foo—AKA Wuzzy. The mausoleum is a wrought-iron dome with six Corinthian columns. A bronze effigy of Wuzzy stands in the center. At her feet are inscribed the words of Byron: "In life the firmest friend. The first to welcome, foremost to defend."

Another famous English pet cemetery is Silvermere Haven. Here are some epitaphs from headstones and monuments there:

> *Scruffy—our little sausage. Love you always.*

> *Pepi—a broken link can never be replaced.*
> *Mummy & Auntie.*

> *Whiskey, Runaway Winkway. Missed by all the family.*
> *Love Mum & Dad.*

> *Cosmo—a gentleman. Help me live without you.*
> *(Written by Cosmo's master, Dai Llewellyn, former*
> *lover of Princess Margaret)*

> *Fritz, a German sausage dog killed*
> *crossing the road near Tonbridge.*
> *His front part crossed safely,*
> *his after end was hit by a Triumph motorcycle.*

EPITAPHS BY THE POETS

Beauty without vanity, Strength without insolence,
Courage without ferocity, and all the Virtues of man
without his Vices.

BYRON'S EPITAPH TO HIS NEWFOUNDLAND,
BOATSWAIN[15]

J ust as the lives of their pets were an inspiration to many
poets and novelists of the age, their deaths moved many to
compose tributes:

WRITER	DOG	EPITAPH
William Wordsworth	Music (hound)	To the Memory of a Dog, Music
Robert Burns	Hoggie (sheepdog)	My Hoggie
Sydney Smith	Nick (mixed breed)	Exemplary Nick
Lord Byron	Boatswain (Newfoundland)	To Boatswain
Robert Southey	Phillis (spaniel)	On the Death of a Favorite Old Spaniel
Robert Herrick	Tracie (spaniel)	Upon My Spaniel, Tracie
Matthew Arnold	Geist	Geist's Grave
Thomas Hardy	Wessex	A Popular Personage at Home

---

[15] Byron left instructions that he be buried beside Boatswain, his devoted (and reportedly rabid) Newfoundland. The poet's wishes were disregarded. He was laid to rest under the altar of the abbey adjoining his home.

THE SPIRIT THAT WAGGED ITS TAIL

Whenever you visit my grave, say to yourselves with regret but also with happiness in your hearts: "Here lies one who loved us whom we loved." No matter how deep my sleep I shall hear you, and not all the power of death can keep my spirit from wagging its grateful tail.

EUGENE O'NEILL, "THE LAST WILL AND TESTAMENT OF SILVERDENE EMBLEM O'NEILL"

THE FURTHER SIDE
TAILS OF THE UNDEAD—II

Without ending the Wild and Woolly Age on too somber a note, it should be mentioned that some of our late great pets may still be with us. To this day the phantom of Lord Byron's Boatswain is seen in Nottinghamshire. Sir Conan Doyle's ghostly Hound of the Baskervilles may be more than a figment of the imagination at Clarow Court, a remote retreat in the English countryside where Sherlock Holmes's creator had an unsettling stay at the turn of the century.

Here now, some documented "Tails of the Undead" from both sides of the Atlantic during the last century and the first part of this one:

• In 1850 a colonel of the Second Dragoons of the Rio Grande, in an effort to solve his Indian problems, bet the Comanches he could bring the dead back to life. The Comanches, not a gullible group, took the wager.

The colonel led an Indian dog into his tent, chloro-formed him, then carried him back out to the chief and cut off his tail to prove he was dead. When the dog didn't move, the chief was satisfied. The colonel then made abracadabra motions, the pooch suddenly jumped to his feet, and the Comanches fled, terrified.

Three years later, the colonel unexpectedly ran into the chief again. The chief showed him the dog's tail, which he had kept as a memento of the resurrection, and told him that since then he had told his braves not to waste their bullets on him since he had such "strong medicine." [16]

• In 1916, Arthur Springer, a retired Scotland Yard inspector, while taking a photo of a garden party in Tingewick, Buckinghamshire, caught the image of a headless ghost dog. The creature is standing beside the hostess, wagging his tail.

• In the same year, Albert Payson Terhune, the famous British writer of dog stories, along with Reverend Appleton Granis and several other houseguests, quite clearly saw the ghost of his deceased mixed-breed, Rex, peering at them through the window.

• At around the same time, one New Year's Eve night shortly after the death of the family spaniel, Chris, John Galsworthy's wife, Ada, had a visitation. Reported her husband:

She saw him quite clearly; she heard the padding tap-tap of his paws and very toe-nails; she felt his warmth brushing hard against the front of her skirt. . . . Had he some message, some counsel to give, something he would say, that last night of the year of all those he had watched over us? Will he come back again?

---

[16] From *Everglades to Canon with the Second Dragoons,* Theodore F. Roden-bough (1875).

Concluding the story, Galsworthy says: "No stone stands over where he lies. It is on our hearts that his life is engraved."

But polter-pets weren't just pooches. In 1909 the Society for Psychical Research received this report from an English lady:

My sister had a favorite cat called Smoky, a pure-bred Persian of a peculiar shade, and small. . . . In the spring she became ill, and died about the middle of June 1909. The gardener buried her and planted a flower over her grave. Shortly before Smoky died, she had been attacked by a dog, and had her ribs broken, so that she walked quite lamely. This injury was the final cause of her death.

On July 6th, my sister and I were at breakfast. I was sitting with my back to the window, when suddenly I saw her looking absolutely scared, and gazing out the window. I said, "What's the matter?"

She replied, "There's Smoky, walking across the grass!" We both rushed to the window and saw Smoky, looking very ill, her coat rough, staring at us and limping across the grass in front of the window, about three or four yards away.

My sister called to her, but she took no notice. I remained at the window and saw the cat turn down a path leading to the end of the garden. My sister ran out after her, still calling. But to her surprise Smoky never returned, and the last sight of her was among the shrubs.

THE LAST REBEL DOG

The most historic conflict of the last century was, of course, the American Civil War. Many good men fell, as did many animals. Though a particularly grim war, it was not without an inspiring pet tale or two that carried all the wildness, heroism, and legend of the age of which it was a part. . . .

In 1864, at Union headquarters in Virginia, Private John Simpson was brought before Colonel Panton on charges of espionage. Though Simpson, a recent enlistee, wore a Yankee uniform, incriminating Confederate documents and identification were found in his possession.

After interrogation, Colonel Panton ordered that the Rebel spy be shot at dawn. When asked if he had any final requests, Simpson said he would like to say good-bye to his dog, Pete, a black-and-white mongrel.

Panton denied the request.

As soon as Simpson was led away to the stockade, Panton's men caught Pete and beat him to death with their rifle butts.

The next morning, when, on his way to the firing squad, Simpson asked the guards where Pete was, they assured him that the dog was being well taken care of. "He's the best buddy I've ever had," said the prisoner, relieved.

Moments later, as the guards lashed him to the shooting post, he looked down at his feet, his eyes went wide, and he exclaimed, "Why, it's Pete!"

Thinking that the condemned man was already delirious, the guards quickly blindfolded him, stepped back, drew their rifles, and waited for the word from their commanding officer. But Colonel Panton, staring now at the same spot where Simpson was, suddenly turned quite pale. Several times he attempted to give the "Fire!" command, but he had apparently lost his tongue.

"Execution deferred!" he finally managed to stammer, and hurried away.

After sundown that day, the Confederates, thanks to Simpson's counterintelligence, attacked the Union hideaway and Colonel Panton was killed.

When Simpson was freed, he told his comrades that Pete had returned from the hereafter to save his life and the Confederacy.

VII.
THE
ROCK 'N'
ROLL AGE

I was desperate. The swine who stole my dog doesn't realize what he did to me!

Hitler, 1917, after a railroad worker in Alsace stole his terrier, Fuchsl

I am accustomed to hearing malicious falsehoods about myself . . . but I think I have a right to object to libelous statements about my dog.

FDR, 1944, in reply to Republicans who accused him of sending a destroyer to Alaska to pick up his marooned Scottie, Fala

It was a little cocker spaniel dog. . . . Black-and-white spotted. And our little girl—Tricia, the six-year-old— named it Checkers. And you know, the kids (like all kids) love the dog, and I just want to say this right now, that regardless of what they say about it, we're gonna keep it.

Richard Nixon, Checkers speech, 1952

The cat is the flashpoint for the invasion of privacy. The photographers don't have the common decency to leave a little girl's pet alone.

Aide to President-elect Clinton, 1992, after members of the press allegedly lured Chelsea Clinton's cat, Socks, out of the Little Rock governor's mansion for a photo op

DECORATED DOGS, DISNEY DUCKS, AND COULEE CATS

After thirty thousand years of cohabitation with our species, most pets can confidently say that they are better off today than yesterday.

They are no longer sacrificed or mummified. The days of the Colosseum are back, but now mascots get to watch from the sidelines in air-conditioned booths. Cats are not burned as witches or dogs as werewolves or moddey dhooes. Pet consumption even among Cambodians and modern adventurers is largely a thing of the past thanks to the advent of alternative options at national franchises such as Chun King and Der Wienerschnitzel.

Things are better from the positive point of view, too.

According to a recent survey, 91 percent of pet owners babytalk their pets, buy them Christmas presents, and, when out of town, phone or send a postcard.

Pets-only hotels, retreats, and restaurants are everywhere. Canine and feline grooming and pedicure boutiques are widespread, as are clothing and accessory outlets. The service industry also prospers: everything from pet dating services, to limo services, to angel services. Pet professionals proliferate: walkers, sitters, nutritionists, psychologists, psychics, and Super Dooper Pooper Scoopers.

Royals continue to treat their dogs well. The duchess of York recently knighted her terrier, Rutherford, with a dinner knife. In 1952 Mahabat Khan Babi Pathan, maharajah of Junagadh, held a state wedding for his golden retrievers, Roshana and Bobbie.

Since the turn of the century, more than one million dogs and cats have been named as beneficiaries in wills. In 1968 oil heiress Eleanor Ritchey left $4.3 million to 161 strays.

In the last decades, pets have diversified in their careers. Whereas historically professional opportunities have been restricted to such areas as hunting, herding, and mousing, now we have canine marriage counselors, TV weathercats, narcotics hounds, and more.

In warfare, our best friends and allies have been decorated with nearly every award except the Purple Heart.

Here are some of the milestone dates of the early Rock 'n' Roll Age that have led to this great pet revolution:

Dateline	**Milestone**
1899 (A. D.)	ACA (American Cat Association) and ACFA (American Cat Fanciers' Association) founded.
1906	Last dog executed for witchcraft in Delemont, Switzerland.
1911	Albert Schweitzer establishes a mission in Africa with his cat, Sizi.
1915	"The Dogs of All Nations Expo" opens in San Francisco, featuring 185 breeds.
1917	A railroad worker in Alsace steals Hitler's terrier, Fuchsl. He vows revenge on the French. (See "Hitler's Fuchsl and Blondie," page 245.)
1918	End of World War I. Seven thousand Allied dogs were killed in action. Many are decorated. (See "Tommy, German Shepherd . . . ," page 241.)
1920	King Alexander of Greece dies of blood poisoning after being bitten by his pet monkey.
1920	Roaring Twenties pet dances become the craze— the turkey trot, grizzly bear, bunny hug, and foxtrot.
1922	Warren Harding's Airedale, Laddie Boy, is interviewed by the *Washington Star*.

1925   Balto, a malamute, leads Gunnar Kasson's team to diphtheria-plagued Nome, Alaska, with antitoxin serum. Later, a statue of Balto is erected in New York City's Central Park.

1925   Clarence Darrow defeats William Jennings Bryan in the Scopes Monkey Trial.

1927   Buddy, the first Seeing Eye, a female German shepherd, begins service.

1927   Walt Disney creates Mickey and Minnie Mouse and later Pluto, Goofy, Donald, Daffy, and Daisy Duck.

1928   Norwegian explorer Roald Amundsen eats his sled dogs in the Arctic.

1929   Admiral Richard Byrd takes his fox terrier, Igloo, on his first Antarctic trip and regrets it.

1930   Cats help in the construction of the Grand Coulee Dam. Strings tied to their tails, they shimmy through drainpipes, connecting ropes to cables.[1]

1932   FDR's police dog, Major, rips the trousers off British prime minister Ramsay MacDonald.

1940   Pont-a-Mouson, France: Last burning at the stake of a man convicted of bestiality (his mistresses: three French heifers).

1941   FDR and his Scottie, Fala, sign the Atlantic Charter with Winston Churchill and his poodle, Rufus, aboard the USS *Augusta*.

1944   General Omar Bradley leads the Normandy invasion with his poodle, Beau. General George Patton liberates France with his bulldogs.

1945   Central Park, New York: Jerome Napoleon Bonaparte (the last American Bonaparte) trips on the leash of his dog and dies of injuries sustained.

---

[1] Twenty years later, a four-month-old kitten scaled Switzerland's Matterhorn (14,780 feet) without ropes.

1945   Eight dogs, three horses, thirty-one pigeons, and one cat receive the highest Allied animal decoration for service in World War II: the Dickin Medal for Valor.

A MESSAGE TO AMERICA'S DOG OWNERS!

Total war has made it necessary to call to the colors many of the nation's dogs. Thousands of dogs, donated by patriotic men, women, and children and trained for special duties with the Armed Forces, are serving on all fronts as well as standing guard against saboteurs at home.

More thousands of dogs are needed. New recruits are being inducted daily at the War Dog Training Centers, rushed into training courses which skill them as sentries, message carriers, airplane spotters, packcarriers—and other tasks which must remain secret.

WORLD WAR II FLIER CIRCULATED NATIONALLY BY U.S. DOGS FOR DEFENSE, INC.

Profiles in Currage
THE BEAGLE HAS LANDED

The twentieth century has seen a dramatic increase in paramilitary pet involvement, particularly from the ranks of canines.

In World War II the Allies drafted almost all breeds, except basset hounds. Some dogs laid telephone wire, others hauled gun carriages and ammunition, others ratted foxholes, others were trained to infiltrate enemy encampments and steal or destroy tactical documents.

Especially critical to our war effort were the antitank dogs. In 1945 *New York Times* Soviet correspondent Ilya Ehrenburg reported seeing one recruit help take out half a dozen German tanks in a single day. There were also the devil dogs, a top-secret marine battalion. So effective were they that when peace was declared, the devils were promoted en masse from privates to corporals.

During the worst years of the Middle East crisis, the Hezbollah was reported to have employed bomb-laden kamikaze donkeys. In defense, the Israeli army deployed exploding Dobermans and Belgian shepherds. The dogs carried dynamite packs into Syrian and Palestinian underground guerrilla hideouts such as those of Ahmed Jibril's Popular Front. Once in, the recruit was detonated by remote control.[2]

Here are some of the most highly gallant heroes from recent wars:

TOMMY
GERMAN SHEPHERD, WORLD WAR I

Mascot of a Scottish regiment, Tommy was wounded three times, gassed, captured, and rescued. At the end of the war, he received the Croix de Guerre medallion for gallantry.

DAISY
RETRIEVER, WORLD WAR II

Mascot of a Norwegian merchant ship torpedoed in the North Atlantic in 1944, Daisy dove into the icy sea with surviving crewmen and throughout the night swam from man to man, licking faces to revive the sailors.

---

[2] In 1992 Andrew Whitley, Jerusalem correspondent for the *Financial Times* of London, reported that Arabs weren't fond of dogs, whereas Israelis liked them.

CHIPS
COLLIE-HUSKY-SHEPHERD MIX, WORLD WAR II

Chips served in North Africa as a U.S. Army battalion guard, participated in the invasion of Sicily, and won the Silver Star for capturing a machine-gun nest during that engagement. Though he was wounded in the effort, he was denied the Purple Heart. Later, Chips bit General Dwight D. Eisenhower. (The Defense Department denied that the incident was related to the rejection.)

BIBER
BELGIAN SHEEPDOG, DESERT STORM

This veteran seventeen-year-old recruit is our most recent war hero. During Desert Storm he was wounded while sniffing out explosives in Kuwait. According to CNN (and confirmed by PNN), he also cut his paw while helping to free the U.S. embassy and took seven stitches. Biber's handler petitioned the Defense Department's MWDA (Military Working Dog Agency) for the Purple Heart. The MWDA denied the petition, stating the precedent-setting case of Private Chips, hero of World War II, also rebuffed.[3]

Biber went on to receive awards from the Lancaster City Council (California), his county government, and his local VFW chapter. He marched in the Antelope Valley parade and also accepted honors from the New York Coalition of Dogs. Finally, he led the Fourth of July parade in Ravenna, Ohio. The parade featured a bagpipe ensemble and a clown act.[4]

Currently construction is being completed on a Washington, D.C., monument to the more than thirty thousand K-9 Military

---

[3] Forcing the hand of the MWDA in Biber's case was the *Air Force Times.* On July 29, 1991, the magazine published a formal protest by Navy Chief Petty Officer Drew A. Solberg. Solberg stated that he could think of "no more degrading issuance than awarding a Purple Heart to a dog." He concluded that issuance of the award would be "a serious insult."

[4] General Norman Schwarzkopf was invited to the occasion but sent his regrets. Barbara Bush and Vice-President Quayle were also invited but did not respond.

Corps dogs that have served our nation in the last five wars. According to the *Los Angeles Times* (June 8, 1991), donations for the memorial have come from veterans such as Joseph J. White, whose platoon was saved in 1970 when a K-9 recruit warned it of a Vietcong ambush. White and others have sold their military decorations to help fund the monument.

ANNE FRANK'S TOMMY AND BOCHE

On July 5, 1942, Anne Frank and her family moved into an Amsterdam warehouse attic. Here the thirteen-year-old schoolgirl found two cats. One was an attic cat, which she named Tommy. The other was a warehouse cat, which she called Boche. She explained her reason for the names in a March 12, 1943, entry in her diary:

> The aggressor is always the warehouse cat. Yet it is always the attic cat who manages to win—just like among nations. So the warehouse cat is named the German, or Boche, and the attic cat the English, or Tommy.

When the Franks' friends, the Van Daans, moved into the attic, their fifteen-year-old son, Peter, brought with him his own cat, Mouschi. The boy often tried to catch Mouschi without getting near the window outside, which German soldiers passed regularly. Anne described the play:

> Peter looks all around—aha, he sees him . . . crawls into the office again and pulls the animal by its tail. Mouschi spits. Peter sighs. What has he achieved? Now, Mouschi is sitting right up by the window cleaning himself, very pleased to have escaped Peter.

WINSTON CHURCHILL, MR. CAT, AND THE MOUSE ARMY

Winston Churchill, the British prime minister, was a great pet lover. At his country residence, Blenheim, palace of the grand dukes of Marlborough since the seventeenth century, he kept goldfish, parakeets, and black swans. But his favorite pet, besides his poodle, Rufus, was undoubtedly Mr. Cat.

The prime minister customarily set a place for Mr. Cat at the table. His nephew, John, recalled one particular meal at Blenheim when Mr. Cat, after downing a slice of cream-covered pheasant at his place "without making a mess," suddenly got the hiccups. "At exactly the same moment my uncle got hiccups as well," reported John, "with the result that the two of them seemed to be gravely bowing to each other. Sarah [Churchill's wife] and I had to stuff our table napkin in our mouths in case we laughed. My uncle noticed and was very displeased. 'What on earth do you think you are doing?' he asked crossly. 'I do not see anything funny at all!' "

John told another story about his uncle and the First British Feline that was particularly historic since the event took place during World War II:

> One evening when the ladies had left the dining room, the curtains moved and Mr. Cat appeared. "Oh, look," said my uncle brightly. "Cat has a mouse." He toyed with his prey, but my uncle was not in the least put out by the drama being played in front of him. The rest of us felt a bit green.
>
> "How interesting to see him exercise control over his victim," he commented. Then, after a tense moment or two, my uncle declared: "Now is the time."
>
> Suddenly the entire mouse disappeared down Mr.

*Cat's throat, head first; he cleaned his whiskers and
silently stepped over to the fire for a nap. A stricken
silence followed.*

*"You see," observed my uncle proudly, "a whole
army destroyed in one move!"*

CELEBRITY PET PROFILE
HITLER'S FUCHSL AND BLONDIE

Churchill's mortal enemy, on the other hand, hated cats.

Like his idols, Frederick the Great and Wagner, Adolf Hitler
was a dog person. Indeed, most biographers agree that the
commander of the Third Reich had only three great loves: Eva
Braun, his mother, and his dogs.

In 1942, during one of his Table Talks, he said: "I love animals, and especially dogs. But I'm not so very fond of boxers,
for example. If I had to take a new dog, it could only be a
German shepherd, preferably a bitch."

While writing pamphlets during the twenties, as well as
newspaper articles for the *Radical Observer,* he often signed
with the pseudonym "Wolf." Later, during the war, he called
his Belgian headquarters at Brûly-de-Pesche, "Wolfsschlucht";
his Prussian headquarters at Rastenburg, "Wolfsschanze"; and
his Russian command post outside Kiev, "Werewolf."

The only thing he liked about America was Walt Disney's *Big
Bad Wolf.* He often watched clips of the cartoon and roared
with laughter, especially when the hero huffed and puffed at
the house of the three little pigs.

Hitler's life had three important pet periods:

THE FUCHSL PERIOD
(1915–1917)

In January 1915 during World War I, a stray terrier jumped
into Hitler's foxhole. Later the future Führer recalled, "He was

engaged in pursuing a rat. He fought against me, and tried to bite me, but I didn't let go." He adopted the dog, named him Fuchsl (Little Fox), and soon gained his trust with treats. "At first I gave him only biscuits and chocolate [he'd acquired his habits from the English]."

Hitler took a keen interest in Fuchsl. "I used to watch him as if he'd been a man—the progressive stages of his anger, of the bile that took possession of him. He was a fine creature."

Soon the little white terrier knew how to behave even when his master was dining. "When I ate, he used to sit beside me and follow my gestures with his gaze. If by the fifth or sixth mouthful I hadn't given him anything, he used to sit up on his rump and look at me with an air of saying, 'And what about me, am I not here at all?' It was crazy how fond I was of the beast."[5]

In August 1917, when a railroad worker in Alsace offered him two hundred marks for Fuchsl, Hitler refused, saying he wouldn't even take two hundred thousand. A short time later, his terrier disappeared and was apparently stolen. He wanted to go after his pet, but his regiment was pulling out.

THE STASI AND NEGUS PERIOD
(1942–45)

In 1929 Hitler met the seventeen-year-old Eva Braun in a photographer's studio. They had an affair, Eva soon hoped for a marriage proposal, but none was forthcoming.[6] In 1935, a few months before attempting suicide, she wrote in her diary: "If only I had a little dog I would be less lonely. . . . I did so want a Basset puppy, and still no sign of one." After the suicide attempt, Hitler rented her an apartment in Munich and gave her a little dog "with bear's fur."

Seven years later, shortly after the outbreak of the war, the Führer gave Eva two Scottish terriers, Stasi and Negus. The pair apparently terrorized the mailman, Georg Otter.

---

[5] He later observed that his pet was "a real circus dog—he knew all the tricks."
[6] Hitler was also involved with his niece, Geli, at the time and until she shot herself in 1931.

THE BLONDIE PERIOD
(1941–45)

In 1941 Martin Bormann gave his commander in chief a German shepherd bitch, Blondie. (Bormann himself was a poodle owner and very protective. One day when his poodle was attacked by another dog, he had the culprit seized, soaked with gasoline, and set on fire.)

Soon Hitler favored Blondie over his other shepherd, Muck, given him by his bodyguard, Ulrich Graf. He regularly walked Blondie at his retreat, the Berghof, and drove her through the fields in his VW. She also often flew with him in his four-engine FW-200 Condor, piloted by Hans Baur, who himself brought along Waldi, his dachshund.

In 1942, the commander of the Third Reich told his architect, Albert Speer, that after the war he planned to retire to Linz, Austria, his childhood home. "Aside from Fräulein Braun," he confided, "I'll take no one with me. Fräulein Braun and my dog."

Meanwhile, as his troops overran Europe, Hitler taught Blondie to jump through hoops, climb ladders, and hurdle walls.

He appreciated that her eating habits were much like his own. "In many ways my shepherd Blondie is a vegetarian," he said. "There are lots of herbs which she eats with obvious pleasure."

Hitler and Eva Braun often teased each other about their pets: he called Stasi and Negus "handsweepers"; and she declared, giggling, "Your Blondie is a calf." But in the end the terriers reportedly had the run of the Berghof.

On his birthday in 1943, the Führer appealed to his mistress for a special favor. "Effie, will you allow poor Blondie to join us for half an hour?"

Eva put her terriers away, and Blondie came out, did tricks, and howled for her master, delighting him.

Blondie had four pups in March 1945. Six weeks later in the Führer's Berlin bunker, the Russians closing in, Blondie was given a cyanide capsule by an SS doctor. Hitler bade her good-

bye in the bathroom, then took a dose with Eva, whom he had
married hours before. The puppies and Negus were shot in the
garden by an SS officer.

According to one account, the dogs were cremated and their
ashes spread with Hitler's and Eva's.

FREUD'S JOFI AND WOLF

W hen Hitler's Nazi army stormed Austria in 1938, the
father of modern psychoanalysis, Sigmund Freud,
fled to England with his chows.

In his biography, *Sigmund Freud: Man and Father* (1959),
Martin Freud, the psychoanalyst's eldest son, says that Jofi was
"the dearest friend of father's later years." The chow attended
all her master's medical appointments and determined the end
of each. Explained Martin: "When Jofi got up and yawned, he
knew the hour was up: she was never late in announcing
the end of a session, although father did admit that she was ca-
pable of an error of perhaps a minute, at the expense of the
patient."

Another extraordinary dog in the household was an Alsatian,
Wolf, who belonged to Freud's daughter, Anna. One day, frightened by gunshots from Nazi soldiers outside the Freud residence in Vienna, Wolf ran out of the house and disappeared.
Anna searched desperately for her pet, but to no avail. Hours
later, the dog returned home—in a taxi.

"According to the taxi-driver," recalled Martin Freud, "Wolf
had jumped into his cab and courteously resisted all efforts to
remove him while, at the same time, raising his nose suffi-
ciently high to permit the taximan to read his name and address
on the medallion hanging from his collar. Wolf must have
thought the man rather stupid in not immediately understanding what he meant. The address, 'Professor Freud, Bergasse 19,'
was plainly written."

The cabdriver was apparently honored to drive the great dog
because when he reached Bergasse 19 and Freud himself came

out, he said, "Herr Professor, for this passenger I have not switched on the taxi-meter!"

But Martin reported that his father paid the cabbie in full and tipped him well.

EISENHOWER'S SECRET WAR: OPERATION SQUIRREL

General Eisenhower masterminded the Normandy Invasion in 1944, D Day, which led to the fall of the Third Reich.

But ten years later, our thirty-fourth president was facing an offensive at the White House that had him at wits' end. The squirrels on the South Lawn were digging holes in his prize putting green. Finally, one day he threatened to shoot them personally.[7]

The Secret Service immediately mobilized "Operation Squirrel Seduction." Hoping to lure the rascals off the presidential putting green, they covered the adjoining lawn with peanuts. The squirrels gobbled up the treats. Then they returned to their project on the putting green with renewed energy.

The Secret Service quickly rolled with Tactic #2: Operation Exodus. The First Squirrels were rounded up and chauffeured to the Lincoln Memorial.

The next day, they were back—on the putting green.

At last the Secret Service prevailed when they relocated the squirrels uptown to Rock Creek Park.

---

[7] The president's wrath did not apply only to squirrels. According to his grandson, David, he kept a shotgun next to his TV at his Gettysburg residence to shoot crows, and his groundskeepers were under instructions to shoot any cat on the property.

CHECKERS TO MILLIE
TO SOCKS

The most important dates in our last pet period revolve around the presidency—especially the Checkers, Millie, and Socks administrations. The events involve not only politics but space shots, rock 'n' roll, mandatory Manhattan poop scooping, stupid (or not-so-stupid) pet tricks, big-time publishing, getting fixed in San Mateo, and more:

Dateline	**Milestone**
1952 (A.D.)	Nixon delivers the Checkers speech.
1956	The King goes platinum with "Hound Dog," topping the charts for eleven weeks. (See "Pet Rock Platinum and Gold," page 284.)
1958	Soviet Samoyed bitch Strelka is shot into space on *Sputnik.* (See "Space Cadet Pets," page 297.)
1962	First issue of *Playboy,* featuring bunnies and pets of the month.
	Cold War begins to thaw: Khrushchev gives to Caroline Kennedy Pushinka, daughter of *Sputnik's* Strelka.[8]
1963	LBJ picks up beagles Him and Her by their ears, causing national outcry from pet owners.
1963	Animal rock groups dominate the charts: Animals, Beatles, Byrds, Monkees, Turtles, Steppenwolf, and so on. Pet dances sweep the United States: the alligator, the pony, the stomp.
1976	California scientists link the DNA of a man and chimp, creating the basis for the "Humanzee."

---

[8] Later, Charlie (the Kennedys' terrier) and Pushinka have four puppies: Butterfly, White Tips, Blackie, and Streaker.

David Berkowitz, AKA "Son of Sam," shoots six women in New York. He later confesses to police that his neighbor Sam Carr's dog "told me to kill."

1978   "Pooper scooper" law enacted in New York City. (Beforehand, 175 tons of pet poo are dropped on the streets daily.)

1980   Stupid Pet Tricks debuts on "Late Night with David Letterman." (See "Not-So-Stupid Pet Tricks: The Top Ten," page 290.)

1982   St. Louis Dog Museum opens (rivaling Europe's great Hundemuseum, or Hound Museum, in Berlin).

1985   The Swedish government enacts the First Sea Monster Conservation Act to protect Storsjoodjuret (the Creature of Lake Storsjon).

1986   Broadway and Hollywood pet hits: *Cats, Batman, Dances with Wolves, Teenage Mutant Ninja Turtles* ... (See "Twentieth-Century Foxes & Felines," page 285.)

Dogue and *Catmopolitan* are published.

1988   Animal Health Insurance Co. of Massachusetts offers the first pet HMO.[9]

1988   George Bush (owner of spaniel Millie) and Dan Quayle (owner of Lab Justie) announce that their opponents for the presidential election, Michael Dukakis and running mate, Lloyd Bentsen, will be facing "a couple of pit bulls."

1989   New York City Board of Health requires that all resident pit bulls be neutered and that owners carry liability insurance of $100,000.[10]

[9] In 1992 Firemen's Fund came out with Medipet Health Insurance (annual premium: $99).
[10] During the same period NYC mayor Ed Koch, in a bid for reelection, asks the city council to ban pit bulls. Councilwoman Carolyn Maloney backs the move until pit owners bring their pets to her office. "I couldn't ban them," she said. "They are too sweet."

U.S. troops invade Panama. All Panamanian K-9 corps defense dogs are shot in their kennels. Included among casualties: Manuel Noriega's personal pet, Zap.[11]

1990   Millie's Book outsells George's.

Spuds MacKenzie makes *People*'s 1990 Best Dressed List.

San Mateo County, CA, Board of Supervisors tentatively approves nation's first law requiring most dogs and cats to be fixed.

1991   Iditarod Trail Committee bars non-northern breeds —especially poodles—from the annual Alaskan sledding competition.

1991   Queen Elizabeth II is bitten by one of her Welsh corgis when she tries to break up a dogfight.

House of Commons passes a bill requiring American pit bulls and Japanese Tosas to be neutered or destroyed.

1992   Boozer, a basset hound from Minnesota, opens a bank account and appears on "Good Morning America." (See "Boozer: History's First Liberated Dog," page 292.)

1993   Chelsea's Socks replaces Barbara's Millie in the White House, becoming the nation's first First Cat since Amy Carter's Misty Malarky Yin Yang.

K-9!

As we have seen, dog sleuthing has a long and rich history. In 400 B.C. the watchdog at the Temple of Aphrodite caught an art thief after a twenty-mile chase. The fourteenth-century medieval mastiff Dragon collared his mas-

---

[11] Months later, the Berlin Wall is torn down, and all K-9 wall dogs are shot.

ter's murderer, Richard de Macaire. In 1888 a hound by the name of Max, belonging to an Englishwoman, Mrs. T. P. O'Connor, reportedly apprehended Jack the Ripper himself but was given the slip by the legendary murderer before the police arrived.

During the 1950s, Scotland Yard kept a force of K-9's that were the envy of the world; the majority were German shepherds, and there were eight Labs that patrolled Buckingham Palace.

Today law enforcement agencies worldwide employ dogs. McGruff, the TV hound in the trench coat, urges Americans "to take a bite out of crime." K-9 collector cards are distributed by many U.S. city and county police departments. In 1993 U.S. Customs Service "All-Star Drug Detecting Dog" cards came in Nabisco's Milk-Bone boxes. Each card featured a two-by-three-inch color mug shot of the recruit and on the back his rap sheet: name, tag number, breed, age, weight, "total seizure value to date," and a brief description of his larger busts. Some California county K-9 cards include a quote from the dog himself. For example, for San Joaquin Sheriff Department deputy Adolf[12] (a ninety-five-pound rottweiler and three-year veteran on the force):

> ADOLF SAYS:
> "The Choice for Me Is Drug Free!!
> So Be a Winner and Just Say No!"

The top K-9's receive decorations from their departments, make public appearances, and are often honored by citizens in the communities they serve. In 1988, the exclusive Manhattan restaurant Sardi's threw a luncheon for Nero, top cop dog for the NYPD (also present was Great Elms' Prince Charming II, a Pomeranian, Best in Show Champion at Madison Square Garden's Westminster Kennel Club Show that year).[13]

Here now are a few of the legendary K-9's of recent years:

[12] Full name: Count Adolf Wolfgang Von Berlin.
[13] Even so, it should be added that K-9's are not popular with everyone. And the way they are handled sometimes causes controversy. In 1991, according to the

ROCKY AND BARCO
BELGIAN MALINOIS DOGS, TEXAS
NARCOTICS DEPARTMENT

In 1987 alone, Rocky and Barco, honorary sergeant majors, made over 250 busts, helping seize contraband valued at $300 million. Mexican drug smugglers put a $70,000 bounty on the head of each.

WINSTON
LABRADOR RETRIEVER, BRITISH NARCOTICS AGENT

So many successful searches-and-seizures has Winston made that Colombian heroin dealers have a million-dollar bounty on his head.

HARASS II
GERMAN SHEPHERD, PRIVATE DETECTIVE,
GALETON, PENNSYLVANIA

Harass, with his trainer, John Preston, freelances for law enforcement agencies nationwide. He has supplied crucial evidence in many criminal investigations. In a recent Florida murder case, Harass matched a suspect, via scent, with a washcloth he used to smother an elderly woman.

RINNIE
RETRIEVER, BURGLARY DIVISION, WICHITA
POLICE DEPARTMENT

Rinnie was an ace detective for the WPD until he was told to surrender his badge for a bogus collar. . . . One night Chuck

---

Los Angeles Times (June 25), civil rights groups filed a class action suit against LAPD chief Daryl Gates and the department's K-9 unit, alleging that dogs attacked more than nine hundred persons without cause.

The year before, a senior Texas prison official, Jerry Hodge, was criticized for training K-9's on inmates, injuring some badly. Since 1982 Hodge had reportedly been asking prisoners to volunteer as prey in hunts that became parties for his friends. (Report: *New York Times,* August 18, 1990)

Smith, a local supermarket accountant, reported that he had been carjacked and robbed of store receipts. The police had Rinnie sniff Smith's car to see if he could scent the escaped robber. After investigation, the dog jumped out of the vehicle and bit Smith firmly in the fanny. Rinnie was dismissed from the case, and his handler, John Judge, discredited. Some time later, though, as a result of new evidence and a polygraph test, Smith was discovered to be the robber after all, having made the original police report to throw investigators off his trail. He was booked and convicted, and Rinnie got a commendation.

KEN-L RATION PUP HALL OF FAME

Not all dog heroes are professionals. Most are ordinary house pets but, when finding themselves in extraordinary 911 circumstances, rise to the occasion.

Many major pet food companies have a hall of fame for such heroes. Ken-L Ration's, established in 1954, is among the oldest. Here are some of its recent inductees:

Hero: Tango, mixed-breed puppy.
Owner: Al Choate, auto mechanic, from Port Townsend, Washington.
Deed: Tango rescued Al from a mad mother cow who mauled him, puncturing a lung and breaking his ribs. Tango bit into the cow's cheek and didn't let go until Al had crawled to cover.

Hero: Leo, a poodle.
Owners: William and Lana Callahan of Hunt County, Texas.
Deed: Leo saved the Callahans' eleven-year-old boy, Sean, and his nine-year-old sister from a six-foot diamondback rattler, throwing himself in front of the snake. Though he took numerous bites himself, Leo pulled through.

Hero: King, German shepherd–husky mix.
Owners: Howard and Fern Carlson, Granite Falls, Washington.
Deed: King gnawed through a plywood door to save the Carlsons from their burning house. Though the hero's coat was in flames at one point, he stayed in the inferno till the end. Said Fern, "He was the last to leave. He wouldn't budge before we were outside."

Hero: Reona, rottweiler.
Deed: When the tremors of the 1989 San Francisco earthquake began, five-year-old Vivian Cooper screamed. Reona, who lived next door, jumped over the fence and into the Coopers' kitchen. She pushed the little girl against a wall, saving her from a toppling microwave oven. After the quake, Vivian's mother said to the dog still standing guard, "Can I have my baby back, please?" Then she reported, "Reona looked at me as if to say, 'Well, if you are calm enough.' Then she just walked out the door."

HUMAN HALL OF FAME

A tribute to pet heroism would not be complete without at least a brief look at the other side of the coin: people who have rescued pets that weren't their own and under circumstances beyond the call of duty.

• In December 1989, police officer Michael Fusco from Shelton, Connecticut, employed the Heimlich maneuver followed by mouth-to-mouth resuscitation to save a Dalmatian that choked on a squash ball.
• In December of the previous year, Patricia Lopes used a similar technique to revive a customer in her pet grooming parlor. Lopes had just given Escape, a thirteen-year-old greyhound owned by Roger Roy of Acushnet, Massachusetts, a routine shampoo and pedi-

cure when the dog suddenly collapsed, seeming to have suffered heart failure. Lopes administered CPR. "After a few minutes," she said, "I heard a cough and then a gurgle." Escape pulled through. But according to *The New York Times* ("Kiss of Life for a Dog," December 11, 1988), Lopes added "she does not mind kissing dogs but would rather not perform mouth-to-mouth again."

Doggerel

BEST FRIENDS

[My boxer] Gangster is the truest friend I can ever ask for.

SYLVESTER STALLONE

A dog is the only thing on earth that loves you more than you love yourself.

JOSH BILLINGS, 1919

The plain fact that my dog loves me more than I love him is undeniable and always fills one with a certain feeling of shame.

KONRAD LORENZ, *MAN MEETS DOG*

With the exception of women, there is nothing on earth so agreeable or necessary to the comfort of man as the dog.

EDWARD JESSE, *ANECDOTE OF DOGS*

continued

> *I like dogs very much indeed. . . . They never talk about themselves, but listen to you while you talk about yourself, and keep up an appearance of being interested in the conversation. They never say unkind things. They never tell us of our faults "merely for our own good."*
>
> **JEROME K. JEROME, THREE MEN IN A BOAT**

> *If you eliminate smoking and gambling, you will be amazed to find that almost all an Englishman's pleasures can be, and mostly are, shared by his dog.*
>
> **GEORGE BERNARD SHAW**

> *It is no criticism of the British way of life to suggest that a British family dog appears to be the most important member of the family.*
>
> **MARTIN FREUD, SIGMUND FREUD: MAN AND FATHER**

POODLE COURT

Modern pet law has evolved since Hammurabi's Lex Talonis, Howell the Good's Magna Cata, and the Wild and Woolly Code of the Colt .44.

The capital of the paw suit is Los Angeles. L.A. Animal Control —seventy officers for about two million pets—currently investigates one hundred thousand complaints annually. Ten thousand are barking dog complaints. Some result in citations, others impoundments, many go to court. Recently an L.A. dog owner was sued for $240,000 by his neighbors, who alleged that his four-year-old wolf shepherd, Parka, barked all day. The suit was settled for $6,000.

Other cases are not so modest. An L.A. Superior Court judge ordered a pet owner to pay two Walnut School District employees $2.6 million after they were thrown from the back of a truck swerving to avoid his unleashed dog in the street. He also had to pay a $46 no-leash citation.

Canine litigation has become so serious in Beverly Hills that the town has created an ad hoc "doggie court." Under a huge backlog of cases, Deputy DA Steven Rood often appoints obedience guru Matthew Margolis[14] to mediate.

Southern California is by no means the only hot spot. Also, litigation goes well beyond the garden-variety bark-and-bite cases. A few examples from jurisdictions throughout the nation:

- Texas, 1980. Max, a six-year-old German schnauzer, was accused of breaking and entering and violating two pedigree Pekingese bitches, Dollie and Sen-le. Their owner, George Milton, sued for damages to his house and the cost of the bitches' abortions. Texas Grand Prairie judge Cameron Grey found Max not guilty on the grounds that the plaintiff had originally identified Dollie and Sen-le's molester as a poodle.
- Illinois, 1987. A high-ranking government official, whose retriever died from eating a tampon, appointed a special prosecutor to investigate. The treating veterinarian was found guilty of malpractice, and his license was suspended for forty-five days.
- Tampa, FL. A Labrador/cockapoo, Ari, sued USAir for $50,000, for mental anguish incurred when the airline forgot to board him on his owner's flight to Washington.
- Lancaster, PA, 1988. Nineteen-year-old Gerald E. Huber, Jr., was sentenced to forty hours of community service for ordering his uncle's pit bull to chew

---

[14] Author of *Good Dog, Bad Dog* and *When Good Dogs Do Bad Things,* Margolis runs a training school in Monterey. Among his star clients with good dogs who occasionally do bad things: Doris Day, Cloris Leachman, Penny Marshall, Jon Voight, George Carlin, Cher, Sheena Easton, the late Frank Zappa.

through thirteen trees on a thoroughfare in downtown Lancaster. (The pit was given a suspended sentence and remanded to the custody of Huber's uncle.)

• Massachusetts. Nineteen-year-old Kevin Deschene was sentenced to six months in jail for kicking and beating his family's German shepherd, Champ. A neighbor took pictures of him committing the battery. This was the first time in twenty years anyone in Massachusetts had been imprisoned for animal abuse.

• Arleta, CA, 1989. Postman Floyd Bertran Sterling shot Skippy, a two-year-old German shepherd, after being bitten by him before. According to the *Los Angeles Times* (December 28, 1989), the L.A. district attorney filed three felony charges against the postman. Sterling was fired from the U.S. Postal Service and allowed to perform community service in exchange for a six-month jail term.[15]

• Staten Island, NY, 1991. A feud between two families over a dog urinating on the lawn ended with a shootout in which twenty-one-year-old Christopher Merola was killed. His neighbor, James Collins, was charged with murder.

• St. Louis, MO, 1992. Finally, on a lighter note, divorced couple Carla and Tony Julius filed a custody suit for their two dogs, each maintaining the other was an unfit guardian. Associate Circuit Judge Dennis J. Quillin rendered a three-part decision: 1. Carla and Tony were each awarded possession of one of the two dogs six days a week; 2. Each got both dogs together every Sunday for four hours; 3. Each was allowed visitation rights for the dog he/she didn't have during any given week.

---

[15] Tougher abuse laws do not apply only to Massachusetts and California dogs. According to *The New York Times* (July 24, 1992), Gerald Yates, a Riker's Island prison guard, dropped a co-worker's cat to its death from a ninth-floor apartment window. He was fined $730, sentenced to three years' probation, and ordered to serve seventy hours of community service at an animal shelter.

PNN EYEWITNESS EXTRA!

DOGNAPPER GETS HIS DUE[16]

OCTOBER 1992—CORONA DEL MAR, CA.

Ginger, a cream-colored pedigree toy poodle, wandered out of her house. That night her owner, Maryetta Selle, a retired psychologist and college administrator, received a phone call from a woman demanding $5,000 for the poodle's return. Selle, on Social Security, succeeded in getting the dognappers down to $3,500, then to $2,500.

A friend of Selle's dropped the cash off in a Huntington Beach phone booth. As prearranged, Ginger's abductors left the poodle's collar there as proof they had her.

The next day, the hostage was delivered to a local pound. The personnel called 911. Responding quickly, the police collared David R. Baker, twenty-five, of Midway City.

The poodle snatcher was taken to Newport Beach jail on charges of attempted extortion. His bail was set at $10,000.

Mrs. Selle and Ginger had a joyful reunion. "She was tickled to death when she saw me," reported Selle. "She was shaking like a leaf; she'd been in so many hands that she was scared to death."

---

[16] Source: "Doggone," *Los Angeles Times,* October 30, 1992.

ALL THE PRESIDENTS' PETS—VII
NOAH'S COLLECTION

Scott's new goat is a success—he hauls Scott all around. The two dogs suit him too. Your mother's cat, dog, and mockingbird give a Robinson Crusoe touch to our mode of life.

PRESIDENT RUTHERFORD HAYES, IN A LETTER TO HIS DAUGHTER, ABOUT HIS GRANDSON

Among the most noteworthy developments in recent pet history is the increasing popularity of alternative species. Pet stores now carry everything from parrots, pythons, and potbellied pigs to iguanas, African Goliath frogs, and Guatemalan red-kneed tarantulas.

As we have seen, exotic pets were nothing new for many great personages in history. Pope Leone had his elephant, Charles X his giraffe, Elizabeth I her bears, General Lafayette his alligator, and so on.

THOMAS JEFFERSON
(1801–9)

When Lewis and Clark returned from the Louisiana Purchase expedition, they brought their employer two grizzly bears. The author of the Declaration of Independence had a cage built for them outside the White House. His opponents, the Federalists, dubbed the grounds "the President's Bear Garden."

ABRAHAM LINCOLN
(1861–65)

He gave his son, Tad, many pets. Among them were a pony and later (after the death of the pony in a stable fire) two goats, Nanny and Nanko. Tad often hitched Nanny and Nanko to chairs and raced through the White House. (When Lincoln him-

self was a boy in Illinois, he had had a pet pig that he rode
regularly also.)

RUTHERFORD B. HAYES
(1877–81)

President Hayes and his wife, Lemonade Lucy, called their own
menagerie "Noah's collection." Aside from their shepherds,
mastiffs, and cats, the Hayeses' White Household included a
goat, a mockingbird, and four canaries.

BENJAMIN HARRISON
(1889–93)

Our twenty-third president gave his grandchildren many dogs
as well as two opossums, Mr. Reciprocity and Mr. Protection.
He also gave them a goat, Old Whiskers, whom they hitched to
a cart. One day in 1891, Whiskers took off through the White
House gates with the First Grandkids in tow, the president in
hot pursuit.

THEODORE ROOSEVELT
(1901–9)

The Rough Rider, big-game hunter, and founder of the progressive Bull Moose party, kept the largest White House Noah's
collection of all. It included Jonathan Edwards, the bear; Bill,
the lizard; Josiah, the badger; Eli Yale, the macaw; Baron
Spreckle, the hen; Maude, the pig; Admiral Dewey, Dr. Johnson,
Bishop Doane, Fighting Bob, and Father O'Grady, the guinea
pigs; and his daughter Alice's garter snake, Emily Spinach.

WILLIAM HOWARD TAFT
(1909–13)

The twenty-seventh president (who weighed three hundred
pounds) insisted on fresh milk and brought his own cows to
Washington: Mooly Wooly and Pauline Wayne.

WOODROW WILSON
(1913–21)

During World War I, the former governor of New Jersey judged a rooster show at the White House and kept sheep on the grounds to mow the grass. The head of the herd was Old Ike, a tobacco-chewing ram.

CALVIN COOLIDGE
(1923–29)

Silent Cal kept a bobcat, a bear cub, a pygmy hippo, a wallaby, lion cubs, antelope, a white goose Enoch, a donkey Ebenezer, and Rebecca the Raccoon. First Lady Grace Coolidge walked Rebecca around the White House on a leash and later found her a husband, Horace.

PNN HARD COPY!
LLAMA KILLER PAYS DEBT TO SOCIETY [17]

JANUARY 1987—EUGENE, OR.

Taz, a malamute/Akita cross owned by Shane Bowlin, was seen "chewing on and biting a llama." He was seized by Deschutes County officials. The charge: "Engaging in the killing, wounding, or injuring of livestock."

The suspect was found guilty as charged and sentenced to "be killed in a humane manner on February 18, 1987."

The execution was stayed when Bowlin appealed on constitutional grounds, saying the conviction violated his dog's Fourteenth Amendment rights guaranteeing him a full adversarial hearing. "Plaintiffs were not permitted to confront and cross-examine the witness," asserted counsel for the defense.

U.S. Appeals Court judge James M. Burns struck down the

---

[17] Source: *Los Angeles Times,* February 11, 1989.

challenge, saying: "Federal courts used to be viewed as austere, even learned tribunals. Not any more. Thanks to the expansion of civil rights jurisprudence, this is now a 'doggie court.' Indeed, this case is an animal 'double-header' since it involves both dogs and llamas."

Taz was put to sleep in February 1989 after Supreme Court justice Antonin Scalia, right-to-life/capital punishment advocate, refused to hear the Akita's appeal in the nation's highest court.

Love in the
Time of Collara—11

THREE MODERN STORIES OF PET LOVE GONE WRONG...

TYLER'S JOHNNY TY

President John Tyler and his wife, Julia, had been looking for a suitable mate for their prize canary, Johnny Ty, for some time. At last locating one in New York, they had it shipped to Richmond by steamboat in 1843. But when the Tylers put his new spouse in Johnny's cage, the canary jumped off his perch and sulked on the floor for days, head under his wing. A week later Johnny had a heart attack.

Later the Tylers discovered that the mate was a male.

GOING APE

In 1976, Guy the Gorilla, star attraction of the London Zoo, died a virgin. Though numerous attempts had been made to breed the ape, Guy showed no interest in the opposite sex. Sources close to the gorilla said he was gay. After his death, Guy was commemorated with a bronze statue.

In the same year, Japanese actress Hitoko Tagawa offered to have sex with a celebrity ape, Oliver, in "interest of science."

Oliver's owner, lawyer Michael Miller, sued Nippon TV, calling the proposition a "publicity stunt."

GOOSE DIES FOR HIS MAILBOX [18]

In December 1992, a group of unidentified snowmobilers from Nassau, Minnesota, raced off after hitting a goose that had taken a mailbox as its mate.

The goose and the mailbox belonged to a local farm couple, Carl and Mary Wildung. Mary Wildung explained to reporters covering the story that their twenty-five-year-old honker had lost his real mate seven years before. Shortly after becoming a widower, on the rebound, he grew romantically attached to the Wildungs' mailbox and began to guard it jealously. He regularly charged the mailman at delivery time and nipped the Wildungs when they went to collect their letters.

Snowmobilers began to "buzz" the goose in early December, but he didn't abandon his spouse.

"He was as faithful as ever and guarded the mailbox right until the end," Mary Wildung said.

Later that month, around Christmastime, the snowmobilers came back when the Wildungs were out and ran him down in front of the mailbox. Said Mrs. Wildung, "When Curt came in and told me, 'They did it, they got him,' I actually had tears in my eyes. . . . "

Though they did not press charges, the couple said they wanted an apology from the snowmobilers.

The Wildungs packed the goose's remains into a snow-filled tub outside. They told reporters they would either have their pet stuffed or would lay him to rest out by his mailbox and install a concrete monument there.

"Let's see 'em try to run that over," Mary Wildung said.

[18] Source: "Goose Meets End Defending Mailbox It Took as Its Mate," Associated Press, January 10, 1993.

... AND TWO MODERN STORIES OF PET LOVE GONE RIGHT

CARUSO AND TIMMIE

The Pussy said to the Owl, "You elegant fowl!
How charmingly sweet you sing!
O let us be married! too long we have tarried:
But what shall we do for a ring?"

EDWARD LEAR, "THE OWL AND THE PUSSY-CAT"

President Calvin Coolidge had a canary called Caruso. A Washington newspaperman, Bascom Timmons, had a cat, Timmie, who was very fond of Caruso. So fond was Timmie of Caruso that President Coolidge at last gave the bird to Timmons. The canary would often roost on the cat's back and sing.

When Caruso finally died, he did so on Timmie's back, after one last song.

THE MAHARAJAH'S ROSHANA AND BOBBIE

In 1952, Mahabat Khan Babi Pathan, maharajah of Junagadh, India, held a state wedding for his golden retriever bitch, Roshana, and stud, Bobbie. The nuptials were attended by fifty thousand guests—government officials, international diplomats, and celebrities.

The groom wore gold bracelets and a silk-embroidered cummerbund; the bride was perfumed and heavily jeweled.

Roshana was said to be in season and ready for consummation. Her husband, Bobbie, reportedly mounted the bitch at the altar before being green-lighted to lick the bride.

After the reception, the couple was chaperoned to the bridal suite by the maharajah himself.

Khan Babi kept hundreds of dogs at the imperial residence. Each had its own suite, with telephone and personal valet.

CALIFORNIA PET PASTOR, DAWN ROGERS

Dawn Rogers, ordained by the Universal Life Church, performed seventeen marriage ceremonies for dogs, cats, horses, goldfish, and frogs in 1986. Cost of nuptials: canine—$500; feline—$300.

INTERVIEW WITH THE PARROT

One of the more important developments in modern pet history is the advent of the animal psychologist.[19] Countless pets have been in analysis in the last decade. All too common feelings of inadequacy, shame, loss, and anger affect behavior and quality of life.

Some current pet psychologists are also psychics. They overcome the language barrier with a patient by telepathically tapping into its problems and concerns and communicating these to the owner.

Penelope Smith is such a professional. She talked to author Joanie Doss's three blue-front Amazon parrots—Pepper, TJ (Tequila Joe), and Magnum (Maggie)—for *Bird Talk* magazine (October 1992).

What follows is a transcript of that chat.

Doss asked the questions. Her birds answered through psychic Smith. . . .

QUESTION: How old are you?

PEPPER: I am very young but very mature—fourteen or fifteen years.

---

[19] According to *The Washington Post* (August, 1993), more than 3,000 pet therapists are currently practicing in the United States. Their fees range from $150 to $400 for a three-hour session.

QUESTION: What sex are you?

PEPPER: I don't lay eggs, so I must be male. It doesn't matter to me.

(Doss's note: I had Pepper sexed about two months before the interview. He is small for a blue-front, but wide in the pelvis.)

QUESTION: Were you an adult or a baby when you were captured?

PEPPER:[20] That was a hurtful time in my life. I was a young bird; I didn't have all my color. I wanted to kill people.

SMITH *(interjecting to bird owner, Doss)*: Wow! Many animals just let go and forgive.

PEPPER *(continuing through Smith)*: They clubbed my parents. They killed my parents! . . . I was really mad at people. I wanted to kill them. . . .

(Doss's note: When I got him Pepper was filled with hatred. He bit me every day for eighteen months. He bit through my lip, tried to take out an eye, and pulled flesh from my scalp.)

Later in the interview Pepper tells Doss, through medium Smith, that he feels better. "You let me get all that out. My life began when I met you, Joanie. . . . I am a happy bird now."

But recently Pepper has refused to learn any new vocabulary. Doss says that when she tries to teach him, "he begins eating or playing or even singing so he can't hear me." Dismayed, she asks the bird about this. Again, the parrot answers through Smith.

QUESTION: Why have you stopped learning new words and phrases?

[20] The psychic, answering for the bird here, begins to weep.

PEPPER: It is boring! Do you think that is all a parrot is about—learning new words and phrases?! . . .

SMITH *(interjecting to Doss):* This is one of the most fun interviews I have ever done.

QUESTION: How is your health?

PEPPER: I know they check me out. I know she worries about my respiratory system. It is fine. I am getting a little older. Although I told you I was young, I am older than I told you.

SMITH *(aside to Doss):* He is now giving me thirty-four.

PEPPER: I am strong. I am healthy. I can still do all my tricks: what more do you want?

The interview now turns to Tequila Joe. Perched next to the psychic, he has been waiting his turn to have the floor.

QUESTION: How old are you?

TJ: I'm a young bird. I'm not as experienced as Pepper. Pepper has been in the forest.

QUESTION: What sex are you?

TJ: I don't think I am a male, but I don't think I'm a female. . . . Pepper talked about not laying eggs. I don't even know what an egg is. Could you explain it to me?

PSYCHIC: The only way I could explain that would be about mating with a female.

TJ: I don't know what you mean. What would I do?

PSYCHIC *(to Doss):* He doesn't need a sex lesson now. . . . *(to TJ)* It's okay, sweetie.

(Doss's note: TJ has never masturbated, regurgitated, or been aggressive. Once, Maggie tried to mount TJ. He came running to me in terror. He truly is innocent.)

SMART-MOUTH BIRDS OVERHEARD

I can talk ... Can you fly?

> BENNIE, A PARROT FROM HEALDSBURG,
> CALIFORNIA, TO FIREMEN WHO CAME TO
> RESCUE HIM FROM A TREE
> HE REFUSED TO COME OUT OF
> (SOURCE: HEALDSBURG SUN, OCT. 17, 1986)

What about the appropriation?

> CALVIN COOLIDGE'S PARROT TO THE
> PRESIDENT WHILE HE PREPARES
> FOR A BUDGET MEETING WITH THE
> DIRECTOR OF THE NATIONAL ZOO

Fuck off!

> QUINCEY, A WHITE COCKATOO,
> TO THE ADORING CHILDREN
> AT FLAMINGOLAND ZOO, ENGLAND,
> WHERE THE BIRD ROLLER-SKATED,
> SANG, AND PLAYED PIANO
> (QUINCEY WAS LET GO FOR THE REMARK)

MODERN AFURISMS

Afurisms have evolved over the last four thousand years, keeping abreast of current attitudes. Whereas in biblical times they had "Don't cast your pearls before swine," we now have the simpler and more practical "Don't have a cow." Where in sunnier times it was "Every dog has his day," we now have the far more realistic "Life is a bitch, then you die."

So afurisms today fit the times: they are geared to the bottom line. And a single afurism usually says it all.

We use them as nouns, referring to a person, place, thing, or situation: a dog, a bitch, a bear, a chicken, a turkey, a skunk, and so on. We also have afurisms for personality types on a sliding scale.

> *GOOD:* Cool cat. Fat cat. Hep cat. Sacred cow. Cash cow. Golden goose. Lucky duck.

> *IN BETWEEN:* Lame duck. Sitting duck. Hellcat. Underdog. Monkey's uncle. Gorilla. White elephant. Fish out of water. Clotheshorse. Horse of a different color.

> *LOW-DOWN:* Snake in the grass. Wolf in sheep's clothing. Dog in a manger. Dirty rotten skunk. Birdbrain. Stool pigeon. Horse's ass. Yellow-bellied sapsucker.

We also use afurisms as verbs: to bully, to badger, to birddog, to bitch, to weasel, to rat out, to ferret out, to pig out, to hog, to henpeck, to horse around, to monkey around, to yak.

We have barnyard activities that are commonly engaged in, too. We can count sheep, get somebody's goat, let the cat out of the bag, play cat-and-mouse, go whole hog, go hog wild, give a goose, have a gander, fuck a duck, feather the nest, eat crow, or talk turkey.

Finally, very common afurisms these days are in a's and as a's:

> *IN A's:* In the doghouse. In the catbird seat. Canary in a coal mine. Bull in a china shop. Bats in the belfry. Pig in a poke. Mud in a pig's, cat's, or dead dog's eye.

> *AS A's:* Stubborn as a mule. Gentle as a lamb. Crazy as a loon (fox or cat). Busy as a bee (or beaver). Pretty as a peacock. Free as a bird. Happy as a lark. Hungry as a bear. Horny as a toad.

PAMPERED POOCH AND PUSSY PRODUCTS
A Nineties Sampler

For 1990 and beyond, I predict the dressing of pets as a tremendous fashion movement.

FASHION FORECASTER BERNIE OZER

In 1991 Americans spent $5 billion on their 120 million dogs and cats. The figure has quadrupled since 1987. Receipts for collars, leashes, toys, apparel, and accessories make up a good percentage of the sum.

Here are some of the outlets for products.

KAREN'S FOR PEOPLE AND PETS
NEW YORK

Known as the Bergdorf Goodman of pet couture. Merchandise includes $140 poodle fur coats and stoles and $120 leather jumpers with optional snakeskin trim and gem-studded collars.

ANIMAL MANORS
NEW YORK

Pet castles and condos from $400 to $5,000. Popular dog model: the French château—$2,850. Top-of-the-line cat model: the Egyptian temple. Also available, the Catmastic: six-foot-tall structure with jungle gym and multiple-tier sleeping platforms.

POOCHI CANINE COUTURE, INC.
NEW JERSEY

Carolyn Parrs's collar, leash, accessory emporium. Prices start at $30.

LICK YOUR CHOPS
NEW YORK

A total pet boutique specializing in gourmet treats.

L. COFFEY LTD.
HAUTE FELINE AND HAUTE CANINE PRODUCTS
NEW YORK

Featuring a fine line of china pet bowls, greeting cards, yummy treats. President/owner Linda S. Coffey began the $1 million enterprise in her kitchen.

ADVANCED AVIAN DESIGNS
LOS ANGELES

Complete line of birdhouses: the Playgym, the Parrotree, the Deluxe Townhouse. Also offers premium hardwood perches, as well as toys, ladders, and Birdie Beanery.

In addition to these outlets, many mail-order companies offer a wide array of conventional and high-tech pet accessories.

- Pet Chime, Inc. offers a device that enables cats and dogs to ring their doorbells to get in and out of the house.
- Canine Concepts, Inc., offers the Silencer, an electronic collar that controls "nuisance barking" by emitting high-frequency sound pulses in direct response to a dog's bark.
- The Bitch-Hitch Company (Burbank, California) sells a "solid-weld construction, fully padded" steel armature that holds a bitch in place while she is being bred. Price: $549.99, plus shipping and handling.
- R. C. Steele (Brockport, New York) provides a full line of pet supplies and specialty items in these important areas:

General Hygiene: the Moose Scoop, the Big Stinky, Wee Wee Pads®, and pet sanitary napkins (available in floral or denim).

Dental Hygiene: Petrodex™ dog and cat toothpaste and breath freshener; Beefeaters Mint Bones; Nylafloss™ Chew Rope.

Bedding: Kitty Kups®; Cat Condos; lambswool Dognappers; and a complete line of dog and cat Cuddlers® (the Plaid Cuddler, Super-Soft, Wicker, Rainbow, and Flexi Cuddler).

Toys: Tammi Tugs™; talking Woof! and Meow! cookie jars; Funny Bones (vinyl squeaker toys in various models: the Clown, the Duck, the Pig, the Vet, the Burglar, the Dog Catcher, and others).

Treats: Smoked pig ears; rawhide shoes; Choo-Hooves (regular and barbecue flavor); Yuppy Puppy™ treat dispenser, Pup Pop Rawhide "Munchies" (the Pretzel, the Taco, the Chop, the Cocktail Frank, the "Pacifier," and others).

Clothes and Accessories: Doggiduds® Dog Ponchos; "Protect My Pet" St. Francis I.D. tags; Blinking Hanukkah and Christmas pet collars, holiday antlers, and Santa hats.

The Japanese spend $2 billion per year on their twelve million dogs and cats. Among the more upscale franchises:

ADACHIYA OF TOKYO

Boutique featuring a complete inventory of doggie designer T-shirts, jumpers, rainboots, bikinis, knapsacks, kitty kimonos (from $300), and mink stoles ($7,600).

ISOROKU KIMURA'S PET DATING SERVICE

Pet résumés, snapshots, video preview; $75 per date.

JAPAN TRIMMING SCHOOL

Aerobic and Jazzercise classes, shiatsu massage, and private yoga lessons ($35 for forty-five minutes).

JIPPO, INC.
MOBILE PET ANGEL SERVICE

Cremation service offering radio-dispatched vans, each with a pink altar and portable incinerator. Deluxe pet "soul launching" by laserium also available at extra charge.

Doggerel

PRIVILEGED POOCHES

My dogs don't travel by boat. And they don't go with me to Paris, London, or New York. But they do go with me to Gstaad and Capri.

RUDOLPH VALENTINO

He knew so many words that my husband and I took to spelling in front of him. Of course, always being treated as a person (he often sat at the table with a napkin around his neck), Fafner considered himself a person. His attitude toward other dogs was a mixture of arrogance and contempt, and he barked furiously whenever he saw one.

BROOKE ASTOR, "OUR FRIEND FAFNER"

Shag was too great a gentleman to take part in the plebeian work of killing rats for which he was originally needed, but he certainly added, we felt, to the respectability of the family. . . . The solitary occasion when he found it necessary to inflict marks of his displeasure on human flesh was once when a visitor rashly called him by the contemptible lap-dog title of "Fido."

**VIRGINIA WOOLF,
"ON A FAITHFUL
FRIEND"**

And there is a certain snootiness; Pomeranians speak only to poodles, and poodles only to God.

**CHARLES KURALT, ON THE
WESTMINSTER DOG SHOW**

EATERIES AND HAIRY HOSTELS

FIDO'S FAST FOOD
TOLEDO, OHIO

• Only drive-through for dogs in Toledo, Ohio.
• Located in a former Fotomat booth.
• Proprietors Jackie Zajac and Sheila Mullan guarantee satisfaction.
• Menu: burgers, Furry Fries, peanut-butter bagels. People bags.

SOGO
YOKOHAMA, JAPAN

• Three-course special ($75): premium steak tartare; unsalted ham, sausages, and cheese; white chocolate for dessert.

BEACH REGENCY RESTO-CHIEN
NICE, FRANCE

* Only dog bistro on the Riviera.
* Full dessert cart featuring Camembert and crème caramel.

MONTROSE PET HOTEL
NEW YORK

* Boast of the management: "So exclusive we don't accept people."
* Fresh table setting for every meal.

HARBOR HOTEL
BOSTON

* 230-room facility located on the historic Rowes wharf.
* Amenities for pooches: chewbones, basketball, Super Dooper Pooper Scooper.
* Amenities for cats: litter boxes (with sanity seal), Whisker Lickin's, catnip, and "traditional" mouse (with bell).
* For all: "Welcome Amenity Basket." Sitters and walkers. Pet psychologist on call.

KINUGAWA KOKUSAI HOTEL
JAPAN

* Japan's Dog Ritz: $150 a night, $7 extra for each pet in the party.
* Amenities: Fido futon mattress, "pets-only mixed bathing," followed by blow-dry.
* Dining room special: milk and low-fat boiled chicken.
(Note: Many pets arrive at Kinugawa Kokusai in hats and kimonos. Owner Keiko Akutsu and staff refer to them as "little boys" and "little girls.")

CAMP GONE-TO-THE-DOGS
PUTNEY, VERMONT

• 500-acre complex with swimming pond, tennis courts, hiking trails, dog dorms.
• Accommodates 250 canines, 120 adult people. No kids allowed.
• Special activities: dog square dancing and lure coursing (chasing a plastic bag on a motorized cable).
• Staff of top canine professionals, directed by Honey Loring.
• Tuition for one-week session: $600.

SUPERCAMP
ENFIELD, NEW HAMPSHIRE

• Located near Dartmouth on the former U of New Hampshire campus.
• Run by Canine Behavior Sciences, welcomes "problem" pooches.
• Recreational activities: herding, tracking, retrieving, fashion modeling.
• Tuition (two-week session): $600–$985.

LAST POST
FALLS VILLAGE, CONNECTICUT

• 37-acre wooded retreat for cats who are elderly or whose masters have died or become seriously ill.
• Founded by Pegeen Fitzgerald, New York radio talk-show host.
• Current proprietress, Jeanne Toomey, says Last Post welcomes "moochers" as well as "affluent" cats. (About 450 are in residence.)
• All care and amenities are included.

KAMER CANINE COLLEGE
LOS ANGELES, CALIFORNIA

- Offers a full eight-week method acting course for tomorrow's Benjis and Beethovens.
- Tuition, room, and board: $4,150.

CAT CHAT

It's easy to understand why the cat has eclipsed the dog as modern America's favorite pet. People like pets to possess the same qualities they do. Cats are irresponsible and recognize no authority, yet are completely dependent on others for their material needs.

P. J. O'ROURKE, MODERN MANNERS (1983)

I'm just a cat on a hot tin roof.

**LIZ TAYLOR TO PAUL NEWMAN,
CAT ON A HOT TIN ROOF (1958)**

The trouble with a kitten is that it grows up to be a cat.

**OGDEN NASH, "THE KITTEN,"
FROM THE FACE IS FAMILIAR (1940)**

The cat is a soft, indestructible automaton provided by nature to be kicked when things go wrong in the domestic circle.

AMBROSE BIERCE

There is something going on now in Mexico that I happen to think is cruelty to animals. What I'm talking about, of course, is cat juggling.

STEVE MARTIN

PNN EYEWITNESS EXTRA!

PET BEQUESTS

Years ago, the first pet wills were contested. The precedent-setting case here involved the cats of a seventeenth-century French harpist, Madame Dupois. She died in April 1630, leaving history's first feline bequest. Her will read: "I desire my sister, Marie Blateau, and my niece, Madame Calonge, to look to my cats. . . . Thirty sous a week must be laid out upon them. They are to be served daily, in a clean and proper manner, with two meals of meat soup."

Madame Dupois's sister, Marie Blateau, contested the will in court and won.

There was a similar case in New York City a few years ago involving Terry Krumholz and her two Burmese, Damon and Pythias. Ms. Krumholz passed away in June 1991 and left ample funds for continued care of the cats at her apartment at 1056 Fifth Avenue until their adoption. But, according to *The New York Times* (September 3, 1991), the building now had a "no pet" ruling. Damon and Pythias were evicted, and doormen blocked their return.

On the brighter side, in 1986 Mary Rossi left her twelve-year-old cat, Minky, $25,000 to provide for her daily menu of boiled chicken and poached cod in parsley sauce, with a side of chopped livers. And Minky got it.

Still, as the stakes increase, so, often, do problems. The beneficiary of the largest modern pet bequest was Toby, a poodle. His mistress, Miss Ella Wendell, died in 1968, leaving him $30 million. The relatives went to court. Meantime Toby—who, while Miss Wendell was alive, had slept on silk sheets in his own bedroom and was served breakfast in bed by a butler—slept in a wooden box in the kitchen and was fed on the floor. Before the will was settled, Toby was put to sleep by the executors.

A few less disheartening cases:

• In 1968 oil heiress Eleanor Ritchey left $4.3 million to 161 stray dogs she kept on her Fort Lauderdale ranch. Her former chauffeur took care of them until the last, Musketeer, died in 1984. The estate then passed to Auburn University Research Foundation.

• Patti, an eleven-year-old English setter, inherited her mistress's entire $600,000 fortune.

• BeBe, a California poodle, also received $600,000 from her mistress, a supper club owner.

• At his death in 1971 German entrepreneur George Ritt left his prize Alsatian, Viking Baron von Heppeplatz, real estate valued at $250,000.

• Sugah, a Kentucky goat, inherited her mistress's entire $115,000 estate.

• Dr. William Grier of San Diego, California, bequeathed $415,000 to his felines, Hellcat and Brownie. After Hellcat and Brownie died in 1965, the money went to George Washington University.

PNN EYEWITNESS EXTRA!

THE $30,000 LIBRARY CAT [21]

PUTNAM VALLEY, NY.

A cat named Muffin once lived in the stacks at the town library. She had been doing so undisturbed since kittenhood, for seven years. Many patrons loved Muffin, especially ninety-three-year-old Marjorie Horton, who was leaving the library $30,000 in her will.

Then one day, after allegedly taking several "unprovoked swipes" at children, Muffin was evicted from the building. She was also reportedly aggravating the allergies of a library trustee and several employees.

A petition of protest to the eviction was submitted to the

[21] Source: "Library Cat Is Out, and So Is Library," *The New York Times,* January 12, 1989.

Putnam Valley Library. It carried three hundred signatures. Among them was that of benefactor Mrs. Horton.

"Everybody loved that cat," she said. "I was furious. I wrote them a nice letter. I'm not some young snotnose. But no one listened. Now, not one penny will go to the library!"

Mrs. Horton drafted a new will, leaving her estate to three animal shelters.

"PAUSE TO REMEMBER" [22]

The *Daily Local News* of West Chester, Pennsylvania, runs a weekly column called "Pause to Remember," a pet obituary. The column was born when Henry, a Rhode Island red rooster, died of influenza.

Writer James Giuliano says of his column, "The challenge is to get beyond their [the pet owners'] bereavement—'Oh, I miss him so much'—to the basics such as age, sex, cause of death, and what the pet did all day."

Henry spent his evenings on a recliner watching TV while eating Fritos. The Rhode Island red's Saturday favorite sit-com was "The Golden Girls."

Among other "Pause to Remember" features:

MOLLY BRIGHTENED FAMILY VISITS
Before passing away, this Siberian husky regularly visited her master, an Alzheimer's patient, and was the only family member he recognized.

SEAGRAVE WILL BE MISSED AT MEMORIAL DAY PARADE
A dalmatian's untimely demise after only one ride in a fire truck.

Also included is the story of Butch, a Manx, who did hat tricks with cards; and Billy Metz's 4-H project, Chipper, the guinea pig, blue-ribbon winner at the 1987 Chester County Round-Up, survived by bereaved cagemate, Oreo.

[22] Source: "Cock-a-Doodle-Doo! Henry, a Pet, Finds Life After Death," *The Wall Street Journal,* June 20, 1989.

At first "Pause to Remember" caused some "raised eyebrows" in West Chester. According to *Daily Local News* editor John DeSanto, "People wondered what we were going to do next—road kills?"

Concludes column writer James Giuliano, "This isn't hurting anybody. Not everybody is going to uncover Watergate."

The paper's circulation (39,000) increased 10 percent since the inception of the pet obituary.

PET ROCK PLATINUM AND GOLD

The modern pet era is not called the Rock 'n' Roll Age for nothing. Groups from the Beatles to the Monkees, Three Dog Night to the Stray Cats, have redefined pop music, and animal hits have dominated the charts. Here are the top ten:

The Platinum

"Hound Dog"	1956	Elvis Presley
"Bird Dog"	1958	Everly Brothers
"Chipmunk Song"	1958	The Chipmunks
"The Lion Sleeps Tonight"	1961	The Tokens
"Wild Thing"	1961	The Troggs
"Horse with No Name"	1972	America
"Crocodile Rock"	1973	Elton John
"Disco Duck"	1976	Rick Dees and his Cast of Idiots
"Eye of the Tiger"	1982	Survivor
"Maneater"	1982	Daryl Hall & John Oates

The following dog, cat, bird, and woolly bully hits also deserve special mention:

The Gold

"Woolly Bully"	Sam the Sham and the Pharaohs
"Muskrat Love"	Captain and Tennille
"Monkey Man"	Rolling Stones

"Foxy Lady"	Jimi Hendrix
"Werewolves of London"	Warren Zevon
"Bulldog Blues"	Cream
"Cat Scratch Fever"	Ted Nugent
"Stray Cat Blues"	Rolling Stones
"Cat's in the Cradle"	Harry Chapin
"Li'l Red Rooster"	Howlin' Wolf
"Free Bird"	Lynyrd Skynyrd
"Jungle Love"	Steve Miller Band
"Bungle in the Jungle"	Jethro Tull
"At the Zoo"	Simon & Garfunkel
"White Rabbit"	Jefferson Airplane
"I Am the Walrus"	Beatles

TWENTIETH-CENTURY FOXES AND FELINES

They tell me a cat can look at a king. Well, I have shaken paws with two Presidents of the United States, one Vice-President, one former Secretary of State, more governors than I can wag my tail at, and the ambassador from Japan. . . . I've worn the same tie to the Tony Awards and to Sardi's restaurant. . . . I guess you'd call me a star.

SANDY (CANINE STAR OF *ANNIE*), *THE AUTOBIOGRAPHY OF A STAR*

It is fatal to let any dog know that he is funny. He immediately loses his head and starts hamming it up.

P. G. WODEHOUSE

Show business pets, as we have seen, are nothing new. Zippico the Poodle performed for Roman emperor Vespasian, Marocco the Talking Horse for Elizabethans, Annone the dancing elephant for Pope Leone I.

But organized show business, in the form of pedigree beauty pageants, did not begin until the nineteenth century: for dogs in 1859 with the Newcastle-upon-Tyne show; for cats in 1871 with the London Crystal Palace exhibition.

Show business became more diversified in this century with the advent of commercial pets: the MGM lion, Nipper the RCA dog, Bingo the Cracker Jack dog, the Borden cows Elsie, Elmer, and Beauregard, and many others.

The transition from advertising to acting came naturally to pets, and so we had Dorothy's Toto, *Our Gang*'s Pete, *The Thin Man*'s Asta, Rin Tin Tin, Felix the Cat, Ol' Yeller, Mr. Ed, and so on. And now, more recently, Cujo, Hooch, Bijou, Beethoven, Clyde the orangutan, and so forth.

Here now the Walk of Fame of some of our greatest recent stars, and their rags-to-riches stories. . . .

BENJI

Originally an orphan puppy at the Burbank Animal Shelter, his big break came with "Petticoat Junction." Later, the mixed breed had his own trailer and makeup man and was regularly swarmed by adoring bitches. His movies grossed over $100 million. He passed the mantel to his son, Benji II.

Both were inducted into the American Humane Society's Animal Actors' Hall of Fame. The two Benjis received Top Animal Entertainer Georgie Awards from the American Guild of Variety Artists.

LASSIE

The first Lassie (there were five, all males) was named Pal. His original owner turned the future star over to obedience trainer Bud Weatherwax because he had a bad car-chasing habit. The collie soon became America's favorite dog on one of the most popular—and, at seventeen years, one of the longest-running —TV series, "Lassie." But there was conflict behind the scenes. Weatherwax's wife divorced him, accusing him of loving Pal more than her. Pal slept with the trainer on a giant bed (as did all future Lassies). When Pal died, Weatherwax scattered his ashes at sea.

RADAR

As a puppy this German shepherd nearly died from distemper but was saved by Dorothy Steves. He went on to become a top TV star in Brazil. *The Times,* a Brazilian newspaper, reported: "Radar is a dog, but people tend to forget this. . . . Even the house servants say 'excuse me' to him when they pass." Radar soon left South America to pursue a career in Europe. Twenty thousand tearful fans showed up to bid him bon voyage. In England he became the star of the popular TV serial "Softly Softly."

MORRIS THE CAT

Morris was twenty minutes from execution in an animal shelter outside Chicago when he was saved by adoption. He became the spokescat for 9-Lives catfood. In 1986 he went on to run for president of the United States as a Democrat. He garnered an impressive list of endorsements, including one from Eleanor Mondale, daughter of the former vice-president.

MIKE

Mike did bit parts in TV commercials until his big break in *Down and Out in Beverly Hills* with Nick Nolte. Following the hit, he did a promo tour, had a suite in the Ritz Carlton Hotel, appeared on "Good Morning America," and earned a star and a paw print on Hollywood's Walk of Fame. He donned Gucci accessories and frequently shopped on Rodeo Drive.

TUNDRA

This Samoyed bitch was the star of "Love Boat." She earned $1,000 a day, had a personal hairdresser and a limo, and ate regularly at Le Dome, Morton's, Burger Ballroom, and Koo-Koo-Roo.

SPUDS MacKENZIE

The spokespooch for Bud Light was dubbed the "Ayatola Partyola, the Guru of Good Times, the Philosopher of Fun." But in reality, he was a bitch named Evie (full name Honey Tree Evil Eye), owned by Stan and Jackie Oles of North Riverside, Illinois. Among the bull terrier's other credits: s/he was guest dogjay on MTV; made *People*'s Best Dressed list in 1990; and starred with Robert Downey in *Rented Lips*. Spuds/Evie died of kidney failure in the spring of 1993 after a quiet retirement in Illinois. The celebrity's neighbor, Priscilla Jasso, thirteen, eulogized, "Spuds was kind to everyone. He [sic] never barked at us."

BERT

The Jack Russell terrier of Hal Gurnee, director of "Late Night with David Letterman," regularly roamed around the "Late Night" set and was the subject of the 1989 People magazine cover story "Bertmania!" Celebrity guests had their photos taken with a snapshot of Bert. Among them were Pee-wee Herman, Johnny Carson, Jerzy Kozinski, Charo, Burt Reynolds, Hugh Hefner, Bill Cosby, Zippy the Chimp. The photo op was declined by Simon and Garfunkel. Barbara Walters declined, then accepted.

THE GOLDEN YUMMY AWARDS

The Yummies go to these pet movies in the following categories:

DOG MOVIES
Lassie Come Home (1943)
Old Yeller (1957)
The Shaggy Dog (1959)
I Was a Teenage Werewolf (1957)

Benji (1974)
A Boy and His Dog (1975)
Oh! Heavenly Dog (1980)
Cujo (1983)
The Dogs of Hell (1983)
K-9 (1989)
Turner and Hooch (1989)
Dances with Wolves (1990)
Beethoven (1991)

CAT MOVIES

The Black Cat (1934)
Curse of the Cat People (1944)
The Pink Panther (1964)
That Darn Cat (1965)
Because of the Cats (1973)
Harry and Tonto (1974)

OTHER

King Kong (1933)
Bambi (1942)
National Velvet (1944)
Daffy Duck: The Nuttiness Continues . . . (1956)
The Fly (1958)
The Birds (1963)
Planet of the Apes (1968)
Pink Flamingos (1972)
Jaws (1975)
Splash (1984)
A Fish Called Wanda (1988)
Who Framed Roger Rabbit? (1988)
Teenage Mutant Ninja Turtles (1990)
Homeward Bound: The Incredible Journey (1992)

NOT-SO-STUPID PET TRICKS
Top Ten from
"The David Letterman Show"

Not all pets have the talent or drive to become the next Lassie, Morris, or Spuds. But many have become stars for at least fifteen seconds on the only major television network program that provided a forum for nonhuman entertainers—"Late Night with David Letterman."

Stupid Pet Tricks debuted in 1980. For over a decade "Late Night" viewers witnessed great performances from most major species: somersaulting canaries, cats that came when they were called, and a horse that did a lip-synch to "Indian Love Call."

The majority of the acts were canine. According to Letterman's pet trick coordinator, Susan Hall Sheehan, each breed seemed to have a specialty: rottweilers—hotdogging on skateboards; West Highland white terriers—attacking TVs; Boston terriers—attacking upright vacuum cleaners; dachshunds—tennis ball tricks; dalmatians—soap bubble stunts.

Here now a tribute to the Top Ten Not-So-Stupid Pet Tricks of all time:

10. FACE, PIT BULL
FRISBEE "DEATH SPIRAL" TRICK

Face gripped one side of a Frisbee in his teeth; his owner gripped the other side in his teeth, then proceeded to spin the dog dervishlike on stage.

9. ANONYMOUS
PRESSED KISSER TRICK—ON GLASS

This performer smashed his nose and slobbery lips against a windowpane and held the pose while NBC studio cameras moved in for a close-up.

8. CAESAR, BOUVIER DES FLANDRES
HIGH-WIRE BROOM BALANCING TRICK

Caesar balanced on a broomstick held at one end by his trainer, at the other by Letterman.

7. MUFFY, YORKY
HEAD-BALANCING TRICK

The terrier bitch perched herself on her owner's head while he twirled a baton.

6. MILO, GREAT DANE MIX
BLIND-DOG BISCUIT TRICK

This performer balanced a treat on his nose, tossed it into the air, caught it, and gobbled it down—blindfolded.

5. CHEE CHEE, COCKAPOO
GROCERY-SHOPPING TRICK

Perched on hind legs, Chee Chee pushed a little shopping cart past grocery items lined up on a display shelf. She pawed selections into the basket as she went.

4. BRUTE, TEXAS CHIHUAHUA
A CAPELLA TRICK

Brute sang bluegrass a capella with his owner. Dressed country style for the gig, the Chihuahua wore a hand-knitted cap and overalls (which matched those of his owner).

3. STERLING, MINIATURE POODLE
TELEPATHIC CARD TRICK

The poodle's owner produced an ordinary deck of playing cards, shuffled them, then had the show host pick a card, any card. The host pulled a card and showed it to the cameras and studio audience, but not the poodle. The owner reclaimed the card, shuffled it back into the deck, then placed the deck on the floor. Sterling sniffed the fifty-two and promptly withdrew the correct card.

2. ANONYMOUS, COCKER SPANIEL
BILLY JOEL IMPERSONATION

The cocker was supposed to do something with a pair of over-size sunglasses but choked. The host placed the glasses on the stub of the cocker's tail, and cameras moved in for a moon shot of the hairy face and wagging nose under the shades.

1. BUDDY, COLLIE/LAB MIX
BEER-BUYING TRICK

Buddy snapped up a six-pack of Bud from a grocery shelf and carried it to a checkout stand manned by Letterman. The pooch removed a ten-spot from his leg, secured with a rubber band, and muzzled it over to Letterman. Letterman broke the bill, put the change in the shopping bag, and Buddy exited with his brew.

BOOZER: HISTORY'S FIRST
LIBERATED DOG

In our review of the present pet age, we have concentrated on exceptional pets. Sigmund Freud's Wolf took a taxi home by himself. The maharajah's golden retrievers, Roshana and Bobbie, exchanged vows. Rin Tin Tin and Lassie kept major Hollywood studios afloat. Morris the Cat ran for the presidency. Millie Bush wrote a best-seller.

But we have also seen how ordinary modern dogs and cats have made history by doing extraordinary things. Rocky and Barco, the Texas narcs, seized more than $300 million worth of contraband. A four-month-old kitten scaled the Matterhorn without ropes. Ari, the Floridian Lab/cockapoo, sued USAir for $50,000. Buddy, the Lab/collie mix, appeared on "The David Letterman Show" and bought his own beer without being carded or short-changed.

In view of all this, the burgeoning animal rights movements of this century, multimillion-dollar bequests, and the multibillion-dollar pet supply industry are no surprise.

So we ask ourselves: What's next?

The answer is clear enough: Pet liberation.

But is the average dog or cat on the street equal to the great challenge of the twenty-first century? Are they ready to handle holding their own papers, calling their own shots?

Let's take a look at a current case, the subject of a feature article in *Dog World*. . . .

Boozer is a basset hound who lives in Marine-on-St. Croix, Minnesota, has his own bank account, and is exempt from leash laws.

But the basset was not always his own dog and the wave of the future.

As a puppy, Boozer was turned over by his owner to the Hennepin County Humane Society, which sent him to the University of Minnesota veterinarian hospital, where he was used in studies. A lab worker adopted Boozer and took care of him until he ate the furniture in her apartment. Then she gave him to her brother Joe, who lived in Marine-on-St. Croix (population 610).

After Boozer moved in with Joe, he took to visiting the next-door neighbors, the Moffits, and playing with their kids. Soon he was over at the Moffits so much, Joe gave him to Claudia Moffit.

But hardly had he moved again than Boozer started visiting other neighbors. He ventured farther and farther on each of his outings, until soon he was a regular at bars and restaurants in town.

After Boozer was arrested by the Marine animal control officer, the Moffits tried to keep him tied up. But he howled until he was let loose. Then he would again set out for local bars, restaurants, and the houses of his friends. Finally the Moffits threw up their hands.

The hound started to come and go as he pleased at that point. But eventually he needed shots, heartworm pills, and a new license.

Claudia Moffit raised the money for this by selling Boozer T-shirts in town. With the T-shirt proceeds she opened a bank account for the basset at the local First National. Then she went to the county clerk and had Boozer listed as his own owner, which exempted him from leash laws.

After becoming a legal independent and a dog of means, Boozer attended all town functions, including the Firemen's Ball, the New Year's Eve dance, and Octoberfest. He had his own float in the Fourth of July Independence Day parade, too.

In 1992 "Good Morning America" did a feature on Boozer, billing him as the first dog who belongs to himself. As a result of the show, the basset's T-shirt sales went through the ceiling. Boozer is reportedly now looking into tax shelters and retirement options.

VIII.
FUTURE
PET

High diddle diddle, the cat and the fiddle,
The cow jumped over the moon;
The little dog laughed to see such sport,
And the dish ran away with the spoon.

Nursery rhyme, anonymous

SPACE CADET PETS

Until the early 1960s we did not know exactly how many G's a man was going to pull on a lift-off, and we were very concerned.

CHIEF VETERINARIAN AT AEROMEDICAL RESEARCH LABORATORY, DR. JERRY FINEG, IN CHARGE OF OVER FOUR HUNDRED DOG, CAT, AND CHIMP ASTRONAUTS

The biggest question was the impact—reentry.

DR. WILLIAM BRITZ, FINEG'S COLLEAGUE, WHO RAN A FLIGHT REENTRY MACHINE, THE BIG BOPPER, RIDDEN BY THE CAREER PET ASTRONAUTS

As we look to the future now, we naturally turn to space exploration. Being the first astronauts, pets have made ground-breaking contributions in this field.

In 1946, from the White Sands Proving Grounds in New Mexico, we launched and detonated eight confiscated German V2 rockets. On board: fruit flies.

So far, so good.

The next important launch occurred on June 11, 1948: Albert, an anesthetized rhesus monkey, reached an altitude of sixty-two kilometers on *Blossom 3*. The mission was a success except for a minor landing malfunction. The parachute on the module failed to open, and Albert saw more than stars.

Reentry technology was perfected in the early fifties. In 1951, eleven mice survived a seventy-one-kilometer shot (though their companion rhesus died shortly after impact). In the spring of 1952, capuchin monkeys Pat and Mike were the first primates to splash down safely.

By the later fifties, the Soviets had launched at least forty-two canines. Then, in a three-year period, they made history with a trio of dog shots.

- **1957** November 3. Two-year-old, eleven-pound Samoyed husky Laika became the first living creature in orbit. She survived six days until her oxygen ran out.
- **1959** July 2. Another husky, Otvazhnaya, plus a companion and a rabbit, were fired up 160 kilometers and returned safely.
(Canineaut Otvazhnaya made five more successful suborbital flights before retirement.)
- **1960** August 19. Aboard *Sputnik V*, Samoyeds Belka and Strelka completed seventeen orbits in twenty-five hours. The dogs were the first creatures to survive orbital flight.

The triumphant Belka and Strelka mission caused the United States to redouble efforts with its own space animals. The crucial unresolved issue was still human survivability.

At the Aeromedical Research Laboratory in New Mexico, thirty-eight scientists and veterinarians were working with over four hundred chimp, dog, cat, and mouse astronauts. Pigs and bears were also involved.

The experimenters strapped the subjects to machines that simulated takeoff and reentry conditions. There were two high-velocity carnival-like rides called the Sled Track and the Daisy Track. They measured a number of variables, including changes in the face of a bear, pig, or poodle pulling ten G's. The other instrument, "the Bopper," was a large slingshot that catapulted mammals up to two hundred pounds. The Bopper was used to study landing impact and post-reentry shock.[1]

---

[1] Though less common today, these studies still continue and have begun to attract the attention of animal rights activists. In 1991 (August 12) the *Los Angeles Times* reported on a controversy surrounding a "Quantum Leap" episode: in it,

By the early sixties, NASA was training sixty chimp astronauts. After rigorous physiological and psychological testing, eight finalists graduated to the *Mercury* program. Among them were the Alan Shepard and John Glenn of chimp space cadets: Ham and Enos.

They piloted our own historic missions.

- **1961** February: Ham was only up for six minutes thirty-nine seconds in suborbital space. But, surviving reentry, he returned to what veterinarian William Britz called "the biggest celebration he'd ever seen."

This, however, did not include a ticker-tape parade. Alan B. Shepard got that three months later for the same mission.

- **1961** November 29: Ham's colleague, Enos, orbited the earth three times.

Enos also returned to a celebration at Cape Canaveral, where he was treated to cake, cookies, and a Coca-Cola. Three months later, returning from the same mission on *Friendship 7*, the current senior senator from Ohio, John Glenn, got the ticker-tape parade.

After human survivability was proved, fewer pets were launched into space.[2]

In 1974 *Skylab 3*, as part of a student experiment, carried two spiders, Arabella and Anita, to see how they spun webs in

---

series hero Sam Beckett inhabited the body of a research chimp set to die in a crash-impact test.

Today, most studies of this nature involve autos, not spacecraft. And activists are resorting to more radical demonstrations. Protesting General Motors' animal car crash testing, activist Lucy Shelton dressed as a pig and handcuffed herself to a Cadillac at a Los Angeles auto show in January 1992.

[2] Unfortunately, dogs, though they pioneered space, have not had a space walk. Nor have they had a moon walk, though they have howled longingly at that body for years.

weightlessness. It was found that they did so normally, without difficulty. In 1975, as part of another experiment, the *Apollo-Soyuz* mission carried fish and discovered that they lost sense of which way was up.

During the eighties, as part of its Shuttle Student Involvement Program, NASA began orbiting school science projects. On mission STS-7, students sent up an ant colony to see how ants burrow in weightlessness. On STS-41C, they tried honeybees to see how they made combs in weightlessness. On STS-51, they dispatched twenty-four mice and two monkeys. This last mission went well until the monkeys' business floated out into *Spacelab*'s main cabin and was snagged, with some difficulty, by the human astronauts.

Finally and more recently, Kentucky Fried Chicken sponsored a mission manned by the "Kentucky Space Chicks."

PNN EYEWITNESS EXTRA!

THE INVISIBLE CAT

On May 26, 1991, the *Los Angeles Times* carried a curious story from Berkeley, California: RADIOACTIVE CAT LEAVES A TRAIL.

The piece began like this:

> *Missing: one radioactive cat. Berkeley police are looking for a feline who apparently ingested a dose of iodine 131 during a visit to the vet and excreted the substance into a box of Kitty Litter.*

The radiation level of the feces was high enough to set off an alarm at the waste disposal site. A team of toxic waste specialists were called in to remove the radioactive Kitty Litter and bury it. The garbage truck that carried the litter was grounded for eight days—the half-life of iodine 131.

But what of the radioactive cat?

In spite of the APB issued by the Berkeley Police Department, the pussy was apparently never located. No follow-up reports were made.

In some circles, rumor had it that he/she had become invisible.

FURRY FUTURE
Pet Predictions

The future of pets is a highly speculative subject. The pet historian does not venture into the realm lightly. Certainties are impossible. One can only project, state probability, based on a sober review of shifts, trends, and undercurrents from the Pyramid Period to the Golden Retriever to the Rock 'n' Roll.

Based on that examination, here now some parting projections:

BUSINESS

• The Kinugawa Kokusai Hotel, Montrose Pet Hotel, and Fido Fast Food will become national chains. Poochi Canine Couture, Animal Manors, Lick Your Chops, and Bitch Hitch, Inc., will be featured by *Money* magazine as hot new investments for the year 2000.

• Great Expectations will buy out Isoroku Kimura's Pet Dating Service. Jippo Pet Angel Service will open satellite offices in Beverly Hills, Ann Arbor, and the Hamptons.

• Carl's Jr. will discontinue their "all-star dog." Der Wienerschnitzel will file a Chapter 11. Tail-o'-the-Pup will be firebombed by covert PETA operatives.

LAW

• Dogs and cats will win class action mental distress claims against airlines that ship them to the wrong destinations or mistakenly serve them vegetarian lasagna instead of chicken à la king.

• The relatives of Ella Wendell's deceased poodle, Toby, will successfully sue for restitution of the original $30 million bequest. Miss Wendell's executors will also be prosecuted for feeding Toby on the kitchen floor, then putting him down.

DAILY LIVING

• The 9 percent of recently surveyed pet owners who denied baby-talking to their pet will admit that they were lying and apologize publicly on "Donahue" and "Oprah."

• Tom Jarriel of "20/20" will locate a lost community in China where sacred Pekingese are still attended by eunuchs and suckled by Manchu women.

RELIGION

• Twenty-first-century people will begin openly worshiping cats as in ancient Egypt. A great Cat Fertility Hall such as that at Bubastis will be constructed by a Democratic president in Southern California or just outside the Beltway. (Here, at the solstice women's groups may play tambourine topless and taunt gathering AKC picketers and Iron John wildman groups.)

• Animal psychics and priestesses such as parrot medium Penelope Smith will return to such areas as Delphi, Cannae, and Malibu and establish 900 exchanges.

• Pope John Paul's successor will issue an apology for the pet inquisition. Annual St. Francis Day Animal Blessings will take place in every major diocese. Pope Leone I's dancing elephant, Annone, will be canonized, as will Cardinal Richelieu's martyred cat, Perruque.

SPORTS

• The Bears will return to the Super Bowl by 2000. The Saints may get licked, but they will not be eaten.
• Army will again kidnap Navy's perfumed goat, Billy XXVI.
• Bowing to pressure from animal rights organizations, the Defense Department will posthumously award Biber, the hero of Desert Storm, the Purple Heart—against the strenuous objections of naval Chief Petty Officer Drew A. Solberg.

POLITICS

• First Animals will continue to occupy the White House, rip the pants off prime ministers, and have accidents on the rug. Some may head important cabinet posts, fact-finding commissions, and task forces.
• *Millie's Book* will be outsold by *Sock It to Me,* the First Cat's tell-all memoirs highlighted by a blow-by-blow recount of her abduction and drugging at the hands of CNN and *USA Today* reporters in Little Rock.

SHOW BIZ

• Still snubbed by celebrity ape Oliver, actress Hitoko Tagawa, wearing only a bikini and Tabboo, will venture into China's Hubei Province National Park Preserve for Big Hairy Monsters. Covering the action: Nippon TV, "Hard Copy," "A Current Affair," and Geraldo Rivera (with a gorilla suit on hand in case no BHMs show).
• Michael Jackson and his chimp, Bubbles, will be frozen cryonically and in the year 2300 revived to reprise "Billie Jean" and the moonwalk.

• Based on the exploits of real-life supernarcs Barco and Rocky, a major motion picture starring Gene Hackman, Beethoven, and Bijou will sweep the Oscars —*The Furry Connection.*

SPACE EXPLORATION

• NASA will bring astrochimps Ham and Enos out of retirement to man the first mission to Mars. On return they will be invited to the White House for cake and cookies with President John Glenn.
• NASA, in cooperation with Carl Sagan and Stephen Hawking, will shoot a calico or Cheshire cat into a black hole, the future will become the past, and pets will return to the Pyramid Period.

The last prediction may not be as improbable as it may at first seem. History suggests that our pets could already be time travelers. Consider it:

• The Soviets and NASA continue to withhold top secret information relating to early missions gone awry. Could it be that many *Sputnik* and *Mercury* dogs are already in the fifth dimension?
• Jippo Pet Angel Service has been launching thousands back to the stars since 1986.
• The radioactive cat that became invisible in Berkeley, California, in 1991 after ingesting iodine 131 still has not been located.

Could they all not be back together in ancient Egypt's Temple of Bubastis now, being worshiped as gods?

BIBLIOGRAPHY

Adamoli, Vida. *Amazing Animals*. Robson Books, 1989.

Baur, John E. *Dogs on the Frontier*. Denlinger's Publishers, 1982.

Bord, Janet and Colin. *Alien Animals*. Granada Publishing, 1985.

Caras, Roger. *A Celebration of Cats*. Fireside/Simon & Schuster, 1986.

Fireman, Judy (ed.). *Cat Catalog*. Workman Publishing Co., Inc., 1976.

Hadden, Celia. *Faithful to the End*. St. Martin's Press, 1991.

Kelly, Niall, *Presidential Pets*. Abbeville Press Publishers, 1992.

Leca, Ange-Pierre. *The Egyptian Way of Death*. Doubleday & Co., Inc., 1981.

Morris, Desmond. *Catlore*. Crown Publishers, Inc., 1987.

Quennell, Peter. *The Colosseum*. Newsweek, 1971.

Riddle, Maxwell. *Dogs Through History*. Denlinger's Publishers, 1987.

Schuler, Elizabeth Meriwether (ed.). *Simon & Schuster's Guide to Dogs*. 1980.

Siegal, Mordecai (ed.). *Simon & Schuster's Guide to Cats*. 1983.

Wallechinsky, David, Wallace, Irving, and Amy Wallace. *The Book of Lists 1, 2, & 3*. William Morrow & Co., Inc., 1977, 1982, 1986.

Winokur, Jon. *Mondo Canine*. Dutton/New American Library, 1991.

NEWSPAPERS AND MAGAZINES

Ad Astra magazine
Cats magazine
Dog World magazine
Los Angeles Times, the
New York Times, The
People magazine
Sports Illustrated
Wall Street Journal, The

INDEX